The
Russians
Aren't Coming

The Russians Aren't Coming

NEW SOVIET POLICY IN LATIN AMERICA

edited by
Wayne S. Smith

Lynne Rienner Publishers • Boulder & London

Published in the United States of America in 1992 by
Lynne Rienner Publishers, Inc.
1800 30th Street, Boulder, Colorado 80301

and in the United Kingdom by
Lynne Rienner Publishers, Inc.
3 Henrietta Street, Covent Garden, London WC2E 8LU

Library of Congress Cataloging-in-Publication Data
The Russians aren't coming : new soviet policy in Latin America /
    edited by Wayne S. Smith.
        p.   cm.
    Includes bibliographical references and index.
    ISBN 1-55587-270-0
    1. Latin America—Foreign relations—Soviet Union. 2. Soviet
Union—Foreign relations—Latin America. 3. Soviet Union—Foreign
relations—1985– 4. Cuba—Foreign relations—1959– I. Smith, Wayne S.
F1416.S65R87   1991
327.4708—dc20   91-28838
                                                              CIP

British Cataloguing in Publication Data
A Cataloguing in Publication record for this book
is available from the British Library.

Printed and bound in the United States of America

The paper used in this publication meets the requirements
of the American National Standard for Permanence of
Paper for Printed Library Materials Z39.48-1984.

Contents

Foreword

Jack Perry

The end of the Cold War forces us to think through our assumptions about world politics all over again—a painful but exhilarating process. The revolution from above that Gorbachev began in 1985, and which has since gone far beyond the bounds he first envisioned, is the third great reordering of European politics in our century. The first was in 1919, when the empires of Hohenzollern, Hapsburg, Ottoman, and Romanov crumbled and a new order of nations was set up in Europe, and then fell apart. The second was in 1945, when Stalin created a new empire in Eastern Europe and the ensuing Cold War divided the world between rival superpowers and their respective allies. This third reordering, well symbolized by the fall of the Berlin Wall, saw Moscow voluntarily give up its sphere of influence in Eastern Europe.

Now we begin to draw the consequences of these momentous happenings. One area to ponder is Latin America. No doubt both US and Soviet political thinkers and doers could be accused of ethnocentrism—or superpower centrism, if there is such a term—in their perception of Latin American history since World War II. Some Latin American observers would say that aside from the Cuban missile crisis and US intervention in Central America, ostensibly to combat communism, the Cold War has been largely irrelevant in the history of the area. The "Soviet threat" may have worried some in the United States, and certainly Castro's Cuba was a bone in their throats, but the factual record shows that overall there was never much of a Soviet presence, never much of a Soviet influence, never much of a "Soviet threat." A peasant in Guatemala or Paraguay or a city-dweller in Brazil or Mexico could very well argue that what mattered in Latin American history after 1945 was influenced very little by the Soviet-US rivalry—or for that matter by the ideological struggle between the two "systems" that true believers on both sides thought to be all-important.

Both Moscow and Washington have some grandiose pretensions to explain. One harmful Soviet pretension was that the "Great October

Socialist Revolution" was a turning-point in human history. In fact, nobody but Soviet Communist party members and their self-seeking followers elsewhere ever saw the events of October 1917 as a momentous event except in determining the rulers of the Russian empire. Charles Bohlen was always meticulous in calling it "the Bolshevik coup d'état," which is closer to the truth. The fact that Stalin's Soviet Union became a world-class power, at least militarily, helped obscure the fact that, as an ideology and a system, Marxism-Leninism was always feeble.

In Latin America, the contradictions between Soviet ideology and the place of the Soviet Union as a global superpower were especially sharp. Strange as it may seem, Marxism-Leninism had little to do with the Soviet-Cuban partnership. The heart of that partnership was Fidel Castro's defiance of the "Yankee colossus" and his turning to the Soviet Union for succor. Communism in Cuba was never a menace to the United States, whether Soviet missiles were or not. It is true that many anti-Communists in the United States, including a goodly number in Congress and the Executive Branch, and particularly in the CIA, saw the world in terms of an ideological struggle. Democracy versus communism was, to them, the fateful issue of our time. With this unrealistic way of looking at world politics, they could advocate US intervention in Guatemala or the Dominican Republic or Chile or Nicaragua as part of a majestic Cold War struggle. In retrospect, although Moscow and Havana no doubt took comfort and hope from the successes of self-proclaimed Marxists, the ideological struggle in Latin America was not between pro-Moscow and pro-Washington forces, but mainly between the forces for change and the forces of the status quo. Moscow can take very little credit, or blame, for the outcome of this struggle.

US pretensions toward Latin America are not totally different from Soviet pretensions; both are rooted in great-power hubris. As the Soviets view the Russian Revolution, we think the American revolution of 1776 was a universal event; thus, we have difficulty understanding why most Latin Americans consider it less than relevant to their history—or why they view the Monroe Doctrine not as a protective cloak but as proof of hegemonic pretensions on the part of the United States. Believing as we do in our own benevolence, we find it difficult, unless we have lived abroad, to grasp that for many people US dominance in the New World or in the world as a whole has not been a matter of benevolence. US preoccupation with the Communist threat in Latin America surely seemed to many Latin Americans the twin to our pretension that what was good for the United States must be good for Latin America. Mistrust (and worse) of the giant neighbor to the north flowed from this set of pretensions and misunderstandings.

Now we are at a new juncture of events. Hardly anyone can talk seriously about a Soviet threat in Latin America. Although the possibility of thunder on the left is always with us, and some may still think in terms of international communism—now a mere figure of speech—in fact, the uprisings, rebellions, and revolutions of the future in Latin America will be indigenous, not imported, and will have little to do with Marx or Mao or Stalin or Lenin except for an occasional quotation. Sendero Luminoso in Peru is a formidable movement, but it has no connection with the Comintern or with whatever our ideologues take to be the successors of the Comintern in more recent times.

When we think of the terrible and growing poverty of millions of people in the countryside and in the slums of Latin America, we must surely expect political turmoil and upheaval, not to speak of unbearable human misery, if present trends continue. In 1950, someone might have said, "That is the breeding ground of communism," and had in mind the hammer and sickle. Some of us today worry about political radicalism in Latin America, but we do not think of Moscow or Havana or Beijing—we think of new varieties of communism, or whatever one chooses to call it. Who would have thought of the Shining Path movement? Who would have thought that brutality would continue to come in so many new guises?

At the same time, for many in Latin America, things are looking up. Some economies are doing better. The Brazilians seem to be coming to their senses about the Amazon rain forests. Democracy has been doing well lately. The idea of a US-Mexico free trade agreement points up the potential of modern international capitalism to spread the fruits of industrialism to new places in new ways. Free trade will spread, and perhaps it will help. A cynic would say that the masses in Latin America will not profit much from these developments, but such changes should not be dismissed as unimportant. What is intriguing is free trade and economic modernization on the one hand, and political decline or even atrophy on the other. If national governments in Latin America are weaker in some instances than their local drug lords, and if movements like the Shining Path can bring a country to its knees, where does this leave the brave new world of multinational corporations and free trade zones?

Whatever framework this new reality in Latin America fits into, it does not fit into the old world of the Soviet-US condominium. For the moment, it is true, US resentment of Soviet support for Castro—exaggerated as it is in its US interpretation—is still a problem between Washington and Moscow. From that viewpoint, the US-Soviet-Cuba triangle deserves the extensive attention it receives in this book. The record of Soviet-US intersection and confrontation in Cuba is immensely important, and the future of Soviet-US relations will not easily be free of the problem that is the Castro regime in Cuba.

But as one looks ahead, is it not clear that the Bay of Pigs, the missile crisis, and Soviet support of Castro are fast receding into the past—and that the Soviet Union, even if it wishes to remain true to past commitments, will have less and less to gain from the sort of client-state relationship it has had with Cuba in the past? As the Soviet Union seeks to carve out a place for itself in a new, post–Cold War Latin America, is it not almost inevitable that that relationship will undergo change, moving toward the sort of perfectly normal relations Moscow enjoys with other Latin American countries?

How large the Soviet place will be in the Latin America of the future is an intriguing question. Although it is no longer a superpower, the Soviet Union, whatever form it takes politically, will surely be a major actor on the world political stage. Its resources, its diplomatic talents, and its military power give it that place. True, the role will be quite different from that of motherland of the Socialist revolution it tried to play under Stalin, Khrushchev, and Brezhnev. The Soviet or Russian role in Latin America must be to some extent as a counterweight to that of the United States, along with the West Europeans. This assumes that both politically and economically the Latin Americans will not be content with living in the shadow of the United States. Making their own way in the post–Cold War world will mean finding alternative partners: if the Soviet Union can repair itself and again become a diplomatic force, it should be an eligible partner. The domestic crisis in the Soviet Union makes this a risky prophecy. But one should reckon with the possibility that Moscow will continue to play a meaningful role in world affairs, including in Latin America.

As citizens of the United States, we should probably welcome the possibility of Soviet and West European counterweights in Latin America. The record seems to indicate that when the United States more or less by fiat rules North and South and Central America, then the conditions in Latin America are not what many Latin Americans would want, and the process of political change is kept in an unhealthy condition by US dominance. No one would advocate neocommunism in Latin America—who would want a Castro system or a Shining Path junta government? Yet do we hope to see the continuation of a power relationship in which the United States can invade countries such as the Dominican Republic, Grenada, or Panama with impunity? Most Latin Americans would presumably wish for a regional system in which US power is balanced at least to some extent by the influence of West Europeans and Japanese—and, yes, even the Soviets—in conjunction with indigenous political power. No one foresees or wishes to see any recolonization of Latin America from Berlin or Tokyo or Lisbon or Madrid or Moscow; the danger the Monroe Doctrine was proclaimed to prevent no longer exists. But the passing of the Cold War, if we are honest, gives us a fresh occasion to reexamine not only that famous doctrine but also the present relationship of the United States with its neighbors.

This volume is a provocative and worthy beginning to such a reexamination.

Preface

Wayne S. Smith

Most of the essays in this book were in final form before the abortive hardline coup of August 1991 in the Soviet Union. That pivotal episode, however, in no way diminishes the relevance or invalidates the basic conclusions of the individual essays or of the overall thesis of the book. Quite the contrary, the failure of the coup and the direction of events in the Soviet Union in its aftermath point up even more clearly just how irreversible is the process of change unleashed by Mikhail Gorbachev's "new thinking." In the final analysis, the coup failed because the Soviet Union is already far different from the country it was ten, or even six, years ago. Then, the hardliners might have imposed their wills upon a passive Russian people. No more. The Russian people are passive no longer. The process of change has passed a point of no return.

As we began putting this book together, there were doubts in some quarters concerning its underlying premises. Some participants at the November 1990 conference that launched its preparation, for example, expressed the view that Gorbachev's "new thinking" was no more than a tactical respite, and that Soviet formulations concerning the end of world revolution were a ruse. But if such doubts were prevalent before the events of August 1991, there certainly can be no room for them now. Clearly, the world revolution *is* over; the Cold War is finished; communism itself is crumbling even in the socialist motherland. The whole ideological construct has collapsed. Enclaves of communism remain in China, Korea, Vietnam, and, yes, in Cuba, but world communism is now a thing of the past.

In the wake of the August coup, the situation in the Soviet Union is more unsettled than ever. Indeed, the country may be entering a state of rapid disintegration. Union republics are dropping away. No one seems certain who is in charge. Turmoil prevails. Thus, the configuration of a situation described today may well have changed by tomorrow. As the need to restore order becomes more pressing, the pendulum may even swing back toward more conservative rule. Even so, the swing will be limited. There is no danger of a return to the Stalinist past. There may be some zigs and zags along the way, but basically the direction of march will be toward liberal reforms.

Certainly rapid changes in the leadership are to be expected for a time. Senior Soviet officials in office today may be replaced by new faces tomorrow, and they in turn by new ones next week. By the time this book is in print, Mikhail Gorbachev may be little more than a figurehead, even have been replaced—or, on the other hand, may have regained a preeminent leadership position. Whatever its form, and whoever is directing it (or attempting to do so), the evolutionary process will continue. It has taken on a momentum of its own. The Soviet Union (or Russia) will not return to what it was before 1985. Much less will it go back to the kind of foreign policy pursued before Gorbachev's reforms.

A word of explanation is perhaps in order regarding the inclusion in this book on Soviet policy of chapters presenting the Cuban perspective. The focus is indeed on new *Soviet* policies in Latin America, but given the charges that Cuba has acted as little more than a surrogate of the Soviet Union in Central America, it seemed necessary to factor in the Cuban approach there as well. In the same way, it seemed reasonable to include the Cuban perspective as well as the Soviet when it came to a discussion of Soviet-Cuban ties, which are at the epicenter of continuing US-Soviet contention in Latin America.

All those who helped in the preparation of this book wish to take this opportunity to thank the Carnegie Corporation of New York for the generous support that made it possible. The effort began with a conference in November 1990 at which many of those whose writings appear in this volume gathered to discuss changes in Soviet policy toward Latin America. It now culminates with the publication of this book. From start to finish, the effort had the full support and cooperation of the Carnegie Corporation. For that we are most grateful.

Finally, the editor also wishes to thank Maria Gutierrez, the indefatigable program assistant at SAIS who prepared the manuscript.

Introduction: An Overview of Soviet Policy in Latin America

_____ *Wayne S. Smith*

The First Decade

From the Bolshevik revolution of November 1917 until the Sixth Congress of the Communist International (Comintern) in 1928, the Soviet approach in Latin America was cautious and low-keyed. At first caught up at home in the civil war against the whites, in trying to spark Communist revolutions in Europe, and then in fending off the interventions of the *Entente Cordial*, the new Soviet government could spare little attention for an area on the other side of the globe. To the extent that it gave any mind to events outside the European theater, the Soviet government instead showed interest in such traditional areas as China, India, Afghanistan, and the Middle East.

To be sure, a few Comintern agents such as Mikhail Borodin, M. N. Roy, and Sen Katayama were sent to organize Communist parties in Latin America, a task accomplished mostly by having existing Socialist and workers parties accept the twenty-one points of faith put forward by the Comintern in 1920 as the prerequisite for membership.[1] Representatives of the Mexican Communist party attended the Second Congress of the Comintern in 1920, and by 1925 parties existed as well in Argentina, Uruguay, Chile, Brazil, and Cuba.[2]

Comintern orders to parties other than in Europe, including those in Latin America, were to concentrate on organization and indoctrination and to cooperate with other progressive forces, including, where possible, bourgeois governments. The Chinese Communist Party in 1923, for example, was ordered to work with the Kuomintang. And in a directive from the Comintern to the Mexican Communist Party in 1923, the former congratulated the latter for its decision to participate in elections. "Parliamentary struggle," the directive pointed out, was simply one means by which the party could grow strong.[3]

Such tactics paid off also in the area of state-to-state relations. On

1

November 7, 1924, for example, President Alvaro Obregón of Mexico rewarded the Communists for their support against an uprising the previous year by establishing diplomatic relations with the Soviet Union. Two years later, Uruguay also established diplomatic relations, and in 1928 Argentina authorized the opening of a Soviet trade mission, a step that was expected to lead to formal government-to-government relations.

The policies pursued by Moscow during this first decade did not produce dramatic results, but they were not designed to do so; rather, they were calculated to avoid trouble in a far-removed region while at the same time breathing life into a Communist movement and preparing for the future. Certainly Moscow's approach succeeded rather well in balancing two contradictory objectives, one essentially conspiratorial—to set up and direct Communist parties loyal to Moscow whose long-term aim was the overthrow of the existing bourgeois governments—and the other more traditional—to conduct business with the governments of the region through normal diplomatic channels in order to advance Soviet state interests. By the end of the period, Moscow enjoyed relations with two other countries and hoped to be recognized by several others. And in a number of countries, the small new Communist parties had gained considerable influence. The Mexican Communist Party, for example, had a warm relationship with the government. And in Chile, the party had won increasing acceptance, especially within the labor movement. In the elections of 1925, two party candidates won senatorial seats and seven were elected to the chamber of deputies.[4]

In sum, a good beginning had been made. It was to be spoiled, however, by the tactical shift dictated by the Comintern at its Sixth Congress in 1928.

The Period of Militant Communism, 1928–1935

Although caution and cooperation with non-Communist forces had worked well, in 1928 Moscow went over to the attack. Communist parties in the so-called colonial, semi-colonial, and dependent countries—that is, those of Asia, Africa, the Middle East, and Latin America—were called upon to increase their struggles against landlord regimes and imperialism. They were to demand the expropriation of large estates, the confiscation of foreign and domestic capitalist enterprises, and the arming of workers, peasants, and soldiers. Guerrilla warfare, rural uprisings, mutinies, and general strikes were all listed as appropriate responses to the new conditions discussed at the Sixth Congress.[5] What were these new conditions? According to the Comintern leaders, Latin America had now come within reach of Communist influence and was ripe for revolution. Not only could bourgeois-democratic revolutions be carried out straightaway, but the way was also said to be open to a rapid transition to the Socialist revolutions that were to follow.[6]

As in the first decade of Comintern activity, Communists might cooperate with other progressive elements, but only during the bourgeois-democratic revolutionary phase. And there was a sharp departure from the spirit of the first period in that they were instructed to regard these forces, even in the midst of joint struggle, as "class enemies," to whom they must not in any event subordinate themselves. It was a matter of accepting the help of these non-Communist forces, but never trusting them. And, of course, as soon as the Socialist-revolutionary phase began, they were to be turned upon and struck down.[7]

As events were to demonstrate quite clearly, objective conditions for revolution had not changed at all. In fact, Comintern leaders probably understood that all along. Despite the inevitable ideological justifications, other calculations were behind the shift in tactics. For one thing, the period of the new economic policy in the Soviet Union ended in 1927 and was replaced by the drive for rural collectivization and forced industrialization. As coexistence with the internal bourgeoisie and foreign capitalists was over, Moscow was expected to take a harder line in the international arena as well.

Second, in 1927, the Kuomintang had suddenly turned on the Chinese Communist Party and, in what came to be called "the Shanghai massacre," murdered thousands of its members and leaders. Might not progressive forces turn on the Communists in other areas as well if given half a chance? The Comintern had thought it was using the national bourgeoisie. After 1927, it was not certain who was using whom, and so new instructions went out urging caution in dealing with these "class enemies."

Perhaps the most important factor of all, however, was Stalin's growing domination of both the Communist Party of the Soviet Union (CPSU) and the Comintern. Lenin had been a master tactician and perfectly willing to make alliances with all kinds of forces. Stalin, however, was not a man to trust those whom he could not control. He had viewed with some suspicion the whole concept of collaboration with non-Communist forces. With his hands now firmly on the controls, he limited the nature of that collaboration.

In keeping with its somewhat increased interest in Latin America (now that the conditions for revolution were supposed to have "matured"), in 1929 the Comintern moved its South American secretariat from Moscow to Buenos Aires, where, supposedly, it would be in a better position to give immediate and more dynamic direction to revolutionary action.[8] In June of that same year, the secretariat held the First Latin American Congress of Communist Parties, a great affair in Buenos Aires attended by representatives of the Comintern, Communists from all over the hemisphere, plus delegates from the Communist parties of France and the United States.[9]

The line laid down was a radical one, in keeping with the program already outlined at the Sixth Congress of the Comintern. It held that the objective of bourgeois-democratic revolution in Latin America was the establishment of worker-peasant governments. Moreover, Communists were enjoined to pursue militant tactics in achieving their objectives. Rather than attempting to win influence with "pseudo-progressive" governments, they were ordered to bend every effort to overthrow those governments. It was even suggested that "Indian republics" be set up in those countries with large Indian populations.[10]

The Mexican Communist Party was the first to put the new line to the test, calling for a peasant uprising almost as soon as the Buenos Aires congress had concluded. The revolt was suppressed within days and brought severe government reprisals against the party. Meanwhile, a significant number of members had resigned rather than accept the new line dictated by the Comintern. Thus, from its previously privileged position, the party now found itself badly divided and driven underground by government forces.

In Argentina, the right-wing military government that came to power in 1930 cracked down hard on the Communists, who were accused of fomenting revolution. The secretariat was forced to move across the river to Montevideo and the Soviet trade mission was closed.

In Chile, Communist agitators sparked a naval mutiny in 1931. This was snuffed out almost as soon as it began. Put down almost as quickly was the uprising called for by the Brazilian Communist Party in 1935. A few soldiers in the Rio de Janeiro garrison joined the revolt, as did troops in Natal and Recife. Sharp street fighting resulted, but within two days the uprising had been decisively defeated. Massive arrests followed and the party was driven underground.[11]

In Cuba, the Communist party called for armed struggle against the brand new government of Ramón Grau San Martín (who, ironically, was being accused by the United States of being a Communist) and for the establishment of soviets of workers, peasants, and soldiers. A number of these were, in fact, set up and lasted several weeks, until Grau was moved aside by Colonel Fulgencio Batista, the new strongman of Cuba. Then they were mercilessly wiped out.

Certainly the bloodiest consequences of the new militant line, however, were seen in El Salvador, where in 1932 the newly organized Communist party, led by Farabundo Martí, touched off a peasants' revolt, joined by small elements of the Salvadoran army. The main body of the army, however, remained loyal to the dictator, General Maximiliano

Hernandez Martinez, who put down the revolt in short order and then took bloody retribution. Hernandez's troops murdered more than thirty thousand peasants as an object lesson. Called *La Mantanza*, or the slaughter, this massacre haunts Salvadoran politics even today.[12]

By 1935, as a direct result of the tactics forced upon them by the Comintern, Communist parties throughout Latin America had been either shattered and driven underground—as in Mexico, Brazil, Argentina, El Salvador, and Cuba—or their influence been reduced to almost zero—as in Uruguay, Chile, and Peru.

By 1935 also, Moscow had lost its official presence in the region. Mexico had broken relations after the Communist-inspired peasant uprising in 1929. The Soviet trade mission in Buenos Aires was closed in 1931, and Uruguay severed diplomatic relations with the Soviets in 1935 after it became clear that the Soviet legation in Montevideo had been instrumental in instigating and directing the Communist uprising that had just taken place in Brazil. Such conduct was impermissible, the Uruguayans insisted, and ordered Soviet diplomats out of the country.[13]

Moscow was now frozen out of Latin America and its local allies were everywhere on the run.

Popular Fronts, 1935–1945

Confrontational tactics had brought nothing but disaster, but it was not the failure of those tactics that prompted a return to popular fronts; rather, it was the rise to power of Adolf Hitler in Germany in 1934. As the Fascist threat in Europe began to take ever more sinister and worrisome form, Moscow realized that if it was to survive to lead the world revolution, it would need the bourgeois governments of the West as allies against that threat. Nor was this a time to shun the Socialists or other non-Communist forces of anti-fascism. Differences with them had now to be put aside in order to focus on the more immediate danger posed by a common enemy. Thus, at the Seventh Congress of the Comintern in 1935, popular fronts were given full endorsement. In typical fashion, however, the endorsement was not phrased as a *new* policy; rather, Comintern leaders criticized the parties themselves for not having properly analyzed events and applied the appropriate tactics. It was *they* who were at fault—not the Comintern, not Moscow, and certainly not Stalin. The Communist party of Cuba, for example, was called on the carpet for failing to differentiate between the camp of counterrevolution and the camp of national liberation. In other words, the Cuban Communists ought to have supported Grau! Never mind what their instructions had been at the time. Other parties too were criticized for their tendency to lump all bourgeois groups together. In one of the last sessions of the Congress, for example, Wang Ming, a Chinese comrade, complained, "Many of our comrades in Latin America have characterized nearly all the bourgeois and petty-bourgeois parties as fascists, thus hindering the establishment of an anti-fascist popular front."[14]

In other words, the parties were taken to task for doing exactly what the Comintern had told them to do. One can imagine, however, that they were so relieved to go back to popular-front tactics (after the nightmare that the period 1928–1935 had been for them) that they were not inclined to question the fairness of the criticisms leveled against them. At last, they could make common cause with other progressive groups and identify themselves with nationalist programs. In Mexico, for example, the party became the enthusiastic supporter of Lázaro Cárdenas. In Chile, the Communists entered into an electoral front with the Socialists and *Radicales* in 1938 to support Pedro Aguirre Cerda for president. To their surprise, he won and they found themselves part of a ruling coalition.

The Cuban Communist Party first tried to make peace with Grau and his *Autentico* party (which only three years before they had called Fascist). When Grau rebuffed their conciliatory gestures, they turned instead to Batista, the power behind the throne in Cuba from 1933 until 1940, and then president in his own right from 1940 until 1944. Batista found their support useful; it enhanced his populist image. In 1938, the party was legally recognized and permitted to participate in the 1940 presidential elections, in which it supported Batista. In turn, Batista appointed two Communists to cabinet posts (one being Carlos Rafael Rodriguez, long a member of the Politburo of the Cuban Communist Party under Castro). It was during Batista's four-year term as president that the Communists were able to increase their strength so notably in the labor movement, and, aided by the improved image of the Soviet Union as a wartime ally, to expand their membership throughout the island. By the time Batista left office in 1944, the Cuban Communist Party had grown to 122,000 adherents.[15]

Parties throughout Latin America had similar experiences during the popular-front period. The signing of the Molotov-Ribbentrop Non-Aggression Pact in 1939, however, resulted in a temporary setback. As the Latin American parties all loyally endorsed and echoed Moscow's policy of benevolent neutrality toward Nazi Germany between August 1939 and June 1941, they again found themselves shunned by other progressive, anti-Fascist groups. The Socialists in Chile, the Liberals in Colombia, and the *Apristas* in Peru all condemned the Communists as trained stooges of Moscow who would supinely praise a pact with the devil himself. Thus, Hitler's attack on the Soviet Union in June 1941 was a stroke of good fortune for the Communists in Latin America. The Soviet Union was on the right side again and popular fronts could be resumed.

As US, British, and Soviet allies linked arms and raised glasses to one another during the struggle against a common foe, so also did relations warm among the Communist parties, the governments, and most other political groups in Latin America to the end of the war in 1945. Anti-imperialism was forgotten. Communists condemned as "saboteurs of the war effort" all those who continued to attack Britain and the United States as imperialist countries. They even discouraged strikes and other harmful activities against British and US firms.

With US objections to greater tolerance of the Communists now put aside, and given the great sympathy that arose for the fighting spirit of the Soviet people (a sympathy that rubbed off on the local Communist parties), it is no wonder that by the end of the war the parties had reached their peak strength. They were legal in virtually every country. There were Communists in the legislatures of Cuba, Colombia, Peru, Ecuador, Brazil, Chile, Bolivia, Uruguay, and Costa Rica. In addition to the two Communists in General Batista's cabinet in Cuba, there were three Communist cabinet ministers in Chile. Indeed, the Chilean Communist Party seemed well on its way to becoming the first ruling party in the hemisphere.[16]

Soviet diplomatic and trade ties with the area also expanded markedly during the war years. An important element in facilitating such relations— inasmuch as the other governments of the world tended to regard the Comintern as the cheering section for their overthrow—was the dissolution of the Comintern in 1943. With this barrier removed, all the major countries of South America, except for Peru and Argentina (both under military governments), opened diplomatic relations with Moscow. Mexico reestablished relations in 1942. Cuba recognized the Soviet government in 1943 and in that same year exchanged ambassadors with Moscow. Costa Rica, Nicaragua, Guatemala, and El Salvador extended recognition but did not exchange ambassadors. By 1945, the Soviets had a diplomatic network in Latin America that would not again be equalled until well into the decade of the 1970s.

The Cooling of the Popular Fronts: 1945–1959

The Cold War began almost as soon as World War II had ended and as the US-Soviet alliance gave way to bitter global rivalry, the good fellowship between the Latin American Communist parties and the bourgeois governments also dissipated. Stalin had little interest in Latin America; it was far away and of little immediate strategic relevance to Soviet plans. To the extent that he thought about them at all, however, his opinion of the Latin American governments was not a complimentary one. Especially galling to him, in the early days of the United Nations, was the fact that the United States could almost always use the twenty-vote Latin American bloc to defeat any Soviet proposal in the General Assembly. In a *Pravda* interview in 1951, for example, Stalin accused the Latin American governments of furthering US aggressive policies in the United Nations. "The United Nations," he complained, "is being turned into an instrument of war, into a means of unleashing a new world war. Its aggressive core is represented by the ten member countries of the aggressive North Atlantic Pact and twenty Latin American countries."[17]

It is hardly surprising, then, to find the same Latin American Communist parties that had until 1945 praised Britain and the United States and cooperated fully with their governments now heaping invective on them all. The United States was again described as imperialist and as the principal threat to peace in the world.[18]

As early as the end of 1945, for example, the Cuban Communist Party declared that it had been wrong in its earlier interpretation of the 1943 Teheran conference. It had based the hope that the conference would lead to peace and cooperation on the belief that capitalism had changed its character. But it now saw that this had been an illusion. Capitalism remained the same old enemy it had always been.[19]

A statement in 1947 by Rodney Arismendi, the leader of the Uruguayan Communist Party, showed as well as any just how abruptly and totally the Communists had changed course. Just before the end of the war, Arismendi had stressed the importance of Pan-Americanism, that is, of US–Latin American cooperation. But now, only two years later, he stressed its uselessness:

> The so-called Pan-American brotherhood, it is clear, lacks social and economic foundations of any kind; only effervescent charlatans, unprincipled Quislings and the power hungry can unabashedly assert that the down-trodden Indian or Creole of Latin America has a communion of interests with the limitless wealth of Wall Street or the millionaire set on Park Avenue.[20]

In Brazil, Luis Carlos Prestes stated that in any war of conflict between Brazil and the Soviet Union, the Brazilian Communist Party would fight on the side of the Soviet Union. The Brazilian government, needless to say, was not amused.[21]

It should not be assumed, however, that the turn away from the popular fronts of the war years implied a return to the hard-line radicalism of the 1928–1935 period. The parties hurled verbal barbs at the United States and its local allies, including the national governments, but they did not launch any uprisings or even think of adopting armed struggle as a tactic. And in some cases they were willing to make deals with dictators and to cooperate with progressive non-Communist groups. General Perez

Jimenez in Venezuela, for example, allowed the Communists a rather free hand in the labor movement up until about 1956 in return for tacit Communist support. And Batista, from his return to power via a coup in March 1952 until almost the end of his regime in January 1959, permitted the outlawed Cuban Communist Party (now called the Popular Socialist Party [PSP]) not only to operate but to exercise a disproportionate influence in the Cuban Confederation of Labor (CTC).[22]

In the United States, the fourteen-year period between the end of World War II and Castro's triumph in 1959 saw the hysteria of McCarthyism and, even on a somewhat more dispassionate level, a determined effort to bar any Communist penetration of Latin America. For example, Allen Dulles, director of the Central Intelligence Agency (CIA) reported to the incoming Eisenhower administration in 1953 that anti-Americanism was on the rise in Latin America, along with "trends in the direction of economic nationalism . . . neutralism, and increasing Communist influence."[23]

Dulles went on to warn that "the Kremlin was exploiting this situation." In particular, he said, "the Communist infection" in Guatemala was "such as to mark an approaching crisis."[24]

In response to Dulles's alarm bell, the Eisenhower administration rushed to map out a strategy to deal with this perceived threat—a strategy that included the introduction of a resolution in the Organization of American States (OAS) describing any form of communism as incompatible with the hemispheric system, and then a clandestine operation carried out by the CIA to overthrow the government of Jacobo Arbenz in Guatemala.[25]

In part, US alarm and reaction to what it perceived as a dangerous threat were fed by the shrill language coming out of the Kremlin—and from the Latin American Communist parties themselves. But in truth there was nothing behind that rhetoric. As stated above, in no case did the parties call for armed uprisings or in any other way threaten the peace. They simply talked. Communist influence was most certainly *not* on the rise in Latin America. Quite the contrary, the Communist parties were increasingly isolated now that they could not identify with nationalist issues. Their membership, which had peaked during the war years, steadily dwindled. And in response to their vitriolic attacks against the national governments, in country after country they were declared illegal. Chile was a case in point. There, the Communists in 1946 were brought into a Radical-Socialist-Communist coalition by President Gabriel Gonzalez Videla, principally because of their continuing strength in the labor movement. But they were no sooner in the ruling coalition than they began to abuse the other members (after all, they were under instructions not to trust or be friendly with non-Communist groups). They demanded the dismissal of the Socialists and in general behaved as if they already enjoyed dictatorial powers—behavior that had the effect of uniting almost the whole Chilean political spectrum against them for years to come. In 1947, President Gonzalez Videla dismissed them from his government and in 1948 declared the Communist party to be illegal.[26]

After that debacle, there was only one country—Guatemala—in which the influence of the party was apparently increasing. The Eisenhower administration chose to interpret the situation in Guatemala as a classic example of Soviet penetration. In fact, it was nothing of the sort; what one had in Guatemala was a nationalist revolution. In 1944 the latest in a long line of military dictators had been overthrown, and Guatemala, soon under the leadership of President Juan José Arévalo, had begun a series of relatively moderate reforms aimed at bringing about a more modern, equitable society. In the presidential elections of 1950, Arevalo was replaced by Colonel Jacobo Arbenz, who, following his inauguration in March 1951, continued the process of modernization by putting forward an ambitious agrarian reform law.

The Communists were really a side issue. Given the more open political spirit in the country, the few Guatemalan Communists, who for years had been forced to operate clandestinely, were allowed to organize openly as the Guatemalan Communist Party (PCG) and in 1949 to hold their first party congress. (This did not sit well in Washington, although the reason for this is difficult to say because the Communist party of the United States had always been legal.) Fewer than one hundred were on hand for this first congress. They had hoped to increase their strength, especially among the peasantry, by supporting the concept of agrarian reform. Unfortunately for them, party leader José Manuel Fortuny had just returned from Moscow with instructions from Andrei Zhdanov to refrain from such support, inasmuch as agrarian reform was not an approved policy for semicolonial countries such as Guatemala. Thus, the party program outlined in 1949 called on members to lead the fight against US imperialism and against war, and to support peace and national sovereignty. But, thanks to Moscow, not a word was spoken about agrarian reform.

Saddled with such left-footed tactics, the PCG found itself not only unable to win new adherents, but actually losing members, who broke away to form splinter parties rather than follow the dictates of the newly organized (and fortunately short-lived) Cominform (the Communist Information Bureau, which was organized in 1947 to replace the Comintern; in 1956 it was disbanded as an idea whose time had never come).

Not until 1951 did Moscow reverse its position on agrarian reform. Thus, at its Second Party Congress in October 1952, the PCG was at long last able to identify itself with the one program and issue dearest to

President Arbenz's heart. From that point forward, its fortunes improved (especially after it changed its name to the Guatemalan Workers Party [PGT] in December 1952). Arbenz soon appointed several of its members to the Agrarian Reform Department and began to consult with Fortuny and a few other Communist leaders. This was by no means to say, however, that the Communists were in control—far from it. There were never any Communists in the cabinet, and only four were elected to the legislature. Moreover, the army and all the other national institutions were intact and for the most part opposed to anything that even hinted at a Communist takeover.[27]

As for the Soviet Union, it did nothing other than to sometimes saddle the local Communist party with unrealistic instructions. It provided neither economic nor military aid, did not send advisers, nor did it even bother to set up a Soviet mission. The Guatemalan and Soviet governments had recognized one another during the war years, but had never exchanged ambassadors or established any diplomatic presence in one another's capitals. Nor did they do so now. PGT leaders on several occasions urged Moscow at least to open a consulate. As one of their number, Carlos Manuel Pellecer, put it: "We knocked on the Soviet's door, but they didn't answer."[28]

As Piero Gleijeses has well documented in his book *Shattered Hope: The Guatemalan Revolution and the United States, 1944–1954*, the idea that Guatemala was a Soviet bridgehead was little short of absurd. This was a nationalist revolution, and the Communists saw benefits in cooperating with it. Guatemala almost certainly would have been far better off today—and during the past almost forty years—if the United States had kept hands off. However, given the McCarthyite hysteria of the times—a reality Arbenz as a national leader had to take into account—Arbenz maneuvered badly and helped to bring about his own downfall. Two factors were of primary importance in sparking the final US reaction. First, a number of Arbenz's followers had urged him to give assurances not to let rising Communist influence get out of hand, hoping that would hold off US intervention. But in his annual report to the Guatemalan Congress on March 1, 1954, Arbenz not only refused to give any such assurances, but, to the contrary, gave the PGT a sweeping new endorsement. Many who until then had supported him concluded that he was losing his perspective and deserted the ship.

Second, after years of vainly seeking to buy arms in the United States or Western Europe, Arbenz sent an emissary to Czechoslovakia and succeeded in purchasing a shipload there, on a strictly commercial basis. On May 15, 1954, these arms arrived aboard the Swedish vessel *Alfhem*. Suspecting that they were intended to arm newly organized peasant militias, the army began to grumble. On June 8, constitutional guarantees were suspended and on June 18, 1954, Colonel Castillo Armas, with CIA backing, led a rag-tag invasion force across the border and headed for Guatemala City. The Guatemalan Army refused to fight, and by June 27 it was all over. Arbenz sought asylum and his government collapsed.

Even before the overthrow of Arbenz, the Soviet Union had given little attention—and even fewer resources—to Latin America. Stalin's death in 1953 had opened the way to a more flexible approach in other areas of the Third World. Stalin's view of the world had been a rigid one: the two blocs confronting one another and eventual victory being decided by how many armored divisions each could put in the field. Given that framework, Stalin saw no role for the emerging nations of what we now call the Third World, regarding them all as either sepoys loyal to the former metropolitan powers, or as bourgeois nationalists over whom Moscow could not exercise effective control.

Nikita Khrushchev, on the other hand, who soon won the power struggle in Moscow and became the new Soviet leader, saw great possibilities in the Third World. Were not the emerging nations, he asked, almost by definition anti-imperialist, and thus likely to feel some affinity for the Socialist bloc, which was also anti-imperialist? And if country after country lined up with the Soviet Union, was that not likely to shift the correlation of forces in the world so much in favor of Moscow that the nuclear stalemate could be broken and the way opened to Communist victory on a worldwide basis? Thus, a corollary to the idea of peaceful coexistence between East and West was that struggle between them would continue, but as a new kind of struggle: one for hearts and minds in the Third World.

Therefore, the Third World became the principal arena in which East-West rivalry was played out, and Khrushchev gave more and more attention to it—except for Latin America. Here, the Soviets saw the imperatives of geographic determinism as holding firm. The area was simply too far from the Soviet Union and too close to the United States for effective action. If there had been any doubts about that prior to 1954, they were dispelled by the ease with which Washington dispatched the government of Jacobo Arbenz. Thus, even as Soviet activities increased in other Third World areas, they declined still further in Latin America. Moscow seemed simply to write the area off and did not really look at it again until after Castro's rise to power in 1959.

Active or not, however, the Soviet Union came out of the fourteen-year period following the war almost as frozen out of the area as it had been in 1935. The parties were everywhere in decline and Moscow itself was left with only three diplomatic missions in all of Latin America—in Mexico, Argentina, and Uruguay. Washington might be ringing alarm bells, but objective observers could only wonder why.

Fidel Castro Calls for Armed Struggle, 1959–1968

Fidel Castro may, as he now claims, have read Marx while he was in the mountains. And certainly he is a sufficiently astute strategist to have all along understood that as his international objectives were likely to result in conflict with the United States, it might be expedient at some point to turn to the Soviet Union for protection. Neither Fidel Castro nor his revolution, however, were initially Marxist/Leninist. Rather, both were nationalist. The Cuban Communist party was decidedly suspicious of Castro's revolution in the beginning and did nothing to assist it until the eleventh hour—until, in fact, it was clear that Castro would win. For its part, the Soviet Union was totally surprised, did nothing to help Castro's revolutionaries, and at first regarded Castro with suspicion even after he had taken power.

Why then Castro's turn to the Soviets and his conversion to Marxism/Leninism? Quite simply because by the end of 1959 Castro saw that conflict with the United States was inevitable if he indeed held to his international objectives—which he fully intended to do. He therefore began to turn to the Soviets for protection against US power. He may or may not at that point have intended to convert Cuba into a Marxist/Leninist state. If not, that decision was virtually made for him in April 1961 as he saw US naval vessels off the south coast of Cuba and realized that an invasion was imminent. Fully expecting to face the full power of the United States rather than only a brigade of Cuban exiles, Castro played the only card he had that might prompt the Soviets to come to his support: on the day before the invaders landed, he declared the Cuban revolution to be a Socialist one.[29] This is a Communist government, he was saying to Moscow, and you therefore have an ideological obligation to defend it.

As it turned out, that was unnecessary. The whole invasion force consisted of only fewer than 1,500 men in the brigade. Castro defeated them easily without needing assistance from anyone. Even so, in a way Castro had probably not expected, it was the Bay of Pigs invasion, or, more correctly, its failure, that opened the way to Moscow's acceptance of Cuba as a Socialist country. Until then, the Soviets had been not only suspicious of Castro but also unconvinced of his staying power in the face of US reaction. Fully expecting that he would meet the same fate as Arbenz, they had not wished to ally themselves to someone doomed to early defeat. The US failure at the Bay of Pigs, however, suggested to the Soviets that perhaps the imperatives of geographic determinism were no longer so overwhelming. Perhaps, after all, Castro was going to survive US hostility, and perhaps now the Soviets themselves could operate more successfully in Latin America. There were still problems to be worked out. For one thing, Cuba was not at that point ruled by a vanguard Communist party; rather, the party in power was Castro's own 26th of July movement. That had to be remedied, for if it were to be considered a Socialist state, there had to be a ruling Communist party. Castro thus began the process of combining his 26th of July with the old-guard Communists to produce a new party, the Cuban Communist party (PCC). With that process begun, and with various other discrepancies on the way to resolution, in May 1962 the Soviets accepted Cuba as a Socialist state, and also decided to position ballistic missiles there.[30] The Soviet-Cuban alliance was now a fait accompli.

Cuba's developing association with the Soviet Union had, of course, further stimulated not only US concerns but those of the Latin American states. In January 1962, the Organization of American States voted to suspend Cuba's membership. Castro's reply was immediate and vitriolic. In what came to be called the Second Declaration of Havana, issued on February 4, 1962, Castro virtually declared war on the other governments of the hemisphere as well as on the United States. Hemispherewide revolution was inevitable, he declared, whatever the United States and its traitorous allies in the region might say or do. He ended with a rousing call to all revolutionaries to "get out and fight."[31] Castro backed up his rhetoric with concrete actions. Guerrilla fronts appeared in Guatemala, Venezuela, Colombia, Peru, Bolivia, and Argentina. These were the products of local conditions and initiatives, but in all cases Castro encouraged their establishment and provided at least some degree of support. The war, in effect, was on.

Castro had expected the Soviets to applaud his revolutionary efforts in Latin America, but he was to be disappointed. They had all along regarded his emphasis on armed struggle with skepticism. Such tactics had never won them anything but trouble in Latin America. On the other hand, it was difficult to argue with success. Castro *had* won with such tactics. Further, in the immediate aftermath of the Bay of Pigs, US resolve may have been in doubt. If so, that doubt was dispelled by President John F. Kennedy's resolute handling of the missile crisis. From that critical moment forward, the Soviets were more certain than ever that they wanted no more confrontations in the area. Thus, rather than aiding Castro's efforts to foment revolution, the Soviets increasingly insisted that he accept their own more cautious tactics and that he work through the orthodox Communist parties, whom he despised, rather than through radical revolutionary groups more loyal to him. This was not at all to Castro's taste. The resulting conflict over tactics and objectives provoked sharp tensions between Moscow and Havana during most of the decade of the 1960s. Castro had become Moscow's ally, but he was determined to go his own way. Marxism, he said, was not a church with an immutable doctrine, a Rome, and a pope. "We can differ on any point with any party," he insisted.[32]

In 1964, in an effort to strike a compromise, the Soviets maneuvered Castro into holding a meeting of Latin American Communist parties. There it was agreed that in six countries (Guatemala, Honduras, Haiti, Colombia, Venezuela, and Paraguay) conditions seemed appropriate for Castro's armed-struggle tactics. Thus, the Communist parties in those countries were to support guerrilla warfare. In all others, however, popular-front tactics were to be followed, and Castro was to work through the orthodox parties.[33]

Most observers doubted that the accord would hold, and they were right. It was honored by all sides more often in the breach than in fact. In Paraguay, Haiti, and Honduras, for example, the Communist parties did not go over to armed struggle. And in Peru, Bolivia, and various other states, Castro continued to work through revolutionary groups and to push confrontational tactics. Further, in less than two years, at the Tri-Continental Conference held in Havana in January 1966, Castro outmaneuvered the Soviets and overturned the agreement altogether. This was to have been a meeting at which "progressive" movements from Latin America would be added to those already comprising the Afro-Asian People's Solidarity Organization, thus making it a tricontinental organization. Moscow's principal purpose here was to outflank Peking by bringing its Cuban ally and various other Latin American groups sympathetic to Moscow into the organization. For tactical reasons, the Soviets left the invitation list and agenda in the hands of a Latin American committee controlled by Castro. That was a mistake. Rather than inviting groups and parties enjoying Soviet approval, Castro invited every radical revolutionary movement he could think of. The orthodox Communist parties were largely bypassed and Soviet positions were ignored. Rather, the conference was turned into a Fidelista circus, with resolution after inflammatory resolution for armed struggle and confrontation with the imperialists on a global basis. The Cubans, moreover, insisted that these resolutions superseded the cautious agreement of 1964 and, to the embarrassment of the Soviets, demanded that they honor them.

As government after government called Soviet ambassadors on the carpet for an explanation of Moscow's apparent endorsement of these calls for their overthrow, Moscow hastily disavowed the resolutions. Without "official" representation at the conference, it insisted, it was not bound by the resolutions. (This, despite the fact that Sharaf Rashidov, an alternate member of the Politburo of the CPSU, had headed the Soviet delegation.)

Castro, needless to say, reacted with scorn to this backtracking on Moscow's part. Whatever others might say or do, he declared, Cuba considered the resolutions binding and would carry them out. Those who did not so regard them, he noted pointedly, were guilty of betraying their people.[34]

Shortly after the conference, Castro began efforts to form an axis with two other small, radical Communist states: North Korea and North Vietnam. Together, he seemed to believe, the three of them might prod Moscow toward a more revolutionary line. What may be regarded as the culmination of this trend came in 1967, when Castro published a major treatise on the question of revolution in which he openly rejected Soviet theoretical constructs and made it clear that he would ignore questions of affiliation with the world Communist movement in his dealings with Latin American revolutionaries.[35]

Then, in January 1968, Castro expelled from the newly reconstituted Cuban Communist party a number of old-line Communists known to be closely sympathetic to Moscow. With this clear affront to his Soviet allies, an open break between Havana and Moscow seemed inevitable. In fact, however, it never came. One reason clearly was that Castro had all along understood that Soviet aid was a sine qua non to his survival. (That may or may not be true today, but in 1968 it certainly was.) He could take his independent position only as far as the Soviets would let him. If ever push came to shove, he would have little choice but to accommodate Soviet concerns. And push did come to shove in 1968 when the Soviets threatened to hold back desperately needed petroleum supplies.

It was not simply a matter of Soviet pressure, however. The fact was that no matter what Castro had said in his treatise of January 1968, by that year he had serious reason to doubt the efficacy of the guerrilla tactics he had so long advocated. They had not produced a single victory. Ernesto "Che" Guevara's defeat and execution (some would say murder) in Bolivia the previous year simply further dramatized this failure. Castro's tactics had failed, but others were working. Soviet popular-front tactics had paid off handsomely. Moscow had established diplomatic relations with Brazil, Colombia, Venezuela, Bolivia, Ecuador, Costa Rica, and Guyana, and soon would have relations as well with Peru and Salvador Allende's Chile. Cuba, on the other hand, with the exception of its ties with Mexico, was isolated in Latin America.

For these various reasons, Castro was disposed to shift tactics, no matter how strong the impression to the contrary only a few months before. The first indication of the change came in a speech on August 23, 1968, in which rather than condemning the Soviet invasion of Czechoslovakia, as most had expected, Castro endorsed it. Signs of a warming trend in Cuban-Soviet relations soon followed. November 1968 marked the first time a Soviet naval squadron made a friendship call in Havana. Later that same year Soviet Marshal Adrei Grechko arrived for an official visit. By January 1969, while noting that there might at times have been disagreements between Moscow and Havana, Castro was expressing effusive appreciation for Soviet aid, which he described as having been crucial for Cuba.[36]

In keeping with his new international approach, Castro also began de-emphasizing the extension of revolution as a policy and armed struggle as a tactic. Cuban assistance to guerrilla groups was drastically reduced and, in most cases, eventually stopped altogether. By 1970, for example, Douglas Bravo, Venezuela's hold-out guerrilla leader, was bitterly complaining of Castro's refusal to provide further support. Rather than heeding the plea, Castro put out peace feelers to several of the same Latin American governments he had once vowed to overthrow, now emphasizing his willingness to coexist with them and to respect their sovereignty if they would respect his.

Moscow could congratulate itself on its adroit handling of its headstrong Caribbean ally. It had managed to maneuver and restrain him without ever letting things come to a boil. And its patience had paid off; it had finally brought Castro around to a supportive position. With the dispute with Havana now resolved, the way was open for more than two decades of relative harmony in Cuban-Soviet relations.

The Cautious Line Restored, 1968–1979

The next eleven-year period began well for the Soviets. Two early developments in Latin America gave new credibility to their popular-front approach and nudged Castro even more closely in behind their lead: (1) the progressive military revolution in Peru in 1968, and (2) Salvador Allende's 1970 electoral victory in Chile.

At first, Soviet analysts believed the military takeover in Peru to be a typical right-wing coup. The Peruvian generals were described as "gorillas who had established [in Peru] a regime of ferocious military dictatorship."[37]

But as the military government instituted an agrarian reform and other liberal economic measures, as it nationalized the US-owned International Petroleum Company, and especially as it expelled the US military mission in 1969, the Soviets concluded that this military government was different—it was progressive in nature. Relations between Moscow and Lima warmed noticeably and soon even included a Soviet military assistance program. The Peruvian army acquired Soviet equipment, advisers, and personal links that endure even today, although the military long since gave up power and Peru has gone through several governments throughout the intervening years.

Especially pleasing to the Soviets was the fact that the Peruvian military government allowed the Peruvian Communist party and various other progressive groups to operate, even though political parties were ostensibly illegal. This enabled the Soviets to attribute the favorable turn of events in Peru to the joint efforts of all progressive forces. It was, in short, another victory for popular fronts.[38]

Even Fidel Castro acknowledged that the Peruvian military regime seemed to be leading the country toward a true revolution, thus for the first time implicitly recognizing that there might be more than one way to bring about revolutionary change. Until that point, Castro had insisted that, at least in Latin America, change could be produced only through the barrel of a rifle. But now here was the very institution he had earlier described as a guardian against change actually bringing change about. The world, it seemed, was more complex than Castro had thought.[39]

With another seemingly popular military coup in Bolivia in 1969, and with General Omar Torrijos, who had taken power in Panama in 1968, moving to abrogate previous agreements with the United States over the canal, Soviet analysts began to speculate that the Latin American military might itself be turning into a force for revolutionary change. Such hopes, however, received a setback in 1971 when the progressive military elements were ousted from power in Bolivia by conservative officers.[40] In a different context, new setbacks were to follow in Chile.

Salvador Allende's 1970 electoral victory in Chile had also fallen into the category of "popular-front success." Allende, the head of the Socialist party, had won, after all, on a coalition ticket formed by the Socialists, the Communists, and various other smaller progressive parties—a popular front by any standard.

The Chilean Communist party, moreover, was one of the oldest, most loyal, and well-disciplined parties in Latin America. Moscow had great confidence in its ability to keep the governing coalition moving along the road that would eventually lead to socialism, but without any rapid departures that might provoke a right-wing reaction. That, however, proved overly optimistic. The Communist party did its best; certainly it was always the most moderate element in the coalition. But neither it nor Allende could control the more radical elements, and especially not the Movement of the Revolutionary Left (MIR), which carried out illegal land seizures and other unauthorized acts that did indeed provoke a reaction not only from the Right but from the center. With confidence in the government deteriorating, and due in part also to certain of the government's own financial policies, the Chilean economy was soon in dire straits. Moscow was willing to provide some economic assistance in the form of credits to buy Soviet goods and so forth, but it was not prepared to mount a concerted economic rescue operation. If the choice was between risking a large sum of hard currency or watching the Allende government collapse, Moscow was prepared to see it collapse. Clearly the Soviets were not willing to foot the bill for another Cuba.[41]

Probably it was wise not to do so, for in 1973 the Chilean army overthrew the Allende government and installed a brutal military dictatorship that was to last for more than sixteen years. Soviet analysts rather forlornly noted in the wake of the military coup that in the "peaceful development of revolution, it is probably easier to seize power than to hold it."[42]

No other Latin American apples fell into Moscow's lap during the next few years, and meanwhile not only Moscow's but Havana's attention turned more to Africa. Even so, the rest of the period saw some new successes, especially for Cuba. Given its policy shift in 1968, several Latin American countries had reestablished diplomatic relations with the island even before the OAS voted in 1975 to lift the prohibition on such relations (with the United States voting in favor). Thus, by 1979, Cuba had full relations with eight Latin American governments plus Jamaica and Guyana. All but the latter were members of the OAS. In addition, Costa Rica had established consular relations and maintained a consulate general in Havana. Even more pleasing to Moscow than Castro's new acceptance in Latin America was the improvement in US-Cuban relations initiated by the Carter administration in 1977. The Soviets had long lived with the fear of a confrontation developing between Washington and Havana—a confrontation that would leave Moscow in the agonizing position of having to abandon Cuba to the United States or come to Cuba's aid and in the process put the Soviet homeland at risk. That Castro's more moderate policies were serving to reduce those fears was, then, doubly pleasing to Moscow.

Also pleasing was the degree to which Fidel Castro now acted as a loyal Soviet ally in such international forums as the United Nations and the Non-Aligned Movement (NAM). In the earlier meetings of the latter, Cuban delegations had frequently and openly criticized the cautious Soviet approach to revolution. By 1970, however, with the first NAM summit conference following Castro's shift (held in Lusaka, Zambia), the Cubans were already beginning to float the concept of a natural alliance between the Socialist and the nonaligned world. And at the next conference, in Algiers in 1973, Fidel Castro himself pushed hard for a resolution recognizing that such an alliance existed. Only the closest cooperation among all the progressive forces of the world, he declared, would give them the strength to defeat the imperialist enemy. Thus, he warned, "Any effort to pit the non-aligned countries against the socialist camp is profoundly counter-revolutionary and only and exclusively benefits imperialist interests."[43]

Even with Castro himself taking the lead, the Cubans were unable to ram the resolution through; there was simply too much opposition from such countries as Yugoslavia, India, and Tanzania, who insisted on a policy of equidistance between the two superpowers. To the extent that he could do so, Castro continued the fight for a natural-alliance resolution right up to the sixth NAM summit, held in Havana in September 1979. At that point, however, realizing that resistance to the idea was too strong to overcome and that in the process he was wasting a good deal of his own political capital within the NAM, Castro gave up. No more was heard of a supposed natural alliance between Socialist and nonaligned countries.

Armed Struggle Briefly Reconsidered—And Discarded, 1979–1985

Cuba's acceptance of the national-front strategy was not the only change registered in 1979. In that year, the Marxist-oriented New Jewel movement, led by Maurice Bishop, took over in Grenada, and then the Sandinistas marched triumphantly into Managua.

The first event had little impact on Soviet tactical formulations. Moscow had nothing to do with Bishop's victory. In fact, the Soviets were only vaguely aware of who he was or where Grenada was located. But Castro certainly knew. He had a standing relationship with Bishop and seemed to have been aware that the latter was planning a takeover. There is no evidence, however, that Castro assisted in that takeover. Indeed, that Bishop won at all is something of a fluke, having as much to do with the idiosyncracies of Sir Eric Gary, the overthrown leader, as with any strengths or doctrinal insights on the part of the New Jewel movement. Sir Eric, in fact, was in New York talking about flying saucers at the time of the takeover.

The Sandinista victory was something else again, for what it had done was to replicate the Cuban revolutionary model. Inevitably, this led to some rethinking on the part of the Soviets and Cubans, and to new apprehensions on the part of the United States and the Latin American governments. Up until that point, the Soviets had refrained from support for revolutionary groups, and even the Cubans were virtually out of the business. Havana had continued to provide some minor assistance to the guerrillas in Guatemala, had offered shelter to the Sandinistas after their initial defeat in Nicaragua, and then supported them when they returned to the struggle in 1974. Elsewhere, however, it had given up on armed struggle and gone over to the popular-front tactics espoused by Moscow. But now that Cuba's original preference for guerrillas and armed struggle had in a sense been vindicated in Nicaragua, might not Havana, and perhaps Moscow as well, vigorously embrace—or re-embrace—those tactics?

At first, there was some reason to think the answer to that question might be in the affirmative. For one thing, during 1980 and early 1981, Cuba—and to a lesser extent the Soviet Union—did provide some material assistance to the guerrillas in El Salvador. For another, Soviet and Cuban theoreticians did for a brief period describe the Sandinista victory as confirmation of the efficacy of armed struggle. The Cubans pointed to Nicaragua as the correct model for other Central American revolutionaries, although they emphasized that each nation must find its own revolutionary path, and they seemed to draw no conclusions regarding the applicability of the Nicaraguan model to *South* American countries.

Soviet theoreticians and area specialists went even further. In a now famous roundtable discussion in Moscow organized by the Soviet journal *Latinskaya Amerika*, Soviet participants were categoric in their conclusions that Ernesto "Che" Guevara had been right all along. One Soviet, Boris Koval, declared that the Nicaraguan experience now confirmed "the correctness of Che Guevara's strategic principles, and [gave] life to his idea of creating a powerful people's guerrilla movement."[44]

Nor did the Soviet participants limit the lessons of Nicaragua to Central America; rather, they concluded that given the conditions in most of Latin America, "the path of armed struggle . . . is the most promising."[45]

In sum, whereas the growing turmoil in Central America was the result of internal causes—poverty, social injustice, and repressive governments—the fact was that Soviet-Cuban actions and statements up until the time the Reagan administration took office suggested that they might try to exploit the situation in an increasingly aggressive manner. Thus, although the administration was unjustified in ringing the major alarm bells that it did, and although it grossly exaggerated the situation in its white paper of February 1981, some uncertainty and therefore concern over Soviet-Cuban intentions were in order. That changed quickly, however. Almost as soon as they had spoken the words "armed struggle," the Soviets had second thoughts. Their expectation had been that the success in Nicaragua would be followed quickly by another in El Salvador, and then perhaps one in Guatemala. And having gained that kind of momentum, guerrilla fronts might spring up again all over the hemisphere.

But it had not worked out that way. When in January 1981 the Farabundo Martí National Liberation Front (FMLN) launched what was to have been its all-out offensive, it was quickly and rather easily defeated by the Salvadoran armed forces. In Guatemala also it soon became clear that revolutionary victory remained no more than a distant dream. The army was simply too strong—and ruthless—for it to be more than that. With these developments before them, Soviet as well as Cuban analysts took another look and decided that they had overreacted the first time around and that the prospects for armed revolution were not nearly so promising as they had seemed in 1979 and 1980. In fact, they were not promising at all. A far more sober tone began to characterize the ruminations of Soviet area specialists, and increasingly they concluded that armed struggle had not, after all, been the key ingredient in the Sandinista victory. Rather, it had been "leftist unity," and it was that which Communist and progressive groups in other countries would do well to emulate.[46]

That, however, by no means resolved the question of how armed struggle was to fit into Communist designs in the region. To resolve it, a major conference of Communist and revolutionary theoreticians was held in Havana in 1982. Strangely, as noted above, the Cubans had been less bullish than their Soviet colleagues in the wake of the Sandinista triumph. No Cuban analyst had taken that triumph to mean that the Guevara line of the 1960s had been right and that all Communist and revolutionary groups should now go back to armed struggle. Havana had been encouraged to think that perhaps the Nicaraguan experience reflected improved conditions for armed struggle in a few countries, but the only two they ever actually mentioned were El Salvador and Guatemala.

By the time of the 1982 conference, redefinitions were limited to those two. The finding of the conference was that although armed struggle remained a valid tactic under certain conditions, in all of Latin America the conditions for armed struggle existed in only two: El Salvador and Guatemala. Honduras, which the United States had, by 1982, turned into a base camp for the Contras, was described as a country in which the conditions for revolution were "developing."[47] In all other countries, Communist and revolutionary parties were advised to adopt other tactics, that is, gradualist popular-front tactics.

Interestingly, Soviet accounts of the Havana conference referred to Georgi Dimitrov, for whom, it was said, conference participants had expressed respect and admiration.[48] The significance of this was clear. Dimitrov had taken over as chief of the Comintern at its seventh meeting in 1935 and immediately presided over the abandonment of armed struggle (the line, it will be remembered, favored by the Comintern during the 1928–1935 period of militant communism) and the reinstitution of popular fronts. By referring to him so pointedly in the context of the 1982 Havana conference, Soviet publications were signaling to their readers what the key significance of that conference had been—a return to popular fronts.

It is worth noting that this shift on Moscow's part took place during 1981 and 1982, *before* the US invasion of Grenada in October 1983. The Reagan administration was fond of portraying the latter as an action so intimidating that it had inspired Soviet restraint. A more accurate assessment would be that after the Soviets had already decided upon restraint, the US invasion of Grenada added new weight to the argument that the chances of success were too remote, and the costs and risks too high, to make revolutionary adventurism worthwhile. In short, the invasion of Grenada was not the turning point the Reagan administration claimed it was, although it may have had some additional admonitory effect.

If there was any doubt that the Soviet line had changed, it was dispelled by articles in Soviet journals in the years after 1982. One by Nikolai Vasetski in the January 1987 edition of *Latinskaya Amerika* dismissed not only armed struggle but its practitioners, both past and present, as well. Argentine *Montoneros*, Uruguayan *Tupamaros*, and the M-19 in Colombia were all labeled "pseudo-radical." The M-19's famous November 1985 attack on the Palace of Justice in Bogóta was called "an act of terrorism." Various other groups favoring armed struggle were written off as "Trotskyite."[49]

Vasetski's piece went further than most in writing off the non-Communist Left as hopelessly undisciplined and radical. Not surprisingly, Vasetski himself was criticized by some of his colleagues for adopting a "Stalinist" approach to those he considered guilty of "infantile leftism."[50]

Others, however, supported Vasetski.[51] The prevailing view of Soviet analysts and area specialists from 1982 forward was most definitely one of extreme skepticism concerning the efficacy of armed struggle. And Moscow's actions matched its rhetoric. The single possible exception in a doctrinal sense was El Salvador. There the Soviets continued to acknowledge that "perhaps" the conditions for armed struggle existed. But even in El Salvador the Soviets in fact refrained from the provision of material support and by 1985 had come around to the view that a negotiated solution was eminently desirable.

The Cubans, in keeping with the conclusions of the 1982 meeting in Havana, would appear to have continued to give some degree of support to the FMLN in El Salvador, although that support was never of the magnitude or importance suggested by the Reagan administration. Further, as we shall see in Chapter 9, as early as December 1981, the Cubans signaled to the United States their support for a negotiated settlement in El Salvador and their readiness to discuss and reach accommodations on the whole issue of outside arms supply. They were to continue those signals for the next eight years, with nary a response from the United States.

This, then, was the situation as Mikhail Gorbachev came to power in 1985. Moscow was pursuing a policy in Latin America that was decidedly less than adventurist. It was not egging on or supporting revolutionaries anywhere in the hemisphere, and in the area of greatest conflict—Central America—it consistently called for a peaceful, negotiated solution. At the same time, it had not foresworn revolutionary struggle; rather, the proper conditions for that struggle simply did not yet exist. Presumably, some day they would, and then Moscow could be expected to go on the offensive. World revolution had not been called off; it had simply been postponed.

Notes

1. The twenty-one points are discussed in E. H. Carr, *The Bolshevik Revolution* (London: Macmillan & Co., 1953), p. 193.

2. One might assume, therefore, that the Mexican Communist party is regarded as the first in the hemisphere. Wrong. The Mexican party represented at the Comintern Congress in 1920 had, of course, not accepted the twenty-one points. Further, its principal organizer, M. N. Roy, soon ran afoul of the vicious infighting in Moscow and was expelled from the Communist party. Thus, the party he organized in Mexico has disappeared from the pages of history almost as if it never existed, and according to Soviet histories, the first Communist party in Latin America was the Argentine, which was led by Moscow's favorite, Victorio Codovilla.

3. Quoted in Stephen Clissold, *Soviet Relations With Latin America, 1918–68* (London: Oxford University Press, 1970), p. 82.

4. Luis Aguilar, *Marxism in Latin America* (New York: Knopf, 1968), p. 23.

5. Clissold, p. 77.

6. Ibid., p. 74. See also Kermit McKenzie, *The Comintern and World Revolution* (New York: Columbia University Press, 1964), p. 82.

7. McKenzie, p. 110.

8. Robert J. Alexander, *Communism in Latin America* (New Brunswick, N.J.: Rutgers University Press, 1957), pp. 51–53.

9. Clissold, p. 12.

10. Aguilar, p. 21.

11. Alexander, pp. 109–111.

12. Aguilar, p. 24. See also Cynthia Arnson, *El Salvador: A Revolution Confronts the United States* (Washington, D.C.: Institute for Policy Studies, 1982), pp. 13–16.

13. Uruguayan Diplomatic Note to the Soviet Legation, reproduced in Clissold, p. 98.

14. *VII Congress of the Communist International* (Moscow: Foreign Language Publishing House, 1939), pp. 302–303.

15. Aguilar, p. 33.

16. Alexander, pp. 25–27.

17. Clissold, p. 157.

18. Aguilar, p. 34.

19. Ibid.

20. Ibid., p. 148.

21. Clissold, p. 184.

22. Ibid., p. 36.

23. Quoted in Stephen Rabe, *Eisenhower and Latin America: The Foreign Policy of Anticommunism* (Chapel Hill: The University of North Carolina Press, 1988), p. 31.

24. Ibid.

25. Ibid., pp. 32–33.

26. Alexander, pp. 200–204.

27. Ronald Schneider, *Comunismo en America Latina: El caso de Guatemala* (Buenos Aires: Editorial Agora, 1959), pp. 81–100.

28. Piero Gleijeses, *Shattered Hope: The Guatemalan Revolution and the United States, 1944–1954* (Princeton, N.J.: Princeton University Press, 1991), p. 186.

29. See the text of his remarks in *Revolución*, April 17, 1961, p. 1. This issue is also discussed thoroughly in Wayne S. Smith, *Castro's Cuba: Soviet Partner or Nonaligned?* (Washington, D.C.: The Woodrow Wilson Center, 1984).

30. *Pravda*, May 2, 1962. For a discussion of the Soviet decision in late April 1962, see James G. Blight and David A. Welch, *On the Brink: Americans and Soviets Reexamine the Missile Crisis* (New York: Hill and Wang, 1989), pp. 238–252.

31. For the text of his speech, see *Cuba Socialista*, March 1962.

32. Quoted in Maurice Halperin, *The Taming of Fidel Castro* (Berkeley: University of California Press, 1981), pp. 178–179.

33. See Wayne S. Smith, "Castro, Latin America and the United States," in John D. Martz (ed.), *United States Policy in Latin America: A Quarter Century of Crisis and Challenge, 1961–1986 (Lincoln: University of Nebraska Press, 1988),* pp. 290–291.

34. D. Bruce Jackson, *Castro, the Kremlin and Communism in Latin America* (Baltimore: University of Johns Hopkins Press, 1969), p. 93. Jackson's chapter on the Tri-Continent Conference (pp. 68–94) remains the best description published in the English language.

35. Ibid., pp. 21–22.

36. See Smith, *Castro's Cuba;* pp. 22–23.

37. The author was serving at the US embassy in Moscow at the time and well remembers the comments of Soviet area specialists. This particular epithet was heard on Radio Moscow, October 4, 1968.

38. Leon Goure and Morris Rothenberg, *Soviet Penetration of Latin America* (Miami: Center for Advanced International Studies, University of Miami, 1975), pp. 81–85.

39. From the text of Castro's speech in *Granma*, July 20, 1969.

40. See Wayne S. Smith, "Soviet Policy and Ideological Formulations for Latin America," *Orbis*, Winter 1972, pp. 1137–1139.

41. Goure and Rothenberg, p. 106.

42. A. I. Sobolev, "Revolution and Counterrevolution: The Experience of Chile and Problems of Class Struggle," in *Rabochii Klass i Sovremennyi Mir*, No. 2, March–April 1979, p. 14; quoted in Goure and Rothenberg, p. 117.

43. Quoted in the *Bulletin of the Cuban UN Association* (1978), p. 18, published in Havana.

44. Boris Koval in *Latinskaya Amerika*, March 1980, p. 78.

45. N. Leonov in *Latinskaya Amerika*, March 1980, p. 37.

46. See, for example, N. Leonov in *Latinskaya Amerika*, August 1981; see also *The World Marxist Review*, October 1984, p. 66; and Sergo Mikoyan in *Latinskaya Amerika*, July 1982, p. 41.

47. *The World Marxist Review,* September 1983, p. 45.

48. Ibid.

49. Nikolai Vasetski in *Latinskaya Amerika*, January 1987, pp. 16–25.

50. See Edmé Domínguez Reyes's excellent discussion of the debate in "Pragmatism and Ideology: Gorbachev's Policy to Latin America and Soviet Academic Discussions Regarding the Latin American Left," a paper presented at the Fourth World Congress for Soviet and East European Studies, Harrogate,

England, July 1990.

51. See the editorial, "About an Article in Our Journal," in *Latinskaya Amerika*, September 1987. Cited by Edmé Domínguez Reyes.

Part 1

The Death Knell
of World Revolution

Chapter 1

World Revolution and Class Struggle: Outdated Concepts?

Georgi Mirsky

We live in times of great change and uncertainty. At this point, the only consequence of that change we can be sure of is that the threat of global nuclear disaster has dwindled away. It is difficult to imagine either of the superpowers now thinking seriously of destroying the other. The Soviet Union, decisively weakened by the virtual collapse of the Warsaw Treaty Organization and by the general decline—if not disappearance—of what used to be called the Eastern bloc, is desperately trying to prevent its own dissolution and to achieve internal stability by implementing large-scale radical reforms. Given that socialism has obviously lost its historic competition with capitalism, no one in Moscow today would dream of trying to undermine world capitalism by installing Third World regimes built on the Marxist pattern.

As to the West, its main worry today is not facing a "red challenge," which has practically ceased to exist, but, paradoxically, promoting stability in the Soviet Union, its former adversary.

All this means that at present neither party to the global confrontation, which for several decades conditioned world events, has any incentive to initiate a military conflict. Mankind may sigh with relief; World War III as the culmination of Soviet-US rivalry no longer appears to be a likely, or even a realistic, scenario.

The combined effect of two major phenomena—the end of colonialism and the end of Soviet-US confrontation—has been profound. What we are witnessing is nothing less than the end of the bipolar world that has existed since the end of World War II.

Until now, all major world events were to a greater or lesser extent concentrated around the axis of East-West conflict. In both Moscow and Washington, all significant developments in the world arena, such as upheavals in the Third World, were automatically attributed to the activities of the CIA or the KGB, respectively. More than that, policymakers and public opinion in the Third World countries constantly took into consideration the likely reaction of the two superpowers to their own foreign policies and to developments in their domestic arenas. Within the framework of the "zero-sum game," every success of Soviet policy or gain for leftist forces in the world was certain to be considered a setback for the United States, and vice versa. Neutrals were looked upon as either actual or potential clients—or enemies. With the exception of some great nations, such as India, the majority of world states had to adapt themselves to this bipolar division, which was the dominant factor in international relations.

Today, all this has changed. Third World countries do not have to face the awkward choice between being "progressive" or "pro-imperialist," between being "pro-Moscow" or "pro-Washington"; the long shadow of the superpowers hangs over them no more. Moreover, the very notion of superpower has come to be questioned. It is arguable whether the Soviet Union, for instance, can still be termed a superpower. Some argue that in order to claim superpower status, a nation must not only have an immense territory and a huge population, combined with the possession of nuclear-missile systems, but also be the head of a major system of alliances of a geopolitical and geostrategic nature, and, very importantly, a kind of spiritual leader of a significant part of mankind. (China, after all, has got the territory, the population, and the missiles, but it is not yet considered to have attained superpower status because it plays a lone game. It has never headed a major world bloc.)

If we agree with this notion, and acknowledge that until recently Moscow met all the criteria for superpower status, we must then go on to note that with the disintegration of the Warsaw Pact and with the worldwide reach of Soviet ideology fatally weakened, Moscow's credentials are now flawed.

It might not be out of place to raise a second question, which flows from the first: If the Soviet Union is no longer considered a superpower, can the United States continue to be one? Can one superpower exist and function without the other? Does not the end of the bipolar system mean the end of the superpowers as such?

It is possible to argue that the superpower pattern was initiated by East-West rivalry and, in this sense, was the child of the Cold War, having been inseparable from the ideological dimension of the global struggle between capitalism and socialism. From this point of view, it would seem that the superpower era was a temporary and abnormal phenomenon in the history of international relations.

Is this natural death of bipolarity and of superpower hegemony a great progressive step for mankind, to be unreservedly welcomed? Perhaps not. A sober and skeptical mind might register some reservations or some grounds for apprehension. After all, any phenomenon is likely to have more than one aspect, and thus although it is a blessing in one sense it may be quite the opposite in another. We need not search far to find dangers in the multipolar world. Bipolarity, with all its evils, did exert some restraining and stabilizing influence, if only in relation to forces inside the opposing blocs. Each superpower, while doing its best to undermine the other's positions, was anxious to maintain stability and discipline in its own camp. In the new world political order now taking form, some of the stronger regional powers, devoid of any fear of being disciplined and punished by the superboss, may develop expansionist and aggressive patterns of behavior to the detriment of the international community. Not likely to be restrained by the UN Charter or by international law or morality, they may feel free to settle old scores and to add to their prestige, and even to their territories, at the expense of their neighbors. Iraq's recent brutal aggression against Kuwait is likely only the first of such aggressions.

Nationalistic, ethnic, religious, and other passions are likely to produce many upheavals in the years and decades to come. Patterns of political strife may be different from what Marx and Lenin envisaged, with their stress on class struggle. Further, the grand idea of a world social revolution fueled by the hatred of the exploited classes for their exploiters, and by the workers' burning desire to destroy capitalism, has not material-ized. However, political battles of a violent and often terribly bloody nature go on unabated in most countries of the Third World, and now this trend is evident in some of the former Socialist states of Eastern Europe, especially in the Balkans. Clearly, this pattern presents a fertile ground for extremism, authoritarianism, violence, and dictatorial trends. Saddam Hussein is not likely to be remembered in history as an atypical figure, an odd kind of leader in a country going through the takeoff stage of develop-ment, just as the Ayatollah Khomeini is in all probability not the last of the fanatical religious prophets and false Messiahs arousing millions of the underprivileged. And the danger inherent in these situations is all the greater due to the progress of science and technology. Nuclear prolifera-tion may be one of the most sinister developments of the foreseeable future, and it would be fair to say that this kind of danger is most likely to originate in the Third World. The receding prospects of a global war originating in the Soviet-US rivalry should not blind us to the real pos-sibility of a nuclear catastrophe resulting from a regional Third World dispute.

Does this imply that the Third World as such may be considered a deadly menace to the rest of the world as well as to itself? No. Such an assertion would be off the mark, even if we admit that it is precisely in Asia and Africa that most hotbeds of upheaval are found today (although this statement may be questioned if we take into account the current precarious state of the Soviet Union itself). Hotbeds are one thing, the sources or causes of conflict quite another, and many (if not most) of the latter are linked to the policies of the industrial countries of the North.

The breakdown of colonial empires has not resulted in an end to exploitation, discrimination, or the demand for privileged status on the part of the industrial countries. The gap between the rich nations and the have-nots continues to grow. Economic inequality and injustice represent no less a serious threat to world security than do internal strife and regional conflicts in the Third World. It is fair to assume that instability and violence in the developing countries stem to a large extent from this global imbalance, this continuing injustice. Autocratic rule, undemocratic practices, despotic trends, and contempt for human rights thrive on the poverty and despair of enormous masses of population in the less developed countries, and the West is to blame for a large share of that poverty and despair.

If hundreds of millions of men and women in the Third World have an annual per capita income equal to the price of a pair of ladies' shoes in a New York shop, the world cannot be a fair and safe place in which to live. The world is one whole and it must live or die as one. Some scholars used to liken the poorest countries to a railway car that had caught fire; because it threatened the rest of the train, it would be best to cut it loose on a siding to burn itself out. But such reasoning is foolish and totally illusory. In reality, one cannot cut loose or isolate any part of the whole.

This applies also to environmental problems. Air and water are inseparable and indivisible on our planet. Deadly winds from Chernobyl blew to Western Europe as well as to the Ukraine and to Byelorussia. In the long run, no pollution can be confined within an isolated locality, be it nuclear waste or AIDS.

The term "global problems" has recently become widespread. Former ideological differences and claims to the superiority of one system over another seem less and less relevant to the real problems of today's world—problems such as economic inequality, food, energy, ecology, regional conflicts, nuclear proliferation, international terrorism, and so on. The value of all sorts of ideological "isms" has been rapidly declining, and it is practically impossible to understand and explain the major problems of our time in terms of socialism and capitalism. A new and unbiased approach is called for.

The cornerstone of Soviet "new thinking" is the concept of freedom of choice. In theory, it had been acknowledged long ago. The difference is that in earlier periods implicit in this idea was its relevance to one group of countries only, namely those of a progressive social orientation. It was never clearly expressed but it was understood that the free choice of people would naturally be in favor of a noncapitalist pattern of development. There was no similar recognition of another possibility: that the people could favor a non-Socialist road. What we have now is a just, equitable, and even-handed approach in which any choice made by any given nation is to be respected.

Further, a new look at capitalism has been in evidence in the Soviet Union during the last year or two. The capitalist system has turned out to be much more viable and resilient than it was thought to be. The end of capitalism is not in sight. It is an official opinion now that the change of social formations will occur within a wider historical space than previously estimated. The prospect that socialism will replace capitalism on a worldwide basis is well beyond the horizons that we can see. The conclusion, therefore, is that Socialist countries will have to live side by side with capitalist states for a very long time. And there is no possibility—other than some suicidal attempt to use force—for either of the two sides to change this situation. Accordingly, peaceful coexistence is no longer considered simply a form or variation of class struggle. The significance of this doctrinal change may elude a Westerner not very well versed in Marxist ideology, but as a matter of fact it is enormous. Class struggle means just that—struggle, and its natural aim is, of course, victory. So the world prior to the introduction of our "new thinking" remained in our eyes more or less rigidly divided; it was, as always, "we" and "they." And although any idea of assuring the victory of socialism by force of arms had been discarded no less than three decades ago in recognition of the realities of the nuclear age, the goal of victory, of defeating the capitalist enemy—even if by means other than military—remained. Peaceful coexistence aimed to create favorable conditions for the victory of socialism in this great struggle.

Now the idea is different. The diversity of the present-day world, the plurality of its forms of development, and the legitimacy of these forms—even of those we do not like—has been recognized. The concept of class struggle, being a cornerstone of Marxist thinking, has by no means been discarded, but it no longer conditions our view of peaceful coexistence between states with diverse social systems. Moreover, peaceful coexistence is regarded now as necessarily being of an active nature in order to permit cooperation in dealing with global problems that cannot be resolved with mutual effort without the participation of all sorts of states regardless of their ideology. Consider, for instance, the problem of environment: air and water know no frontiers and it would be foolish to refuse aid to the ideological adversary in trouble in the ecological sphere. But paramount, of course, is the nuclear danger, which cannot be put aside by "passive" coexistence without dialogue with the opposing side and without permanent negotiations on disarmament. And in order to achieve meaningful results in this field, you have to deal with an interlocutor, not an "enemy"—not with an adversary who must ultimately be defeated, but with one with whom one must reason and compromise. Even if we disagree over basic ideological tenets, we must come to terms in the settlement of global problems so that mankind can live on.

And this is where the de-ideologization of interstate relations comes in. It is impossible to cooperate in tackling global problems or regional conflicts while retaining the traditional spirit of ideological intransigence. A line must be drawn between the two spheres: class struggle, including ideological struggle, is one thing, and relations between states are quite another.

In his speech at the United Nations on December 8, 1988, Mikhail Gorbachev said: "We do not renounce our convictions, our philosophy, our traditions and we do not demand that others renounce theirs." Pleading for the "honest struggle of ideologies," the leader of the CPSU stressed that this struggle "should not apply to relations between states." The contrasting spiritual values of both competing world systems have to be put to the test in different fields, including the international one, but not in the sphere of interstate relations. The two terms are not identical. International relations cover a much wider field—they include the whole network of relationships between parties, movements, and so on, which cannot logically be deprived of ideological content. You cannot refuse people, parties, classes, or states the right to feel sympathy for groups or movements ideologically and spiritually close to them. Relations between states is quite another matter. They should be free from ideological debate, because our world in the nuclear age is too fragile for ideological differences to be settled by states in the ways reminiscent of religious wars. The problem is to get rid of the old confrontational approach to peaceful coexistence.

In the nonaligned movement we have perhaps the first example of the practical realization of this goal—namely, the de-ideologization of interstate relations. The fact is that within this movement diverse and often contradictory forms of social and ideological organization have managed to establish a working model of cooperation and have been living side by side for decades. India and Cuba, Yugoslavia and Iran, Vietnam and Morocco—just to mention these states is to realize the enormous heterogeneity of nonalignment. Incompatible and even diametrically opposed ideologies have not prevented the member states from fruitfully cooperating in dealing with numerous problems facing Asia, Africa, and Latin America. If anything, the nonaligned movement proves that interstate relations can be de-ideologized.

What about the attitude toward the movement itself on the part of the superpowers? Some say that both of them are trying hard to woo the nonaligned. Of course, at present no one can afford to belittle or downplay the influence of this movement—its vitality and staying power, and its important place in the life of the international community. The movement has become a permanent, stable, and powerful factor in world affairs. Is its role diminishing in the new psychological climate emerging in the field of international relations?

It is possible to advance arguments in favor of such an assumption. First, the end of the East-West confrontation tends to diminish the importance of the Third World, which ceases to be a valuable prize in the game of world politics. Neither the United States nor the Soviet Union any longer regard the developing areas, in this new period of détente, as the soft underbelly of its opponent, or as a gray zone where relatively minor effort can bring considerable dividends in enlarging its zone of influence.

Second, the new Soviet emphasis on dealing directly with the West, especially with the United States, and on establishing a kind of partnership relationship, means that the bargaining power of third countries is about to weaken.

Both arguments are correct only to a certain point. Although it is undoubtedly true that the ability of the Third World to play on contradictions between the superpowers diminishes as new détente sets in and the division of the world into spheres of influence becomes obsolete, one should bear in mind that Soviet-US competition is not likely to disappear altogether. Nonconfrontation is not synonymous with noncompetition. Presumably, neither side will try to gain more military facilities in the Third World or to create bases or bridgeheads with the aim of encircling the other, but at the same time neither is likely to give up attempts to strengthen its political influence, to encourage friendly regimes, or to prove the advantages of its system in dealing with the problems of backward countries. It would be premature to assert that the days of Soviet-US rivalry in the Third World are over. Also, it would be rash to assume that, with the advent of the new détente, the Third World has altogether ceased to be a prize. It is only the meaning of the prize and its ultimate use that have changed.

In regard to the diminishing value of third forces in the context of direct US-Soviet dialogue, the issue is rather ambivalent. One may argue that the Soviet Union, in order to deal with such a tough and unpredictable (not to say capricious) partner as the United States, needs serious additional bases of support and will welcome reliable friends.

Generally speaking, the networks of international relationships in the present-day world are bound to become more rich and complex. Having rejected the primitive black-and-white, friend-or-foe vision of the world, the United States and the Soviet Union are likely to find it necessary to conduct more flexible and subtle foreign policies, to play more themes and instruments than before, to seek new alliances, and more and more to look for compromise solutions. The world picture has become multicolored; instead of two hostile monoliths facing one another across the globe, many independent actors have entered the stage.

And so, in conclusion, in view of all that has been said about world revolution and class struggle, are we to conclude that both of these concepts are dead?

The first one, world revolution, is very much so. It is not only outdated, it is simply dead. A world Socialist revolution is neither probable nor even desirable. Socialism will live on as an idea and as an ideal, as a noble and humane goal, and as an expression of the urge toward social justice and collective effort and toward the brotherhood of men. But as a concrete form of societal organization, socialism has been a definite and total failure.

It can be foreseen that in many countries of the Third World, Socialist slogans will be raised again and again as young revolutionaries, disillusioned with the bitter fruits of local capitalism, look for alternative patterns. Because the principal alternative to capitalism has long been considered to be socialism, doubtless more than a few revolutionary upheavals will occur under the Socialist banner. But the idea of the worldwide transition from capitalism to socialism has certainly lost any attraction, vitality, or relevance.

The same cannot be said of class struggle. It may be argued that the founding fathers of Marxism grossly overestimated the importance of class struggle in human history and just as grossly underestimated the hold of nationalism and religion. In fact, the failure to understand religion and its role in the life of the individual human being and of society as a whole has been a glaring and fatal flaw in Marxist thought. But this does not mean that the very notion of social classes is wrong or obsolete. Indeed, social classes exist in every society and they are engaged in struggle with each other. Marxism's fundamental error has been to single out and emphasize just this side of the dialectically complex relationship between classes. Marxists saw only struggle while overlooking cooperation and collaboration within society. They were fascinated by concepts of struggle, class hatred, and violence. Probably this obsession with the struggle of the oppressed against the oppressors and with the violent transformation of society lies at the root of the historical failure of Marxism. Society cannot be built on negativist and sterile concepts of hate, struggle, and violent change. But this is not to deny that in many poorer nations—in Latin America, for instance—the underprivileged sectors, driven to desperation by social injustice, may see struggle against those in power as their only hope of breaking out of intolerable misery and hopelessness. Class struggle in diverse forms, then, is likely to be with us until a harmonious and just society is created in the world—and we are very far from that today.

Chapter 2

The End of World Revolution in Latin America

Wayne S. Smith

As we saw in the introduction to this book, Soviet policy in Latin America, except for one disastrous period between 1928 and 1935 (and, one might argue, perhaps again for a few weeks in the fall of 1962), has been neither adventurist nor confrontational. Rather, on grounds that the objective and subjective conditions for revolution did not yet obtain, the Soviets urged the local Communist parties to eschew armed struggle in favor of popular front tactics. The parties were called upon to strengthen their cadres through proselytizing and political indoctrination, to cooperate with other progressive forces, and to get along with the bourgeois governments. In most countries, the parties participated in elections and in other ways acted as legal (if rather unimportant) participants in the national political process. True, Revolution (writ large) remained on the agenda, but for some distant time when the all-important conditions for it had emerged—if they ever did. At least until 1959, popular-front tactics produced, more than anything else, a series of Communist parties that were more interested in survival, in collecting membership dues, and in debates over arcane points of doctrine than in revolution. Badly burned by their brief resort to armed struggle back in the period 1928 to 1935, most of them wanted no part of such adventures again. But then along came Fidel Castro, who having won power with such tactics, urged their adoption throughout the hemisphere. Moscow was reluctant, but once it had accepted him as an ally, it attempted to strike a compromise by authorizing a few Communist parties to go over to armed struggle, most notably in Venezuela. By 1968, however, this half-hearted experiment had ended. In most countries, guerrilla movements had been defeated. Che Guevara had been captured and executed in Bolivia and Communist parties throughout the hemisphere were returning to popular-front tactics. Even Fidel Castro himself soon gave up on efforts to turn the Andes into the Sierra Maestra of Latin America. He gradually halted his support to most of the remaining guerrillas in the region and began reaching out to establish diplomatic and trade relations with the same governments he had once vowed to overthrow.

As we have seen, there was indeed a brief flurry of reassessment after the 1979 Sandinista triumph in Nicaragua. Soviet and Cuban analysts asked themselves: In view of the Nicaragua experience, was not armed struggle, after all, the one true path to power? And, if so, should it not be pushed as the proper tactic all over the hemisphere? But no, the failure of the so-called final offensive of the guerrillas in El Salvador soon pointed up the fallacy of such thoughts, and Soviet and Cuban analysts quickly concluded that what the Sandinista victory really pointed to was not the efficacy of armed struggle but the need for unity among all progressive forces. In other words, the old popular-front tactic had been right; it only needed to be carried out on a greater scale.[1]

By and large, any remaining debate over tactics was put to rest at a meeting of Communist and revolutionary parties held in Havana in 1982. Here, it was agreed that armed struggle remained a valid tactic *so long as the proper conditions obtained*, but that in fact those conditions existed in only two countries: El Salvador and Guatemala.[2] Conditions in Honduras were said to be "ripening," but they did not reach fruition, so Honduras was never added to the list. And Guatemala was removed from the list following the elections there in 1985. Thus, El Salvador became the only country in which Soviet and Cuban analysts agreed that it might be doctrinally correct to support armed struggle. As will be shown in the following chapters, the Soviets nonetheless refrained from such support, and the Cubans soon came to the conclusion that the only feasible way out in El Salvador was via a negotiated settlement.

Tactical Delay as Opposed to Abandonment of Revolution

Still, until Gorbachev's new political thinking, Soviet and Cuban aversion to armed struggle remained tactical in nature, for clearly if one takes the position that armed struggle is inappropriate because the conditions for it do not exist, then by implication one is saying that if the conditions *did* exist, it ought to be tried.

As were Soviet-Cuban tactics, so too were their goals dictated by objective conditions. In a doctrinal sense at least, what they aimed for was not the creation of Socialist states patterned after Cuba, but of full democracies. Strictly speaking, of course, the creation of Socialist states could not be the objective, or at least the immediate objective, because socialism, according to Marx, came about as the result of an inexorable historical process. One could not skip stages along the way. Capitalism grows out of feudalism, and socialism, in turn, would flow out of the class struggle resulting from the internal contradictions of capitalism. As few countries in Latin America were considered to have fully achieved capitalism and bourgeois democracy, the achievement of that stage had to be the immediate objective. Only then could they push on to the construction of socialism.

True, under Khrushchev the Soviets did for a time forget this law of history. In a sense they were forced to do so by the Cuban revolution. Cuba had been considered a semifeudal country ruled by a dictatorship. Yet, without passing through the capitalist-democratic phase, it had, by 1962, been recognized by the Soviet Union as a country already constructing socialism. In order to accommodate the Cuban phenomenon to the doctrinal framework, and to make room in it for other developing countries that might repeat the Cuban experience, the Soviets came up with something called the "non-capitalist path to socialism." It was now possible to bypass the capitalist stage, said Soviet theoreticians, because of the growing strength of the Socialist camp and the consequent change in the correlation of forces in the world.

This distortion of Marxism/Leninism was, it is fair to say, a product of the euphoria of the Khrushchev period with respect to the possibility of crucial gains in the Third World. Like most moments of euphoria, it passed quickly. A number of countries were said to have been on the noncapitalist path to socialism, but with the exception of Cuba none got there. Hence, under Brezhnev's more orthodox stewardship, the whole concept of the noncapitalist path was abandoned. Soviet Latin American area specialists returned to the formulas of the past.[3]

But as the Sandinista victory prompted these specialists to reexamine the tactical prospects for armed struggle, so too did that same event lead Soviet analysts to take another look at objectives. At least a few Soviet area specialists were sufficiently encouraged to argue that a speedy transition to socialism in Latin America might now be possible. They did not argue that the capitalist-bourgeois-democratic stage was unnecessary; rather, their position was that although the immediate objective was indeed full democracy, changed conditions in Latin America had accelerated the historical process and perhaps made it possible to continue on to Socialist revolution in one uninterrupted movement.[4]

Such arguments soon met the same fate as those in favor of armed struggle: they ran up against the reality that neither material conditions nor the correlation of forces had improved so as to place Socialist victory within reach. References to the possibility of rapid transition to socialism in Latin America soon disappeared from Soviet journals. Such a transition was not even deemed possible in Nicaragua. Thus, after one lone reference in *Pravda* in 1983 to Nicaragua's "socialist orientation,"[5] Soviet descriptions of that country slipped back to "democratic," and finally to no more than "progressive."

Cuba had long been described as "an inseparable part of the socialist community of nations."[6] Clearly, Nicaragua was not considered to be part of that community or necessarily even on the way to becoming part of it. Valery Nikolayenko, then Soviet ambassador to Nicaragua, made that absolutely clear. Nicaragua's revolution, he said, was a pluralist one, as contrasted with Cuba's Socialist revolution. Nor, he went on, did Moscow have any interest in drawing Nicaragua closer to the Socialist bloc.[7]

If transition to socialism was not on the agenda even for Nicaragua, much less was it seen as a feasible objective for the rest of Latin America. By 1985, Soviet area specialists were again virtually unanimous in their statements that the objective was full democracy. Transition to socialism was relegated to the category of a distant possibility. Speaking of the Third World in general, for example, a discussion group organized in 1985 by the *World Marxist Review* concluded: "At the present time, the peoples of the developing countries are not fighting for the immediate advent of socialism, although socialism is often viewed as a *feasible historical prospect* [emphasis mine] . . . . Their goal is democracy."[8]

From something that had been seen as a historical inevitability, perhaps even in the near term, the advent of socialism had now dropped back to something that was "often" considered to be "feasible" in a future so distant as to retreat into the abstract. And with Gorbachev's new political thinking, it was downgraded even further. With the events of August 1991, the whole idea has been erased from the Soviet lexicon.

Interestingly, the Cubans had all along been more realistic on the question of socialism as an immediate objective. Fidel Castro himself, for example, was known to have urged the Sandinistas to maintain a pluralist society and a mixed economy, to have good relations with the church, and to keep their lines out to the capitalist West as well as to the socialist East.[9] One may argue that this advice was tactical in nature, and also that the Sandinistas did not always, or even usually, follow it. The point is, however, that it was hardly the kind of advice Castro would have given had he been pushing the idea of immediate transition to socialism.

Nor did other Cuban leaders appear to have been tempted to think such a transition was possible in Central America. In 1983, for example, Cuban Vice President Carlos Rafael Rodriguez stated flatly that "transition to socialism is not today on the agenda in Central America . . . the objective conditions for it . . . do not exist."[10]

Still, as suggested above, until Gorbachev's new political thinking, all this was simply a matter of tactics and an elongated timetable. The conditions for Socialist revolution did not yet exist—nor even the conditions for armed struggle to bring about full democracy—but at some point, it was believed, those conditions *would* develop. The class struggle inherent in the capitalist system would inevitably bring about its downfall. Socialism eventually would triumph all over the world. World revolution and universal communism remained the ultimate goal; it would simply take longer than Marx and Lenin had thought. Thus, Soviet foreign policy, while not pushing for revolution, much less the communization of the hemisphere, for the foreseeable future continued to be based on assumptions of class struggle and the eventual triumph of socialism. World revolution remained on the agenda, however distant its projection.

Abandonment of World Revolution

But as Georgi Mirsky so eloquently argues in Chapter 1, today all that has changed. Soviet leaders have stated categorically that their foreign policy will no longer be based on assumptions of class struggle.[11] Class struggle may continue, but will not necessarily lead to revolution or to socialism, and in any event is the internal affair of the individual country. Moscow is out of the business of trying to extend the Socialist system by force, or, for all practical purposes, by any other means. As former foreign minister Eduard Shevardnadze put it, Soviet foreign policy will henceforth be based on the interests of the Soviet people themselves and will aim for the universal enhancement of peace. The political systems of other countries are none of Moscow's affair; rather, each country must determine its internal arrangements in its own way and without any external pressures. Moscow will remain sympathetic to peoples struggling for national liberation and self-determination, but the last phrase is the controlling one: they must themselves make their decisions and, in the final analysis, win their own fights.[12]

President Gorbachev, moreover, has often reiterated that the Soviet Union will conduct its foreign policy strictly in accordance with international norms and the Charter of the United Nations. It no longer claims to be the instrument of a higher law of history, and thus above the Charter.

In short, as Mirsky has stated in Chapter 1, the world revolution is indeed over. Nor is this simply rhetoric. Moscow's deeds match its words. Even before the reformist victory over the hard-liners in August 1991, there was no evidence that it was fueling regional conflicts, shipping arms to guerrilla groups, or in any other way trying to extend the Socialist system by force or intimidation. Quite the contrary, it had accepted the collapse of socialism in Eastern Europe and allowed those countries to go their own way, even agreeing to the reunification of Germany. As of the end of August 1991, socialism is collapsing in the Soviet Union itself.

Tactical Retreat or Irreversible Change?

Might this not be simply a respite, at the end of which Moscow will return to its quest for world revolution? Hardly. Were it but a tactic, one might point out, it would be perhaps the most expensive in history. But it clearly is not. Once cast down, the ideological tenets cannot be easily restored. Having once acknowledged that there is no "scientifically proven" law of history at work here, that there is no inevitable process leading the world to communism, and thus having undermined the whole foundation of the doctrine, one cannot reverse its collapse with a simple stroke of the pen. And on a different level of perception, having acknowledged that socialism in fact does not work even in the Soviet Union, how can one then hold it up as the standard to which others must strive?

Nor are these the only formerly sacrosanct tenets that have collapsed. Indeed, virtually every ideological spar on which Marxism/Leninism rested has fallen. Perhaps the most central was the theory of the irreversibility of the historical process. The fact that until 1988 no ruling Communist party had ever fallen from power was pointed to as "scientific evidence" that progression from capitalism to socialism could not be reversed and, indeed, as evidence of the validity of the whole doctrinal construct. It is fair to say that the legitimacy of the CPSU's right to rule rested in part on this all-important tenet. Yet that tenet now lies in shreds, its invalidity demonstrated for all to see by the collapse of Communist governments in Eastern Europe and their replacement by democratic ones striving to reinstitute private enterprise. The tenet has collapsed and there is no way to rebuild it. The CPSU itself is now on the way out.

No, the changes wrought by Gorbachev's new political thinking are anything but tactical; they are historic and irreversible, especially in the wake of the abortive conservative coup in August 1991. The idea of world revolution is finished. The Cold War is over. The bipolar world no longer exists. The implications of all this are enormous, not just for the Soviet Union, but for the United States. For more than forty-five years now, "the Russians are coming" has been the cry, and virtually everything the United States has done in Latin America or, for that matter, elsewhere in the world, has been geared to its bitter global rivalry with the Soviet Union. Now that rivalry is over. The kind of security considerations that have shaped US policies since 1945 are no longer relevant. The challenges that once galvanized the United States to action are no more. Thus, US policy, the moral principles on which it rested, and its objectives, are all in need of sweeping review and revision. It is indeed time to throw over Cold War thinking and begin to think in terms of a new world order based on rule of law and strict adherence to the UN Charter. The United States has not yet formed that new mind-set, as evidenced by the 1989 invasion of Panama, which was a blatant violation of the charters of both the United Nations and OAS, and which was condemned by both international bodies. There is more recent evidence, however, to suggest that at least a certain amount of rethinking has begun (such as the President's Enterprise for the Americas Proposal). An excellent way to give such a change of mind impetus would be for the United States to respond in kind to Gorbachev's new political thinking by announcing categorically that henceforth it will conduct its policies toward Latin America in accordance with the UN and OAS charters. Without the security concerns imposed by the Cold War, the United States can now afford to base itself on rule of law, letter, and spirit. If it wishes to retain any claim to moral leadership, it can do no less.

Notes

1. See, for example, Sergo Mikoyan, "Concerning Particular Aspects of the Nicaraguan Revolution," *Latinskaya Amerika*, July 1982, p. 41.

2. *Prensa Latina* dispatches of April 27 and 28, 1982.

3. See, for example, Boris Koval in *Latinskaya Amerika*, No. 6, November–December 1975.

4. The symposium at which such discussions took place is reported in the *World Marxist Review*, October 1984, p. 66.

5. *Pravda*, June 13, 1983.

6. See, for example, the description in *Pravda*, April 8, 1981.

7. *The Washington Post*, November 6, 1988, p. A-42.

8. *World Marxist Review*, December 1985, p. 71.

9. Wayne S. Smith, *The Closest of Enemies* (New York: W.W. Norton, 1987), p. 181.

10. Quoted in *The New York Times*, January 1984, p. 4. See also Jesús Montané Oropesa, in the *World Marxist Review*, November 1985, p. 14.

11. See, for example, the fascinating article by Y. Plimak in *Pravda*, November 14, 1986, in which he calls for a sweeping review of Soviet thinking and says "the need for profound changes is also applicable to the Marxist theory of class struggle." See also *The Washington Post*, October 6, 1988, p. 41.

12. Based on the Russian text of the Schvernadze statement of August 12, 1988.

Chapter 3

Superpowers, the United Nations, and the Post–Cold War Era: More than a Blue Fig Leaf?

Thomas G. Weiss

The Soviet Union has terminated its long-standing support for revolutionary struggles in Latin America and virtually everywhere else in the Third World. Moreover, it has even gone so far as to abandon the basic rationale for involvement in developing countries. The debate among policymakers is spirited, but it is between those who would maintain a limited role for the Soviet Union based on pragmatic calculations of national interest and those who would withdraw immediately and completely from the Third World.[1] Virtually no one argues any longer that the woes of developing countries are part of some heroic patterns of "national liberation" that earlier had provided the pretext for Moscow's involvement. As Robert Legvold has written, "The Soviet Union's revolutionary vocation, greatly transformed over the years, has at last been buried."[2]

However, this generalization resembles others dealing with Moscow's recent changes of heart and policy because it specifies clearly what is *not* Soviet policy. Coming to grips with what Soviet policy actually *is* in Latin America and the Third World is important because so few observers appreciate the extent to which the Soviet Union is surrounded by Third World countries. Indeed, the Soviet Union itself has a number of republics that would definitely qualify for membership in this "club."

What will replace support for world revolution and class struggle? Instead of fomenting instability and vying with Washington for pyrrhic victories in the Third World, three issues have been driving Moscow's policy since Mikhail Gorbachev's ascent to power in 1985. Domestic matters are always a factor, but the Soviet Union is extraordinary at this time because of the extent to which internal concerns are virtually the only explanation for changes in foreign policy. The three domestic elements

44

contributing to the "new thinking" in Soviet foreign policy all reflect a country on the brink of collapse: a burning desire to reduce the costs of empire, the urgent need to concentrate on the governance structure within the union, and finally the public relations requirement to find an appropriate role for a former superpower on the world's stage.

The first two points are no longer debatable and have been addressed consistently by many commentators on both sides.[3] This chapter will address the implications for US foreign policy of the third determinant behind the transformation in Moscow's foreign policy. The Soviet Union has chosen the United Nations as the primary means to remain a player in a drastically altered geopolitical context.

The host of Soviet proposals to rely on multilateral solutions to global problems are genuine,[4] but the principal thrust is to emphasize the Security Council of the United Nations, where Moscow's permanent seat and prominence, like Britain's and France's, is hardly justified by the present global configuration of power. The Soviet Union remains a superpower only because of its nuclear arsenal. What then are the pending problems with a US response to the Soviet desire to make increased use of the world organization, particularly for resolving regional security problems?

The underlying assumption here is that increased Soviet-US cooperation on regional security in the United Nations is in US interests. The momentous changes of 1989 and early 1990 in Eastern Europe and the Soviet Union had temporarily relegated regional conflicts to the periphery of US security calculations, but Iraq's brutal annexation of Kuwait abruptly changed such myopia. The virtuoso diplomacy to construct and maintain the international coalition against Saddam Hussein was only the most dramatic illustration of the UN's utility. Other new peacekeeping operations begun since the end of East-West tensions also met the articulated goals of Washington's foreign policy: removing the Soviets from Afghanistan and the Cubans from Angola, ending the carnage between Iran and Iraq, helping to install a more democratic government in Nicaragua, and securing independence for Namibia.[5]

Rather than repeating in depth how US interests could be served by responding to Soviet overtures in the United Nations and making recommendations about appropriate responses from Washington,[6] this chapter will concentrate on unanswered questions in Washington that impede a more sanguine view about an enhanced UN role in regional security in the 1990s.

The United States is often accused of having too little sense of history. It is worth recalling just how far the United Nations had sunk into the doldrums only a few years ago. A serious possibility of bankruptcy was accompanied by mindless declarations from senior US officials about gleefully waving goodbye to foreign diplomats from the port of New York.

Expectations are now rising much faster than capacities. And the United Nations could fall flat on its face even though cooperation has replaced class struggle as the dominant form of Soviet-US relations in Latin America and the Third World. The euphoria of the last three years—the host of new operations, the 1988 Nobel Peace Prize, the central role in the Gulf and being regularly featured on page one of *The New York Times* and *The Washington Post*—could turn quickly into disillusionment. Ironically, the successful preoccupation with the Gulf—twelve resolutions in the four months after August 1990 moving in a crescendo toward the revival and enforcement of Chapter 7 of the UN Charter—tends to paper over fundamental questions emerging from the UN experience managing regional conflicts over the last four decades.[7]

The remainder of this chapter concentrates on five questions. The author's inability to provide unequivocal responses to them provides a note of caution amidst the flight of doves surrounding the revival of serious discussions of a collective security regime for the Third World.

Does the UN Have Adequate Resources?

The first query relates to a host of rather mundane issues, namely whether the UN will have adequate administrative and financial resources to carry out its peacekeeping tasks professionally. The enormous recent growth in demand on a system that was already overstretched is, to say the least, dangerous. Without adequate attention to management, the UN's reputation will undoubtedly be tarnished and ultimately have a negative impact on possible future assignments in a troubled Latin America and Third World.

The civilian and military sides of the UN secretariat greatly need strengthening. It probably suffices here to say that the peacekeeping budget has increased about fourfold and personnel doubled in the last three years, and there has been no comparable increase in the wherewithal in headquarters to monitor and support operations.[8] The United Nations has been stronger on the political rather than the military aspects of multilateral soldiering. However, as operations become more complex and dangerous, far more attention than at present needs to be paid to the UN's lack of military expertise and independent intelligence-gathering capacities. The United States must reverse its Gramm-Rudmann-Hollings obsession with reducing the UN's conflict management machinery.

Moreover, the lack of adequate financing is now a legendary manifestation of Washington's attempt to keep the United Nations on a short tether.[9] In fact, the world organization has gotten used to juggling what amounts to a year's budget. Over half of the cash-flow problem for the comptroller's office is US arrears. Although Presidents Reagan and Bush have pledged to repay, and there have even been some positive rumblings in Congress, a forthcoming failure or a resolution that irritated a powerful lobby or members of Congress could well lead the United States to renege again on its debts or cut back future UN allocations. International legal commitments, including financial obligations for the United Nations system, have been taken far too lightly by the United States in the last decade.[10] There is little indication that paying its dues is once again viewed as an international obligation rather than a means to ensure that the United Nations behaves according to Washington's expectations. And in relation to financing, all of these problems are acute even before a possible operation in Cambodia, which alone would probably triple the present peacekeeping budget.

Will the UN Advocate Use of Force?

The second question relates to whether we will witness an effective evolution in the traditional UN rules related to the minimum use of force. The range and destructive potential of weapons readily available to governments, rebels, and even rag-tag groups of drug lords provides them with superior firepower over the UN soldiers in blue helmets, whose equipment consists only of light arms to be used in self-defense and as a last resort. Some peacekeeping cognoscente would argue that the United Nations has failed if it resorts to force. But the world organization is being called upon to undertake dangerous assignments. An increasing number of situations into which UN troops are deployed require more first-rate troops, including those of the permanent members.[11] In the past, traditional peacekeeping operations have been staffed mainly by foot soldiers from small and neutral countries.

Moreover, the move toward UN enforcement action actually requires the major powers. Too frequently, the discussion about peacekeeping and enforcement assumes a continuity between the two. In reality, they are very different creatures. Whereas it may be possible for some time to avoid adjusting the rules related to the use of force by traditional peacekeepers, enforcement means the effective projection of military power, as the Gulf crisis so dramatically illustrated.

It is worth noting that military might was not irrelevant when the UN Charter was drafted. Quite the contrary, it was supposed to distinguish the

United Nations from its defunct predecessor, the League of Nations. Secretary of State James A. Baker poignantly recalled this fact while presiding over thirteen other foreign ministers when the Security Council approved resolution 678 and "all necessary means" against Iraq. This international resolve indicated the onset of a new era in which enforcement action against a blatant aggressor may be, for the first time in the postwar period, a viable option. In this context, the use of force by permanent members' troops will be very different from peacekeeping's past.

Can the Security Council Expand?

The third question growing out of the increased reliance by Moscow and Washington on multilateral cooperation in the United Nations rather than on competition in the Third World is whether the Security Council will be able to expand its membership and play a central role in Third World stability. Now that the maintenance of international peace and security is back in fashion, membership in the Security Council will become more pertinent. The only previous constitutional change in the UN Charter occurred in 1965, when membership in the Security Council was augmented to reflect the momentous changes in world politics with decolonization and the birth of the Non-Aligned Movement.

The post–Cold War period certainly rates as an equivalent historical moment that has been ushered in by the collapse of communism in the Soviet Union and Eastern Europe and by the concomitant end of support for revolutionary struggle in the Third World. Japan and a reunified Germany are on the outside of the Security Council, as are such other Third World giants as India, Brazil, Egypt, and Nigeria. A better reflection of twenty-first–century political and economic power will be necessary if the Security Council extends its position as the guarantor of international peace and security anticipated when the Charter was signed more than four-and-a-half decades ago.

In fact, Japan has floated informally a proposal that would call for more permanent members, albeit without veto. Although a constitutional convention to amend the Charter sends chills up the spines of international lawyers and irritates the permanent members, it will become increasingly difficult to finesse or avoid this issue. Facing the new world order that has begun to emerge with the demise of the Cold War will necessitate maturity and foresight from the permanent members, who have enjoyed a monopoly of decisionmaking power that no longer reflects geopolitical realities. There would also be a beneficial demonstration effect in increasing permanent membership along the lines suggested by the Japanese by rewarding countries that have attained great power status without nuclear weapons.

What Will Be the Role of the UN Secretary-General?

The fourth question is whether the UN secretary-general and secretariat itself will be in a position to play an increasingly independent and autonomous role as well as whether governments will tolerate it. On the one hand, UN leadership must say "no" if governments ask the impossible. The United Nations is an *intergovernmental* organization, but there is no need to be slavish, as has often been the interpretation given to the international civil service.[12] In the post–Cold War era, there is need for an augmented capacity in UN headquarters to throw cold water when political, financial, or logistical conditions prohibit professional conduct. The embarrassment resulting from the decision to proceed with the deployment of the UN Transition Assistance Group (UNTAG) in Namibia in April 1989, in spite of inadequate financing and preparations, almost resulted in the unraveling of the first UN operation in Africa since the 1960's ill-fated one in the Congo.

Shoestrings are not the basis on which to conduct business, and the proposed Cambodian operation could well be the new litmus test in this regard.[13] The secretary-general must be willing to stand up to governments and refuse to proceed until all details—political, financial, and logistic—are satisfactorily ironed out. Otherwise, the reputation of the world organization will be tarnished by a fiasco that will ultimately make it less effective in responding to future needs.

In a related way, proposals related to UN efforts to fight drugs and terrorism are much too cavalierly bandied about. The United Nations is not going to be better than great powers at counterinsurgency and at forcefully fighting the plagues of illicit narcotics and terrorism. The secretary-general and his staff must be categorical about their limitations.

On the other hand, they might well expand other tasks more quickly than governments would like. Whereas there remains a reluctance among states, the secretary-general might well lobby actively for an expansion of many highly professional activities. This logic applies particularly to monitoring elections and applying lessons from handling refugees, peacekeeping, and mediation to the challenges in Eastern Europe and even in the Soviet Union.[14] There is greater room for a more extensive and imaginative definition of the acceptable roles for the secretary-general and the secretariat than has been the case before the post–Cold War period.

The next secretary-general will be elected in the autumn of 1991. He (probably not she) should be equipped to be more entrepreneurial and aggressive than his recent predecessors. It is the duty of the United States, the Soviet Union, and other permanent members to be more accepting of outstanding and independent-minded candidates than some of the mediocrities of the past.[15]

What Will be the US Attitude Toward Multilateralism?

Underlying the previous four questions is the fifth and very critical query: What will be the attitude of the United States toward multilateralism, which only a few years ago, and somewhat prematurely it turns out, was pronounced dead?[16]

The momentous changes in the Soviet Union and its policies have been striking. And the United Nations has been a dramatic lens to examine the repercussions on the Third World. In fact, declining support for national liberation struggles and world revolution has accompanied Moscow's embrace of the United Nations, which has led directly to Washington's recent return to the multilateral fold after the unproductive Reagan years of UN-bashing. But there are still serious problems about US expectations and attitudes.

Florence Nightingale was once asked by a royal commission about how to improve hospitals during the Crimean War. She responded that first, hospitals should stop spreading disease. Thus the improved Soviet-US relationship and increased cooperation through the UN's security apparatus is a necessary but hardly sufficient step toward increased Third World stability.

Contrary to the expectations of the architects of the UN Charter, great power entente cannot ensure peace and security in a world where power is diffuse. The events in the Gulf and Panama indicated dramatically that reduced superpower tensions mean neither less conflict nor less intervention by the United States. The fundamental causes of conflict in the Third World are poverty and the nonviability of many governments and elites.[17] These will not disappear simply because of a new warmth between Moscow and Washington.

Most important, neither the US public nor Washington's decision-makers have yet understood the costs of working through the United Nations, although the benefits have become manifest. Alas, the first cost is financial. The United States must be willing to pay—in fact, to pay considerably more and in a more timely manner. There is margin for increases with a per capita US expenditure of a dollar-and-a-half for the UN's regular and peacekeeping budgets combined. Washington's preoccupation with cost cutting appears particularly derisory when the benefits redound so clearly to US foreign policy, as has been the case in Afghanistan, Central America, Iran-Iraq, southwestern Africa, and now the Gulf.

These US foreign policy goals had been pursued unsuccessfully without UN cooperation. Multilateralism is a bargain compared to unproductive and expensive covert and overt operations, not to mention the suffering and lost development prospects of persons caught in proxy wars.[18] The additional costs for one month of Operation Desert Shield— before the aerial bombardment began—were about $1.5 billion; this was the same as one day of combat in the Gulf after the ground war started. This figure is about four times the contribution by the United States to the UN's regular and peacekeeping budgets for all of 1991.

The second cost is some loss of autonomy. US efforts to employ international institutions to roll back Iraqi aggression provide the most striking illustration of the enhanced potential for cooperation to serve US foreign policy. But on several occasions, the Bush administration came very close to exploding the international consensus because of a desire to go its own way. There was the initial rapid deployment, and only afterwards the realization that a blue fig leaf was necessary. And on several occasions since, there has been a palpable impatience with the frustrations of the Security Council. The true test of commitment occurs when one loses, and this is bound to happen sooner or later.

Another way of asking this fundamental question is whether the United States is capable of employing the new methods necessary for this new era. Multilateral diplomacy is slow, public, and inefficient. Compromise is the means and half-loaves are the result. Having international support to reverse Saddam Hussein's adventurism requires the kind of coalition-building and patience that would normally be characterized as "un-American," and certainly not the typical mind-set at the Pentagon or the White House.

Moreover, international standards are meant only to be uniformly applied. Washington continues to maintain an official position that the Iraqi occupation of Kuwait was distinctly different from the Israeli occupation of the Gaza Strip, the West Bank, the Golan Heights, Jerusalem, and southern Lebanon; but such double standards do not sit well. If one is to condemn intervention and occupation, future Grenadas or Panamas are going to create problems. If international law is of consequence, then judgments by the world court in favor of Nicaragua cannot be expediently ignored.

These represent for some the "downside" of multilateralism. The Bush administration and the US public have yet to come to grips with the implications of the post–Cold War world where Third World crises will be solved or exacerbated by multilateral institutions.

Notes

1. For an example of each, see Andrei Urnov, "The Third World and the USSR," *International Affairs*, August 1990, pp. 69–72; and Andrei Kolosov, "Reappraisal of USSR Third World Policy," *International Affairs*, May 1990, pp. 34–42.

2. Robert Legvold, "The Third World and the Superpowers in a Different World," draft paper for a conference organized by the Institute for International Studies of Brown University, December 1990, p. 32. A revised version of this paper, along with others on this theme, is published in Thomas G. Weiss and Meryl A. Kessler, eds., *Third World Security in the Post–Cold War Era* (Boulder, Colo.: Lynne Rienner Publishers, 1991).

3. For a discussion, see Thomas G. Weiss, ed., *The United Nations in Conflict Management: American, Soviet, and Third World Views* (New York: International Peace Academy, 1990); Thomas G. Weiss, ed., *American, Soviet, and Third World Perspectives of Regional Conflicts* (New York: International Peace Academy, 1989); and Mark Katz, *Gorbachev's Military Policy in the Third World* (New York: Praeger, 1989).

4. Edward C. Luck and Tobi Trister Gati, "Gorbachev, The United Nations, and U.S. Policy," *The Washington Quarterly*, vol. 12, no. 4 (Autumn 1988), pp. 19–35.

5. Augustus Richard Norton and Thomas G. Weiss, *U.N. Peacekeepers: Soldiers With a Difference* (New York: Foreign Policy Association, 1990).

6. For an extended discussion, see Thomas G. Weiss and Meryl A. Kessler, "Moscow's U.N. Policy," *Foreign Policy*, No. 79 (Summer 1990), pp. 94–112.

7. For in-depth analyses, see Alan James, *Peacekeeping in International Politics* (London: Macmillan, 1990); John MacKinlay, *The Peacekeepers* (London: Unwin-Hyman, 1989); and a special issue of *Survival*, vol. 32, no. 3 (May/June 1990).

8. For discussions of these problems, see Norton and Weiss; James O. C. Jonah, "The Management of UN Peacekeeping," in Indar Jit Rikhye and Kjell Skjelsbaek, eds., *The United Nations and Peacekeeping: Results, Limitations and Prospects* (London: Macmillan, 1990); and F. T. Liu, *United Nations Peacekeeping: Management and Operations* (New York: International Peace Academy, 1990).

9. Susan R. Mills, *The Financing of United Nations Peacekeeping Operations: The Need for a Sound Financial Basis* (New York: International Peace Academy, 1989), Occasional Paper No. 3; and Alan James, "The Security Council: Paying for Peacekeeping," in David P. Forsythe, ed., *The United Nations in the Global Political Economy* (London: Macmillan, 1989), pp. 13–35.

10. David P. Forsythe, *The Politics of International Law: US Foreign Policy Reconsidered* (Boulder, Colo.: Lynne Rienner Publishers, 1990); and Daniel Patrick Moynihan, *On the Law of Nations* (Cambridge, Mass.: Harvard University Press, 1990).

11. For discussions of the changing military demands of peacekeeping, see Gustav Hagglund, "Peace-keeping in a Modern War Zone," *Survival*, vol. 32, no. 3 (May/June 1990); and John MacKinlay, "Powerful Peacekeepers," *Survival,* vol. 32, no. 3 (May/June 1990), pp. 233–250. For an alternate civilian view, see Robert C. Johansen, "UN Peacekeeping: The Changing Utility of Military Force," *Third World Quarterly*, vol. 12, no. 2 (April 1990), pp. 53–70.

12. For a discussion, see Thomas G. Weiss, *International Bureaucracy* (Lexington, Mass.: Heath, 1975); and David Pitt and Thomas G. Weiss, eds., *The Nature of United Nations Bureaucracies* (London: Croom Helm, 1986).

13. See John MacKinlay, "A Role for the Peacekeeper in Cambodia," *RUSI Journal* (Autumn 1990), pp. 26–30.

14. For an extended discussion of these possibilities, see Thomas G. Weiss and Kurt M. Campbell, "The United Nations and Eastern Europe," *World Policy Journal*, vol. 7, no. 3 (Summer 1990), pp. 575–592.

15. For a discussion of necessary reforms by former senior UN officials, see Brian Urquhart and Erskine Childers, *A World in Need of Leadership: Tomorrow's United Nations* (Uppsala, Sweden: Dag Hammarskjold Foundation, 1990).

16. Thomas L. Hughes, "The Twilight of Internationalism," *Foreign Policy*, no. 61 (Winter 1985–1986), pp. 25–48.

17. Joel Migdal, *Strong Societies and Weak States* (Princeton, N.J.: Princeton University Press, 1988); and Mohammed Ayoob, "The Third World in the System of States: Acute Schizophrenia or Growing Pains?" *International Studies Quarterly*, vol. 33, no. 1 (March 1989), pp. 67–79.

18. Anthony Lake, *After the Wars* (New Brunswick, N.J.: Transaction Publishers, 1990).

Part 2

New Policy
from New Thinking

Chapter 4 _____

An Official Statement of the New Soviet Policy in Latin America
_____ *Valery Nikolayenko*

Any analysis of contemporary Soviet policy toward Latin America should begin with the principles on which it is based, the cornerstone among them being what has come to be called "new political thinking." One of the basic elements here is that of making relations between states less dependent on ideology. In practice, this means that, while we do not repudiate our own views and beliefs, we respect those of other states and wish to join them in building a new world order based on equality of rights, mutual respect, priority of human values, and freedom of choice—in other words, a world order based on principles that have equal significance for all nations regardless of their social and economic systems.

We have already witnessed more than once that any other approach hinders, or even blocks, resolution of today's most important issues, such as promotion of cooperation, the rational use of the fruits of the scientific and technological revolution, overcoming economic backwardness, and, most certainly, liquidation of tensions, removal of nuclear threat, and elimination of militarism.

Today the Soviet Union reaffirms these principles by its actions in Latin America. Our country pursues a policy of friendship and cooperation with Cuba, and values and augments in every way its relations with Mexico, Brazil, Peru, Argentina, and Nicaragua, as well as with other Latin American countries. Eloquent testimonies to this commitment have been visits to the Soviet Union last year by President Collor of Brazil and President Menem of Argentina, reestablishment of diplomatic relations between the Soviet Union and Chile, and establishment of relations with Honduras. Nor is the door closed to diplomatic relations with other Latin American countries.

Although not recognized officially, in the past in Latin America as well as in the other regions there existed a de facto political and ideological face-off between the Soviet Union and the United States. But now confrontation yields more and more to cooperation, above all in the defense of the main human values—the right to life, freedom, and democratic development.

In Latin America, this kind of cooperation has been manifested in the joint Soviet-American efforts to promote political settlements of the Central American conflicts. The main credit for the progress achieved so far, of course, goes to the Central Americans themselves, as well as to Latin Americans in general. But the contribution of the Soviet Union and the United States has also been significant because it led to the creation of appropriate conditions for such a settlement. Characteristically, in recent years our contacts with the US side on Central America have come a long way from a mere exchange of opinions and information to the establishment of constructive interaction and even agreement on a number of critically important aspects of the settlement. The Soviets also have established good communications on these matters with many Latin American and West European governments. Recognition that further confrontation holds no prospect, that it is imperative to find points of mutual understanding and a balance of interests, and, finally, that interaction is necessary has become a common denominator for actions by Latin America, the Soviet Union, and the United States. This applies to the approaches to the improvement of the situation within and around Nicaragua, and now to efforts aimed at a negotiated settlement in El Salvador.

The Soviet Union's constructive position on the Central American issue, and the absence of any self-interest there on its part have contributed to the noticeable enhancement of the prestige and credibility of Soviet foreign policy in Central America and beyond.

From the very beginning, we have assumed that the role of the extraregional states is to help in preparation of regional accords and to ensure the most favorable external conditions for their implementation. Taking that into account, from the beginning the Soviets supported the peacemaking efforts of the Contadora "eight" and, later on, the decisions adopted in Esquipulas and at the subsequent presidential summits of the five Central American states.

The Soviet Union has put forward a number of specific initiatives aimed at the complete cessation or substantial reduction of arms transfers to Central America. As is well known, since the end of 1988 the Soviet Union has unilaterally stopped its supplies of weapons to Nicaragua. Even before the elections there had taken place, we declared our readiness to recognize the outcome, whatever it might be, and to carry on the policy of equitable, mutually beneficial cooperation with the Nicaraguan state. The Soviet side encouraged by every possible means a more active and effective role for the United Nations and for its secretary-general in the process of working out a regional settlement.

The Soviet Union proceeds from the understanding that at this stage—with the elections in Nicaragua having been held, the new government there having been installed, and the problem of the contras having been practically resolved—the center of regional tension has shifted to El Salvador. Thus, we believe that the main thrust of efforts toward a settlement should be aimed at finding ways to stop armed confrontation and at ensuring reliable guarantees for insurgents who lay down their arms. We also believe that the Geneva and Caracas accords provide the basis for this, if the conflicting parties will only recognize the need to make mutual concessions and reasonable compromises. We have sought to convey this point of view both to the FMLN leadership and the Salvadoran government, with which we have established direct contacts.

We believe that for political settlements in the region to become irreversible, an urgent solution has to be found also to the problem of providing Central American nations with effective international assistance to rebuild their economies. In that regard, we express readiness to continue and expand our bilateral cooperation with Central America as well as to take part in the multilateral efforts, aimed at reaching the aforementioned goals. For example, we participated in the donors' conference on Nicaragua in Rome, and we have raised the level of our participation at the next meeting, in Paris.

Similarly, we see real possibilities for the nonconfrontational resolution of other conflict situations in the region, including first of all the US-Cuba face-off, as well as the territorial dispute between the United Kingdom and Argentina. The Soviet Union is ready to assist and support such solutions however it is able.

We are actively assisting in the demilitarization process in Central America, and we fully support the proposal to create a zone of peace, security, and cooperation there as well as in the South Atlantic. We also advocate nonproliferation in Latin America. At the same time, we share the opinion expressed by many Latin American leaders, among them President Callejas of Honduras, that the genuine security of a nation is not limited to its military component, but also involves economic, social, and ecological aspects.

In more general terms, our experience in Latin America proves that the end of East-West confrontation has brought greater trust and openness and removed a number of irrational obstacles to dialogue and cooperation. It has, in short, had a decidedly positive impact in the international community. We are in favor of freedom of choice, but we believe that this freedom should not be taken as an excuse to act irresponsibly or violently, whatever the religious, nationalist, or ethnic pretexts.

I would like to stress that democratization processes in Latin America enjoy our full support, wherever they take place—in Chile, Paraguay, Haiti, or other states—because these processes create the necessary conditions for adequate political, social, and economic development, and help the countries to incorporate themselves more actively into various spheres of international associations and interaction.

Within the context of human values, we view the whole issue of human rights as being of great importance. It is the totality of rights that we are talking about—the totality that is not subject to any exemptions or "double standards" in evaluating the human rights situation of a country. In the past, we were reluctant to discuss this issue when it concerned our country, and, at the same time, we were extremely cautious about the issue as it applied to other countries. The motives were simple: not to interfere in the internal affairs of other nations, or even in purely ideological considerations. Sometimes also it reflected a reluctance to damage our bilateral relations. That is exactly the reason why we did not emphasize the human rights situation, for instance, in Argentina, when the previous military regime openly trampled on human rights. Now the issue of human rights is no longer taboo in Soviet foreign policy. It is discussed as a natural component of bilateral relations and as a way to find common approaches that can ensure the real implementation of all pertinent norms of international law. This certainly reinforces the thesis that foreign policy is the extension of domestic policy.

Artificial barriers to the discussion with Latin American countries of other issues, such as terrorism, narcotics, and mutual guarantees for investments, also are being removed.

Our understanding of the present stage of the revolutionary movement in Latin America, that is, of the popular struggle for freedom, democracy, and social progress, is as follows. First of all, one has to note that the world we now live in is drastically different from that of, for instance, forty years ago. And this process of change goes on. Deep social changes have brought to life new political forces, new social movements, and new currents in ideology. They reflect an aspiration for independence, democracy, equality, and social justice. These ideas have transformed themselves into real and powerful factors in world politics. They cannot but evoke sympathy and support.

Clearly, the process of democratization and revolutionary change in different countries is of varied scope, orientation, and results. We must keep in mind that the revolutions in Cuba and Nicaragua had their roots in the social and economic conditions of those countries. The people came forward to build a just and humane society, which they thought would guarantee a decent living and freedom from outside interference and pressure.

Regrettably, the realization of this noble purpose was from the very start subject to acute political battles and internal and external confrontations. All that could not but influence the forms and ways by which the set goals have been realized as well as the degree to which they have been achieved. Moreover, it led to a "besieged fortress" situation, or to certain self-isolation. This undoubtedly lowered the ability of these countries to perceive the new aspects of international life and to react adequately to the current realities.

Practice shows that today, be it in Latin America or in other parts of the world, it is almost impossible to maintain a "closed" society. On the other hand, the unjustified claims of the right to dictate to the peoples—to create around them artificial barriers of a political, economic, or any other nature aimed at changing their societies—should be dropped. To help them integrate fully into regional and global associations is a far more noble and rewarding task, worthy of the modern civilized world community.

Regarding relations with Cuba—we value our friendship with this country and we plan to develop further our historically established links with it. The Soviet-Cuban summit in Havana in April 1989 and the Soviet-Cuban treaty of friendship and cooperation signed there provided new impetus to these links. The treaty, of course, does not jeopardize the interests of any third countries.

Concerning the US trade and economic blockade of Cuba, already an anachronism and practically the last outcry of the Cold War, the Soviets continue to be the main support for the Cuban people in the area of economic development, although there have been miscalculations and mistakes in that regard. At the same time, we openly speak of our intention to move this cooperation to a new level, adequate to the imperatives of today. Our economic relations with Cuba will be streamlined to ensure maximum mutual benefits for both parties. This should not be taken as the consequence of attempts to exert influence on us from outside.

Soviet military cooperation with Cuba is a consequence of the external threat to the security of that country. That is why the nature and the scope of our military assistance to Havana will depend on the degree to which this threat will decrease—on whether the normalization of Cuban-US relations will begin.

Our relations with Cuba are, in fact, undergoing a complicated process of adapting to new conditions, but it would be completely wrong to say that some kind of crisis is breeding in them.

One more point needs to be stressed. We are gratified by the fact that in many countries, particularly in Latin America, there is growing understanding that it is necessary to increase efforts aimed at lessening tension around Cuba and normalizing Cuban-US relations. I believe that such actions are in the interest of all countries of our modern interdependent world, including the United States.

One of the most notable characteristics of the political and diplomatic setting in Latin America today is, undoubtedly, the dynamic development of regional integration. A growing number of nations are joining the process because they believe, and justifiably so, that this opens up additional possibilities for joint solutions to the difficult social and economic problems and helps create conditions for the accelerated development of the region.

This is a positive phenomenon, which, to our mind, increases the prospects for solving Latin America's economic, financial, trade, and ecological problems. It also contributes to the forging of international links in the Western Hemisphere and in the world at large. With that in mind, it is interesting that Washington appears to have launched its own search for a new, adequate approach to inter-American relations and its role in them. At least that is an impression one gets from analyzing the Enterprise for the Americas proposal put forward by President Bush. Time will show whether it is true, but already it is possible to agree with many Latin Americans who view the US initiative as a starting point for an equitable inter-American dialogue.

The evident strengthening of multilateralism in the diplomacy and external economic policy of the Latin American countries quite naturally refracts into the ever-growing diversity of our contacts with the region and into our desire to develop mutually beneficial cooperation not only with individual countries but with their groupings as well. Our involvement in the developing dialogue between the countries of Eastern and Central Europe and the nations of the Rio group is a new and important element of our relations with Latin America. Within that framework our foreign ministers have already met twice, in Budapest and in New York; the next meeting is planned for 1991 in Buenos Aires. There is a consensus that the further exchange of opinions, ideas, and proposals creates an impressive platform for our foreign policy and for financial and economic interaction to assure progress and the resolution of global problems.

Our intention to establish mutually beneficial cooperation with one of the oldest regional organizations—the Organization of American States—has the same perspective. It results logically from the positive accomplishments over recent years in our bilateral relations with the OAS member countries. We also give credit to the constructive processes within the organization itself, which reinforce its potential to be the central political forum of the Americas and the principal instrument of inter-American accord, and which have involved all the countries of the Western Hemisphere without exception in mutually advantageous dialogue and cooperation. We are convinced that the OAS can complement and reinforce the efforts of the United Nations to build a structure of global security.

Regarding the general aspects of Soviet policy in Latin America, the following important consideration must be mentioned. With all the movement toward integration in many parts of the world, be it in Latin America or in Europe, it seems that there is a growing comprehension that regional integration should not isolate and dissociate nations. That is exactly the reason why we see in the experience already gained in interregional contacts the contours of future links between the two continents— America and Europe. From this point of view, the dialogue between the Rio group and the European Community is important. It is conceivable that the approaching quincentennial of "The Encounter of Two Worlds" may very well give an additional momentum to bringing the two continents together. We hope that within that framework we will join the nations of the Americas in discovering new horizons of cooperation in today's interdependent world.

Strengthening the channels of interregional cooperation presents us, I believe, with one more area where mutual involvement by the Soviet Union and the United States is quite promising. It is already a matter of record that our countries have accumulated substantial experience in working together to advance the European process and to build new structures of security and cooperation in Europe. So there is reason to believe that the Soviet-US effort could help to find meeting points of the "common European home" and the new inter-American system that will enable us to create a lasting and effective foundation for global, political, trade, and economic interaction.

The processes under way in the international arena have dramatically changed the political map of the world. Increased attention is drawn to the Pacific region where an intensive regrouping of forces and interests is taking place. A system of international cooperation is emerging there, and it draws into its orbit virtually all the nations of the Pacific region, including the Latin American countries, many of which border the Pacific.

This tendency calls for new approaches to international relations in this part of the world, based on the concept of the unified Pacific area. Certain ideas on the matter have already been developed. These include the widely known speeches of President Gorbachev in Vladivostok and Krasnoyarsk and the documents of the international meeting of experts in Vladivostok.

We believe that the foreign policy vector of many Latin American countries turns to the Pacific. It is our opinion that on the issues of ensuring peace and security in the region, on arms control, ecology, and combating illegal narcotics trafficking we should support the positions they take within various international organizations, particularly at the Conference on Economic Cooperation in the Pacific.

The evolution in recent years of our views on the problems of the world economy involved certain changes in our approach to bilateral trade and economic cooperation in general and with the Latin Americans in particular. The Soviet Union finds it necessary to move away from ideological confrontation over the issues of social and economic development and toward universal interaction aimed at perfecting international economic relations. We are talking about implementing the principles of global consensus on the development of multilateral economic cooperation in the interest of all nations. Hence, it is only logical that the Soviet Union applies the same principles of balance of interests, justice, and mutual benefit to its bilateral economic relations with Latin America.

In order to arrive at this position we had to discard the dogmatic views that were predominant in our policy in the past. In many ways, the changes in Soviet policy are similar to the changes taking place in Latin America. In that sense, the objective conditions exist for the useful exchange of experience and for establishing cooperation and interaction in various fields. The steps toward making the Soviet economy more open and market oriented favor that process.

We are reviewing many previous approaches to external economic links, such as the import of capital. Today we think that with due regulatory measures by the state, the Soviet economy could fruitfully use financial inputs as well as the technological and administrative experience of foreign companies. Already we are putting into practice the principle of granting foreign investors the same privileges as Soviet members of the business community. This creates good options for the development of new models of economic partnership between Latin American countries and the Soviet Union, for the establishment of joint ventures in our countries, and for multilateral investments by Latin Americans in the Soviet economy. Naturally, the agenda of our relations with Latin American nations includes the issue of working out the agreements on mutual guarantees for investments.

At the present stage of deep reforms in the economy of the Soviet Union and of many states of Latin America, the development of external economic cooperation runs into considerable difficulties. But there is mutual understanding that these are the difficulties of growth. With the deepening of reforms, real possibilities for extending cooperation into new spheres will appear. That is why we understand our task to be one of seeking new perspectives, forms, and tendencies in various spheres of economic, trade, scientific, and technical research.

The integration of the Soviet Union into the world economy creates favorable conditions for economic and financial cooperation between various groups of states and for Soviet–Latin American cooperation. At the same time, there are those who say that the improvement of East-West relations may adversely affect the economic situation of the developing countries, leading to the reduction of the credits and investments received by these countries.

Our country, however, does not intend to "develop on credit," counting on foreign assistance to do wonders and solve all our problems. On the contrary, we intend to draw on external support only as an auxiliary—but not decisive—element of national development, the basis of which remains the effective utilization of our domestic potential.

According to our estimates, the commercial credits and loans that the Soviet Union is receiving today cannot and should not significantly influence international financial markets and the total level of liquidity. That would be contrary to our interests. At the same time, these credits and loans objectively contribute to the formation of a new consumer market in the Soviet Union, which, in turn, could be used—and is already being used—by many countries of the world including the Latin American nations.

If there were mutual Soviet and US interest in doing so, our two countries could possibly agree to cooperate on trade and economic issues in Latin America. And that could extend to the establishment of joint ventures in Third World countries, to the coordination of development assistance to Nicaragua, and so on. The results and benefits for the Latin American, US, and Soviet participants in such a joint effort might be most interesting.

In concluding this review of Soviet policy in Latin America, I would like to note that regional problems are on the agenda of the developing Soviet-US dialogue: they feature prominently in our contacts at the highest level as well as between our foreign policy institutions. For a long time, and for obvious reasons, our consultations have focused on Central America. Meanwhile, there exists a natural interest in widening the scope of our exchange to cover the whole specter of problems of Latin America, particularly its role in world affairs. We are open to productive exchange of ideas on this subject. We also believe that it would be useful to supplement the steps by our governments in this direction with wider contacts between our academic communities. This would enable both sides to work more productively and profoundly on their respective foreign policy approaches and to analyze more thoroughly those processes in the Western Hemisphere that have a growing influence on diplomacy and the world economy.

Chapter 5

A New Soviet Perspective
Karen Brutents

The Soviet Union is now reviewing its Latin American policy, as well as its foreign policy in general. This has already brought significant changes, but the process is by no means finished. There is certainly no question of having second thoughts about such principles as respect for the independence of other countries, equality of rights, noninterference in their internal affairs, and support for the aspiration of Latin American countries to play a more substantial role in the world. These principles will remain central to our policy.

What is being undertaken is to overhaul that policy on the basis of universally accepted human values and to abandon approaches based on ideology, narrow alliance commitments, and global strategies, which were very important in the past but are no longer important. The aim now is to adapt Soviet policies to the realities of the modern world and engender them with a new world outlook.

But before we proceed to analyze the outcomes of these shifts in political and ideological outlook, there is a need to describe the setting for the Latin America policy of the Soviet Union and our current assessments of the situation in Latin America. These assessments have also undergone change.

Latin America has long been considered as part of the Third World— and is considered so now by many specialists. This perception is open to argument, all the more so because the very notion of a Third World seems now to be up for critical review.

To a significant degree, the idea of a Third World was born of a world divided into two competing blocs. Presently, we witness the disintegration of this pattern of international relations and a new realignment of forces in a world that appears to take on a multipolar shape. Besides, this notion is also being critically tested by current economic processes.

However, Latin America is still characterized by all the typical Third World problems, including economic underdevelopment; explosive demographic processes; glaring social antagonisms; difficulties in adjusting its culture and civilization to modern science, technology, and morals; and an unfulfilled aspiration to national self-assertion and independence. Regrettably, during the 1980s these problems had not been resolved; nor, indeed, had decisive progress been made toward resolving them. In fact, some of them have been exacerbated, and new difficulties and even dangers have arisen. In spite of that, this part of the world, like all other regions—for all the zigzags and reverses, for all the difficulties and even convulsions—is experiencing the irrepressible development of processes in the course of which a new Latin America is being born that is likely to occupy a much more prominent place in the world than it does today.

The diversity of Latin America makes it impossible to devise general formulas that would be valid to assess processes taking place in all the countries of the continent. There is nonetheless good reason to identify a number of general dimensions and peculiarities special to the new situation and that are characteristic of, and common to, these processes.

One of these is the strong and still growing tendency toward the democratization of state administration and society. The 1980s saw a transformation of the continent's political scene with the military dictatorships in Chile, Argentina, Uruguay, Paraguay, Bolivia, Guatemala, Honduras, and Haiti ousted from power and a civilian government established also in Brazil. The sources of this tendency are the growth of the middle class and skilled manpower, plus the moral, political, and sometimes economic bankruptcy of dictatorships, and the influence of the democratization wave that has swept through many countries across the world. An important factor is that in the past the Soviet-US confrontation had led the United States to support the most macabre of dictatorial regimes.

At present, and probably for the first time in history, constitutional governments have been formed in nearly all countries of Latin America. Although in many cases democratic procedures are seriously flawed, this biggest and, on the whole, most irreversible shift has ushered in a new period in the life of Latin America and will undoubtedly have a profound effect on the overall development of the continent.

The bourgeois politicians who have risen to power in the continent's leading countries have a number of significant traits in common. All of them come from the opposition and have campaigned under democratic slogans that brought them victory in elections. Many are dynamic and strong willed, pragmatic in tackling complicated issues, good mixers, and possess an image that is attractive to the people.

Certainly, the establishment of civilian rule does not eliminate the sharp political divisions, including those that relate to the fundamental principles of state organization. Even now the continent's various political forces often hold totally divergent views about how their countries should develop. Indeed, democracy itself becomes the arena where these differences reveal themselves. The views about essential elements, functions, goals, and limits advocated by the usually neoliberal ruling elite differ to a large degree from those held by the left-center and the right-center, to say nothing of certain sections of the middle class, the working class, and fringe groups. Nonetheless, the constitutional order—and this is an especially important new element—creates the necessary political environment for the evolution and reconciliation of these differences, for abandoning the Latin American tradition of settling matters through the use of force, and for the setting up of conditions for reaching a widely based consensus on key issues. If these conditions are taken advantage of, and the democratic process develops in a sustained manner, then it will be fair to say that the continent has entered a phase in which forces across the political spectrum have abandoned armed struggle as a method of attaining their goals.

In recent years, determined efforts have been made in Latin America to develop the area's productive forces through the achievements of the technological revolution. Experts differ in their assessments of the results obtained in the 1980s in this area. Some believe that this period has been a lost decade, citing the growing indebtedness, runaway inflation, and the plight of the poorest nations. In the view of others, the region, in spite of profound economic and social crises that hit it in the early 1980s, has made unquestionable progress.

The latter point of view seems to be more correct. Latin America accounts today for approximately half of the industrial output of developing countries. Although it has not as yet been deeply involved in the technological revolution occurring today and has been only superficially affected by the information revolution, the continent has already built up highly developed electronic, aviation, and motor industries, and as well has been involved in the newest branches of chemistry, pharmaceuticals, and biotechnology. Half of the direct foreign investments in the Third World have been made in Latin America. Several Latin American countries, with Brazil and Mexico in the lead, are among the ten capitalist countries with the largest gross domestic product (GDP), and these countries are taking the first steps to cross the line separating their still "slow" (a term used by Alvin Toffler) economies from the "fast" Western economies. Some of the other countries of the region, although lagging somewhat behind, have developed their own industrial base, and their national industries have firmly established themselves in the domestic and external markets.

For all that, the economic sphere is also beset by serious unresolved contradictions. Alarm is voiced in Latin America, often not without reason, at the fact that the neoliberal development model, implemented according to scenarios written by transnational corporations, primarily serves the interests of the latter while neglecting the needs of the nations themselves. Alarm is fueled by the fact that Latin American countries have shown increasing technological and financial dependence on transnational corporations and unilateral attachment to the US market. Also of concern are the excessive role of foreign investment and the huge profits exported by foreign investors. To sum it all up, the point at issue is that the nature and ways of Latin America's economic development are as yet determined to a large degree not by Latin Americans themselves but by the world economic and financial power centers (especially given the region's immense foreign debt). Therefore the continent's integration into the world economy is taking place on an inequitable basis.

Another equally important point is that the economic progress of the 1980s was achieved at a high cost. It aggravated imbalances in the continent's development and placed an increasingly heavy burden on the bulk of a population that already faced virtual social regression.

The countries of the region have accumulated some experience with economic integration. The Latin American Economic System, which is the first economic organization in the Western Hemisphere without US participation, is increasingly active. At the initiative of Brazil and Argentina, an agreement has been signed that envisages the setting up of a "common market" whose other members are Uruguay and Paraguay. Attempts are under way to revive the Central American Common Market. A similar tendency has become apparent in the Caribbean. All this warrants the conclusion that a new level of regional economic integration and cooperation is emerging.

Greater emphasis on economic ties with Japan, Western Europe, the countries of the Asian and Pacific region, and Africa is further evidence of the intention to consolidate the basis for independent development, expand and diversify foreign economic ties, and assume a role in the international division of labor that would correspond to the potential of Latin America.

Greater cooperation is apparent in the political sphere as well, as evidenced by the activities of the Group of Eight and the Group of Central American states, among others.

We are by no means overestimating the advances made in the process of economic integration; we are aware that it is unfolding with difficulty, hindered by "national egoisms," different levels of development, the various specific features of the economies of individual countries, and, finally, by certain external resistance. Also, a difficult question arises with respect to the interrelation and connections between the process of Latin American integration, which is already under way and will have as its end result the establishment of a "common market," and the US-advocated plans to set up an "area of free trade" encompassing both Americas. The continent's political leaders and experts are understandably worried about the place the Latin American states, with their as yet considerably smaller economic potential, would have within such an "area."

The democratic processes in Latin America, combined with the acceptance of the neoliberal development model, result in more open economic relations. This gives Latin American countries significant advantages, but it appears also to make them more vulnerable to their stronger economic partners. There exists, though, the point of view that this kind of dependence is inevitable and, in any case, preferable to the cruder and harsher forms it assumed in the past.

Important changes have occurred in Latin America's foreign policies. It is now anything but the "province of the world." The isolation of the countries of the region within the Pan-American system, which had persisted over many decades, as well as their noticeable isolation from the mainstream of international life are now things of the past. The increasing tendency of Latin American countries to expand, diversify, and globalize their international ties, while reflecting their growing potential, is at the same time clearly motivated by their eagerness to enhance their independence.

Latin Americans are now effectively involved in the discussion of all major issues of world politics. Characteristically, of the six nations that have launched internationally publicized initiatives in the field of nuclear disarmament, two—Mexico and Argentina—are Latin American.

Both political circles and the peoples of the continent are increasingly aware of the connection between, on the one hand, safeguarding their right to their own political and social choices in addressing such evils as poverty, famine, and illicit traffic in drugs, and, on the other hand, strengthened peace, international security, and the democratic restructuring of international relations. Latin American governments are pursuing a more clear-cut policy in support of the principles of national self-determination, noninterference in other countries' internal affairs, and peaceful settlement of conflicts.

The greater independence of Latin American states has been strikingly exemplified by their concerted policy to bring about a peaceful Central American settlement. It has also been reflected in the way the Group of Eight is becoming an influential force in the Western Hemisphere. The meetings of the Group may be seen as an important stage of identifying the sphere of common interests of the region's leading countries seeking to draw up common foreign policy approaches. There is reason to believe that the acquired positive experience of successful joint actions, as well as the region's needs related primarily to efforts aimed at attaining a more fair status of the continent in the world economy, will continue to stimulate a Latin American consensus.

North-South relations will continue to occupy a prominent place in the foreign policy priorities of Latin America. While welcoming East-West rapprochement, Latin Americans are expressing apprehension lest it result in diminished attention to their problems. They point out that the North-South dialogue has not as yet received sufficient impetus, let alone yielded tangible results. Latin Americans would like to see a balance between the interests of the East, the West, and the South.

It would seem that as the world grows increasingly aware of its global interdependence, the role of Latin America will be felt more and more clearly. The lungs of our planet, after all, are situated in the Amazon basin.

Latin America's increasing activity in the sphere of foreign policy has not been smooth by any means; rather, it is impeded by a number of adverse factors. Among them are the unabated rivalry between some countries of the continent, the long-standing tradition of regional isolationism, the scarcely developed habit of reconciling different views, and finally the tendency, observed especially after the war in the Gulf, toward the establishment of the so-called "one-pole" world.

As is clear from the above—which is far from a comprehensive account of all the important issues of today's Latin America—there are now many new developments in the life of the continent that coexist with old contradictions and evils. It is this singular combination of dynamic new elements, with still powerful old elements, that marks the peculiarity of modern Latin America. Casting a shadow over all are its continuing social ills, such as the poverty of the bulk of the population and the lack of progress in resolving such vital social problems as education and health care. It is obvious, for example, that the movement toward a more democratic and humane society remains a fragile process, which could be cut short at any moment if it is not underpinned by sustained economic growth leading to a gradual improvement in the standards of living of the people.

An acute problem for Latin America is posed by the narcotics business. However, in this case as well—apart from the role of the United States, which is the main market for the drugs and therefore stimulates this deadly trade—the issues to be addressed are, above all, social; that is, the pauperized peasants who are the principal producers of coca, marijuana, and opium poppy must be assured some other mode of existence. One other increasingly pressing problem—ecology—likewise has a social motivation. The underlying reasons are both internal, as in the plundering of natural resources, and external, as in the transfer of environmentally hazardous processes from the developed capitalist countries.

All this notwithstanding, and being fully aware of the existing difficulties, complexities, and contradictions, we nonetheless proceed from the assumption that Latin America has become involved in an irreversible process of change and will at an ever more rapid pace be drawn into the mainstream of international life as an important and active participant. More than that, we should believe that Latin America will become one of the regions from which the new superpowers of the twenty-first century will emerge.

The pace of this process and its very nature will, of course, depend not only on Latin Americans themselves, but also on the approaches of the world community, primarily the North, to the problems of this region. Latin America will have to endure a sort of a competition with time itself. It faces the danger of falling irrevocably behind the group of leading countries. However, it has the necessary prerequisites to achieve success.

Throughout the Cold War period the policy of the Soviet Union in Latin America, as, indeed, in other regions of the world, was guided by two sets of motivations: the global confrontation with the United States and ideological commitments. At the practical level, these were closely linked to one other and were interrelated, although differing in importance in different specific cases and in different periods.

This can be illustrated, for example, by the line taken by the Soviet Union with respect to the independence of Latin American countries. As a matter of principle, and in conformity with our ideology, we showed solidarity with the national-liberation and nationalist aspirations of Latin American countries and supported their policies aimed at the strengthening of state independence. Practical considerations guided us in the same direction. As a superpower that sought to counter the pressure of the United States and at the same time contest its global ambitions and positions, the Soviet Union understandably believed that it was in its interests if Latin American states achieved greater independence and freed themselves of the dominating influence of the Soviet Union's rival. In this context we of course had great sympathy for the anti-US feelings that were common enough on the continent and were closely related to nationalist sentiments. Like the United States, we at the time believed that everything that was bad for our rival was good for us.

Certainly, this singular harmony of ideological and practical geopolitical considerations did not occur very frequently. Often one kind of consideration took precedence over the other. It must be stressed that the geostrategic component our relations with Latin America had with respect to the United States had an effectively defensive character. It was not a question of seeking to establish ourselves on the continent to secure some kind of bridgehead, but rather of undertaking diversionary maneuvers, attempting to neutralize or to offset the activities of the United States in other regions. The Latin American states were quick to grasp the essence of this game and the ensuing advantages to be enjoyed. If the Soviet Union, by drawing the attention of the United States to its presence in the region (which, by the way, was not very significant), wanted to lessen the US pressure, Latin American countries, for their part, sought to use the "Soviet card" to get extra room for maneuver and to obtain concessions from their northern neighbor. In short, important fundamental principles—the recognition of the right of nations to self-determination, independence, and equality; special treatment of countries that had experienced colonial or semicolonial domination; and, finally, a firm policy of supporting social progress—certainly played a positive role in determining the content of the Latin America policy of the Soviet Union, and in the final analysis served the interests of the Latin American countries.

On the other hand, our belief in the universal applicability of our ideology and our desire to prove its superiority over the ideology of the rival and his "henchmen" in the Western Hemisphere—all this resulted in the fundamental postulates of our policy sometimes being used without adequate analysis of the nature of the processes occurring in some Latin American countries. These same motives led us in some cases to turn a blind eye to the striking discrepancies between the course of events in these countries and our own ideological precepts. This was especially the case if this or that government began to behave in an anti-US manner.

Also, we must recognize that not all forms of our support for progressive movements proved effective in the final analysis, especially when they followed only the logic of force inherent in the development of internal processes in Latin American countries. At the same time, we must firmly dismiss allegations about the notorious "hand of Moscow", which were widespread enough at the time and are even now sometimes repeated. The Soviet Union has never been and could not have been the "parent" of any political movements or parties in Latin America. Neither did we choose the form of struggle that was used.

The relations between states were much less affected by the ideological orientation of our policy than were contacts with various nongovernmental organizations, such as, for instance, solidarity movements, peace activists, and feminist, youth, or trade union movements. But even in these cases, it would be a simplification to see nothing but the wish to "tease Uncle Sam." However it may sound today, we were motivated by a sincere commitment to the ideals of national freedom and social progress. As for the comparatively well-established cultural and humanitarian ties, the main motivation was to use wide exchanges to encourage efforts to preserve original cultural values in the face of an onslaught of US mass culture.

An overall assessment of Soviet-Latin American relations in the 1970s and 1980s shows considerable expansion in almost all spheres. The number of countries with which the Soviet Union enjoys friendly ties has grown, the level of political cooperation has risen, mutual understanding has become deeper, and a coincidence of the points of view on a number of key international issues has been identified. The Soviet Union's views on the maintenance of peace and the setting up of a comprehensive system of international security are particularly in concert with those of Latin America. There also has been an upsurge in the efforts to find ways of expanding economic relations. Although those efforts have not always met with success, a number of agreements have been signed.

A peculiar situation has taken shape in this area. Trade and economic ties have remained at a low level. A number of exceptions have been the Soviet purchases of agricultural products from Argentina, our fishing in Peruvian waters, shipments of Soviet military materiel to Peru, as well as purchases of small amounts of bananas and coffee from Latin America. At the same time, the absence of competition between the products of the Soviet Union (except petroleum) and of Latin America in the markets of other countries ruled out any trade conflict and strengthened the chances of cooperation in the world arena. In other words, in the area of trade and economy, a situation exists in which bilateral relations are not so important as concerted actions in the multilateral arena.

The Soviet Union's current policy in Latin America is and will be guided by its considerably changed motives. We have effectively banished from our political and diplomatic practice those elements that only recently were inseparably linked with the image of a superpower: ideological messianism, global confrontation with the United States and its allies, excessive armaments, and the view that force was central to the conduct of international relations.

With respect to Latin America, this means that we no longer consider it, or the other regions of the world, as the object of confrontation with the United States (and we are hopeful that the United States will pursue the same line). Although this part of the world has suffered to a smaller degree than others from East-West confrontation, such a shift will undoubtedly have a positive impact even here. The Soviet leadership has declared that it has no strategic interests in Latin America and will resolutely follow this course.

At least two events in the process of perestroika may be considered as key indicators with respect to Latin America and to the United States. The first such event is the statement by Gorbachev during his April 1989 visit to Cuba—his first visit to Latin America—in which he said that "the Latin American continent, as, indeed, all others, must not be an arena for rivalry between East and West."

The other event occurred later, during the summit meeting on Malta in December 1989, when we finally made the difficult acknowledgment that the Soviet Union no longer considers the United States its enemy.

We are stripping our policy of ideological patterns and laying down instead human values as our policy foundation. But this does not necessarily mean that we will abandon or somehow depart from such principles of intergovernmental relations as equality, mutual respect, noninterference in domestic affairs, nonuse of force, and solidarity with aspirations of national independence. On the contrary, we will adhere to these principles more closely than ever in our relations with the Latin American countries.

At the same time, recent experience shows that priority in our policy will be given to such aspects as support for peaceful efforts in solving regional problems, clear-cut commitment to political settlement of disputes and conflicts, and a businesslike approach toward economic cooperation. This is seen clearly in the attitude of the Soviet Union regarding elections in Nicaragua and in the active Soviet efforts to bring peace to El Salvador and to Central America as a whole.

Democratization of social and political life on the continent—the unfolding of perestroika and new political thinking in the Soviet Union—pave the way for revitalizing international intercourse between the Soviet Union and Latin American countries.

The increased role of public opinion in the Soviet Union constitutes a new feature in shaping relations between our country and Latin America. Our partners in Latin America as well as in other regions of the world will now have to take heed of the view expressed by our parliamentary institutions, mass media, and the population itself as regards our relations with them. A deeper understanding of our policy on the part of the Soviet population will undoubtedly strengthen the basis for more solid and enduring relationships between our country and others.

The active policy pursued by many Latin American states to eliminate the nuclear threat and prevent an arms race in outer space, their willingness to democratize international relations and to reject policies based on force, and the harmony of views between these states and the Soviet Union on the external debt problem—all these factors provide a good basis for furthering our relations. The Soviet Union intends to work closely with the Latin American countries to address more effectively problems that are generated by planetary interdependence, such as environmental protection. This interdependence may become a key element in the relations between the Soviet Union and the Latin American countries in the not so distant future. And, finally, it is also important that the improvement in Soviet-US relations creates a more favorable environment for the rapprochement between the Soviet Union and Latin America.

Of course, the trend for bettering the international and regional climate will not remove all problems and obstacles between the Soviet Union and Latin American countries. In this connection, the evolution of the domestic processes in the Soviet Union will be of special importance, determining in large measure its capabilities in the field of external policy.

At a time when the Soviet Union is quite justifiably seeking to assimilate the most sophisticated technology and expand its contacts with major Western countries, one might assume that our commercial and economic relations with Latin America might go through hard times. However, one cannot totally discard the possibility that new forms of cooperation and new partners may emerge, thus strengthening our overall relationship.

Friendly Cuba stands out among our partners in Latin America. The Soviet Union and Cuba are linked not only by close ties but, more importantly, by major political and moral commitments. Present changes will undoubtedly affect these relations. And it will take more than one year to restructure them on a mutually beneficial basis. Much depends on the course of developments in the Soviet Union, in Cuba, and in the world as a whole.

The above reflections lead to the conclusion that in the near future Latin America is not likely to move upward in the priority scale of Soviet foreign policy. At the same time, this is likely to be a period of experimentation and search for new kinds of engagement.

When addressing readers in the United States about the multifarious world of their southern neighbors, one can't help pointing to two things: the role of the Latin American region in Soviet-US relations, on the one hand, and the projection of these relations on the social and political being of the peoples to the south of the Rio Grande, on the other. It would be helpful if we took into consideration the present moment, which by all accounts marks a turning point not only for the interaction of two major powers but for the world community as well. The essence of these changes in Soviet-US relations emerged clearly at the Soviet-US summit in June 1990. Now, with benefit of hindsight, one can appreciate how succinctly Mikhail Gorbachev formulated this essence: "from confrontation and rivalry toward mutual understanding, interaction and partnership."

And as the Soviet president pointed out: "Following this formula we've recently covered a greater part of the road and apparently we are somewhere at the beginning of interaction, although there already exists the elements of partnership. The trend is easily traced."

Soviet policy toward Latin American countries has been given rather extensive coverage. As far as the US policy toward Latin America is concerned, the United States must have a good idea of all its ups and downs, as well as the specific features of its recent evolution. It would be fitting, therefore, to present our most general vision of it. As far as we understand, the United States, in shaping its policy toward Latin America, was guided by the so-called "imperative of strategic denial." It was based on two major postulates: First, although the states in the Western Hemisphere are not strong enough to threaten US interests, their weakness may be used by some extracontinental force. The United States, therefore, must prevent the interference of any other power in the affairs of the hemisphere. The second postulate, which is closely linked to the first, reveals its bottom line—the United States must ensure its hegemony over the hemisphere.

During the Cold War, this imperative was mainly reflected in concentrated efforts to keep the Soviet Union out of Latin America, and to counter nationalist and sometimes democratic movements—which were groundlessly portrayed as the result of communist plots—in this area of the world. At the same time, natural social and political processes in certain Latin American countries, aggravated by desperate misery and US interference guided by the same "imperative," were often represented to the US public as the result of "Soviet machinations." Well-known events that took place in Cuba and later in Nicaragua were ordinarily viewed by Washington in the light of confrontation with Moscow. One cannot but note that the perception of both Cuba and Nicaragua as major external "nuisances" for Washington was created and, so to say, bred by the United States, which had for many years backed notorious antipopular and antidemocratic regimes.

Of course, we are not going to teach the United States how to treat others, especially how to deal with Latin America. But it would be only natural if the United States also underwent changes in accordance with the requirements of the current peaceful period in modern history. Certain positive developments in the US approach toward the problems of Latin America are already discernible: President Bush's "Enterprise for the Americas" and the 1989 Brady plan. Of course, these haven't yet gotten into high gear; it is therefore too early to judge their results. But they seem at least to point to certain shifts in the priorities of US policy in Latin America—a shift from security issues to greater attention to economic relations (also with the purpose to meet the challenges of the European Economic Community [EEC] and Japan).

Unfortunately, we also witnessed a display of the old thinking in the invasion of Panama. No matter why it was carried out, this act ran counter to international laws, to provisions of the UN charter, and to norms of the OAS. Some well-known experts would agree with Wayne S. Smith's assessment:

> With the exception of the "Enterprise for the Americas" initiative which is so far only a point of light on the horizon, the Bush administration has taken little advantage of the tremendous possibilities created by the end of the cold

war and the beginning of a new era in which there is no enemy to threaten the United States from Latin America.[1]

And the Brady plan, as Smith puts it, has turned out to be "just a band-aid measure, and not a very effective one at that."[2]

I think that the weak and the strong sides of these plans are well known to the United States and its neighbors in the hemisphere. Let us then turn to the possibilities of our cooperation in the solution of Latin America's problems. It is well known that in June 1990 these possibilities were seriously discussed during the Soviet-US summit meeting. The character of these discussions was determined by the desire of the presidents of both countries to use the benefits of US-Soviet regional cooperation to consolidate relations of partnership between the two countries and to protect the legitimate interests of other states. But not all the differences have been overcome. They still prevail in such issues as lessening tensions between the United States and Cuba.

By the way, it was the Cuban problem, which still remains a thorn in US-Soviet relations, that, during the Caribbean crisis in 1962, taught both sides the first lesson of great significance—how to balance conflicting interests. It is the very same lesson that for many years remained unheeded by the leaders of our countries and that we are perhaps only now learning. Almost thirty years ago, the breaking of the missile stalemate proved the possibility of comprehending and "separating" the interests of our countries. It has taken us a long time to follow up on that first step.

There is no doubt that such decisions require competence, mutual flexibility, and personal courage on the part of policymakers. In October 1962, these very qualities, displayed by both sides, helped to change drastically the destructive momentum of the conflict.

It seems that the search for a balance of interests in any situation must become, and is now becoming, the proof of "new thinking" in US-Soviet relations. As President Bush said at the summit meeting: "In Nicaragua we showed that we can work together to promote peaceful changes." We believe that the search for balance of interests on the settlement of regional conflicts in Latin America has brought Soviet and US policymakers to a number of common approaches, which could make this difficult work much easier. First, we should mention the need to give up ideological preferences. By this we do not mean likes and dislikes, but the fact that the Soviet Union and the United States must give preference to the rules of international law. Second, the countries must recognize that forcible measures will not lead to the achievement of satisfactory results. Even if considerable military superiority and obvious "successes" in this sphere are achieved, the political and social effects of such measures may be destructive. And last but not least, the mechanisms and capabilities of the UN system must be used more actively for the settlement of regional conflicts.

But in the current political reality nothing is as easy as it may seem. The fact remains that there are still certain forces in the United States that look with suspicion at everything the Soviet Union has done or has proposed to do in Latin America. These are the forces that continue to see Latin America as their "backyard."

It was chance that made the peoples of North and South America neighbors. We understand why the United States takes such a keen interest in everything that happens beyond its southern borders. But in our high-tech century, the distances in the world are continually being "shortened," thus changing the very notion of "neighborhood." Now the Soviet Union can very well be regarded as a Pacific neighbor of the United States and Latin America, or, if you wish, as a neighbor sharing the planet with them. Hence, we are changing our approach toward the interests of other countries.

From this point of view, we can regard Latin America in the context of concerted US-Soviet efforts to create a new world order under the auspices of the United Nations and in coordination with other states. The maintenance of a nuclear-free regime and conventional arms limitations in Latin America have been brought to the foreground of modern political life. A special role for the Soviet Union and the United States in this process is well understandable.

Only the international community as a whole can answer the global challenges that face us: to bridge the gap between the developed and the developing countries, to establish a new and more just economic order, to further intercontinental integration, and to protect the environment through different multilateral programs. The environmental challenge is based on the fact that the largest oxygen-generating zones of Amazonia and Siberia and the biggest reserves of fresh water are to be found in Latin America and the Soviet Union, whereas the United States and the industrial countries of the West have at their disposal modern soft technologies. Incidentally, the Heads of States and Governments Conference of the United Nations Environment Program (UNEP), scheduled to take place in Brazil in 1991, offers a good opportunity to reach important agreements. And, finally, the joint US–Latin American fight against the illicit trafficking of narcotic drugs will require broad international support.

The new approaches toward the solution of Latin America's problems first of all demands that we consign to oblivion the ideological priorities of the old military blocs and their rivalry for new spheres of influence, and replace them with the values common to all mankind with a concern for the interests of the continent and its vital needs. Support of various democratic processes in the countries of the continent is also in the common interest of the Soviet Union and the United States.

Wayne S. Smith, whom I quoted above, states at the end of a recent article in *Current History*: "It's time for the U.S. to move out of the 19th century and to start moving toward the 21st."[3] I think these words apply not only to the United States.

Notes

1. Wayne S. Smith, "The United States and South America: Beyond the Monroe Doctrine," *Current History* (February, 1991), p. 90.
2. Ibid.
3. Ibid.

Chapter 6

Comments on the
New Soviet Course

Ilya Prizel

Latin America was always a low priority area for the Kremlin. In no other region of the world, however, did Soviet forays—or perceived forays—so disturb the US sense of insularity and security. If indeed the Soviet goal was to distract the United States from vital international arenas through activism in Latin America, it was eminently successful. From 1947 on, with the outbreak of the Cold War, every US administration has vowed to defend the hemisphere from Soviet penetration. Thus although in fact the economic and the geostrategic importance of Latin America to the United States has declined since the end of the Korean War, every potential Soviet "encroachment" into the hemisphere was perceived as a mortal threat to the national security of the United States, and thus provoked a massive and disproportionate response. In an era of intercontinental missiles, the geographic proximity of Latin America was largely irrelevant, and US trade with much of Latin America has declined dramatically. Even so, perceived Soviet expansion into Latin America was—and is—considered an affront to US prestige. For example, although the US administration scarcely noted the "loss" of Ethiopia to communism—despite the fact that Ethiopia was one of the largest African countries and a long-time ally of the United States—the "loss" of tiny Nicaragua created a massive US furor and was an important factor in the defeat of the Carter administration in the 1980 elections. Given the extreme sensitivity—almost, indeed, the irrationality—of the United States when it came to extrahemispheric presence in Latin America, the two chapters in this book written by Valery Nikolayenko, of the Soviet Foreign Ministry, and Karen Brutents, formerly of the International Department of the CPSU—both with a history of strong commitment to Soviet involvement in Latin America—make for interesting and stimulating reading.

In his "official statement," Valery Nikolayenko expands on the fundamental change that has taken place in Soviet policy toward Latin America since 1987 when the doctrine of "new political thinking" was promulgated by the Soviet government. According to Nikolayenko, current Soviet foreign policy toward Latin America has been completely denuded of ideological content; Moscow's main goals in the region are now to guarantee stability and ensure a climate that will enable the Soviet Union to expand its links with Latin America without provoking tension either within the hemisphere or with the United States. Nikolayenko's description of contemporary Soviet policy toward Latin America is, on the whole, correct and indeed borne out by the facts.

However, Nikolayenko's discussion of the Soviet-Cuban relationship is more problematic. For one thing, he insists that Soviet-Cuban economic ties must continue, but there are many Soviet citizens—including deputies in the Supreme Soviet—who disagree with him. For another, his assertion that Soviet military aid to Cuba is merely a reflection of the threat that Cuba is facing from the outside may be somewhat misleading. Nikolayenko fails to mention that the United States, in the wake of the 1962 missile crisis, committed itself not to invade Cuba. Nor does he mention that the Soviet military depends on its eavesdropping facilities in Cuba to monitor the United States and thus, at least for the moment, has an incentive to continue to supply Cuba with its military needs. Another curious point in Nikolayenko's chapter in this book is his statement that Soviet economic development will not require massive foreign aid. President Gorbachev's more recent indications that such aid may indeed be necessary either contradict Nikolayenko's statement or at least suggest it is out of date.

Karen Brutents, in his chapter describing the Kremlin's post–Cold War policy toward Latin America, gives a succinct and largely accurate description of Moscow's former policy toward the hemisphere—a mix of Soviet ideological messianism as well as utilization of the turmoil in the hemisphere as a means to distract the United States from more vital areas of the international arena such as Europe and the Middle East. Yet, despite the fact that the article is written in the spirit of post–Cold War cooperation, some habits die hard and at times the author cannot resist an occasional Cold War–style jab. For example, in covering the litany of ills to befall Latin America, Brutents asserts that "in the past the Soviet-US confrontation had led the United States to support the most macabre dictatorial regimes." This statement is overly simplistic. Although it is true that the US record in support of democracy in the region is not exemplary, nevertheless the Kennedy and the Carter administrations did much to foster democracy in the hemisphere. Further, in its day, the Soviet Union has supported its own share of dictators. And it is more than passing curious that in the United Nations, Moscow consistently blocked efforts to raise the Argentine military government's human rights record.

In discussing US–Latin American economic relations, Brutents appears not to have entered the era of "new thinking." He ascribes the currently fashionable "neo-liberal" economic doctrine to an alleged conspiracy of multinational corporations, when in reality neoliberalism owes its roots to US and British academia and has actually been detrimental to many multinationals who in the past benefited from the protected environment of the Latin American market. Furthermore, Brutents sounds the alarm over the fact that the region has become exposed to the "excessive role of foreign investment and the huge profits exported by foreign investors." In this case the author appears to have gotten it backwards. The greatest anxiety to befall the Latin Americans does indeed concern the role of foreign capital. However, the main anxiety in Latin America is not that foreign capital will devour its independence, but rather that such money will fail to come. With the demise of communism in Eastern Europe and major privatization campaigns taking place around the world, Latin American intellectuals are increasingly alarmed that the change in the international environment will lead to growing marginalization and, as Jorge Castañeda put it, the "Africanization" of Latin America.[1]

Another Marxist-Leninist tenet that Brutents seems unable to put to rest is the notion that foreign investors derive "huge profits" from their investments in Latin America. There is no doubt that profit is the main motive for investment, but the sad truth is that Latin America by and large proved to yield rather modest profits to investors. This explains the continued decline in the ability of the region to attract foreign capital. Most transnational investment occurs within the developed world (Canada alone has attracted more foreign capital than all of Latin America combined), and because of the modest profits along with substantial risks that both equity and capital investment in Latin America entails, the presence of foreign capital there is smaller than in any part of the world except for sub-Saharan Africa. Brutents's allegation that the excessive foreign capital presence in Latin America is responsible for the region's economic plight is not borne out historically, or empirically. It should be noted that the prosperity of societies such as those of the United States and Canada was attained through the massive utilization of foreign capital. Even in Brutents's native land most historians agree that the period of fastest real economic growth occurred between 1880 and 1914, when Russia was able to secure massive access to the international money markets. What Latin America needs today is more capital, not less.

Brutents's analysis of Latin America's prospects in the coming decade is far more optimistic than my own. He sees Latin America as having made important gains in the 1980s, and believes it will continue to build on these gains during the coming decade. He is particularly encouraged by the reemerging interest of many Latin American countries in the revival of

the various regional "common markets" as well as Latin America's growing economic ties with Japan, the European Community, Africa, and the
Pacific.

While it is true that some Latin American countries (primarily Chile)
have attained impressive growth and diversification away from monocul-
tural export, the 1980s were dismal for most Latin American economies.
Aside from facing a mountain of debt, the world price for most of the
region's exports declined, and, in fact, with a few notable exceptions, most
of Latin America's economic growth has failed to keep up with its increase
in population, causing an absolute decline in the standards of living.
Furthermore, despite occasional movement by Japan and the European
Community to expand their links with Latin America, the sad reality is
that the marginalization of Latin America within the international division
of labor has accelerated. Japan, despite massive trade surpluses, opted to
invest most of its funds in either Western Europe or North America. To
the extent that Japan did invest in the Third World, its investment was
targeted almost exclusively in the Pacific rim of Asia, with Latin America
attracting an insignificant share of Japanese trade and capital. Similarly,
the European Economic Community, as it moves toward 1992, is becoming increasingly introspective, with little will to commit resources to a
region as remote as Latin America. Western Europe, with its parochial
policies such as the Common Agricultural Policy (CAP), has in fact not
only excluded Latin American exports to Europe, such as Argentine
leather to the Italian shoe industry, but actually has become a competitor
of Latin America, annually dumping millions of tons of highly subsidized
meat, grain, and sugar, and thus causing severe damage to the economies
of Latin America. Despite persistent talk of the EEC playing a greater
global role, the fact remains that the European Community's concerns are
very parochial; aside from the Maghreb, the Middle East, and lately
Eastern Europe, the Economic Community shows no inclination to play
either a political or an economic role that would be helpful to Latin
America. Nothing perhaps illustrates the marginalization of Latin
America within the international system more than the fact that Japan has
cut its loans to Latin America from $10 billion to $4 billion (and redirected
the remaining $6 billion to Eastern Europe).[2] Similarly, although the
European Community agreed to cut Poland's debt by 70 percent, it
showed no inclination to help Latin America ease its debt burden or to
expand the access for Latin American goods to Europe's protected
markets.

Brutents may also place more hope in the various regional common
markets than they warrant. Although the emergence of various regional
markets in Latin America is indeed a welcome development because these
markets are an expression of a growing political and economic solidarity,

the potential economic impact of most of these is not likely to be great. Most of these market partners often trade in similar primary commodities or semimanufactured products, and much of Latin America's industrial output is technologically backward as well as expensive; therefore, it is doubtful whether these markets will ever serve as the economic catalyst to induce growth in the region's moribund economies.

Furthermore, I disagree with Brutents's suggestion that most Latin Americans fear and oppose the creation of a common market with the United States. It would seem that most Latin Americans have realized that access to developed markets is the ultimate guarantor of economic growth; it was this realization that led the Mexican government to reverse its half century of self-defeating nationalism and actively strive to create the North American Free Trade Association (NAFTA) with the United States and Canada. This action by Mexico, far from provoking fear in Latin America, actually led to an ever-increasing number of other nations that aspired to consummate a similar relationship.

Finally, sadly, I do not share Brutents's belief that the democratic changes that have taken place in Latin America during the 1980s are permanent and irreversible. It may well be true that most Latin Americans prefer a democratic form of government over others, but it is equally true that many Latin Americans, much like the East Europeans, believed that a democratic transformation would lead to rapid economic improvement as well as greater integration into the international economic system. As these hopes for rapid economic improvement fade, the Latin Americans' faith in democracy may deteriorate. One can argue that the reason democracy in Peru continues to limp along is not due to the strength of its democratic institutions but is rather because neither the political Left, nor the Right, nor even the army have any idea how to lead the country out of its political crisis and have thus made no attempt to overthrow the fragile democratic regime.

Although on the whole, I am far more pessimistic than Brutents about the future of Latin America and its standing in the international system, I am somewhat more optimistic about the future of Soviet–Latin American economic relations. I fully agree with Brutents that the Soviet Union will strive to attain most of its sophisticated technology from the developed capitalist countries, but I believe there is a great deal of room for expansion in Soviet-Latin American trade. First of all, many aspects of the Soviet economy are not capable of absorbing the most sophisticated technology generated by the West. The Soviet Union's decision to hire Spain's Telefonica to upgrade the Soviet telephone system indicates Moscow's cognizance of the limited ability of its own infrastructure to effectively utilize state-of-the-art technology.

Furthermore, Latin America is a producer of many consumer goods, which, although they may not meet international standards, will be welcome in the Soviet Union's undersaturated markets. Latin America's willingness to engage in "counter trade" makes it a desirable partner for the cash-strapped economy of the Soviet Union. It is likely that the Soviet Union and Latin America will develop an active economic exchange, utilizing the model of Soviet-Indian trade, which enabled India to export items it could not place globally while allowing the Soviet Union to increase the variety of consumer and industrial goods available to its public without expending scarce hard currency.

Brutents ends his chapter by citing a statement by Wayne S. Smith calling on both superpowers to leave their nineteenth-century policies toward Latin America and move into the twenty-first century. I heartily agree with my colleagues that Latin America should cease being a battlefield between two ideologies, and I am optimistic on that score. It seems quite certain that the era of "new thinking" will indeed revolutionize the Latin American policies of both Moscow and Washington. Whether Latin America will find a new role within the international system, however, remains an open question.

Notes

1. Jorge Castañeda, "Latin America and the End of the Cold War," *World Policy Journal* (Fall 1991).
2. Ibid.

Part 3

The Soviet Union
in Central America

Chapter 7 —————————————————————

On the *Real* Soviet Policy Toward Central America, Past and Present

————————————————— *Kiva Maidanik*

This chapter examines Soviet policy toward Central America from my personal perspective—the perspective of an autonomous Soviet witness, but one largely influenced by the Latin American Left. I thus present a vision that is of both "Eastern" and "Southern" extraction.

During the first two decades after the triumph of the 1959 Cuban revolution, the Soviet Union did not have a coherent policy toward Latin America.[1] There were no clear regional goals, no short-term plans, no long-range strategy, and no high-priority targets. The Soviet government was not interested in obtaining political power in the region, nor did it view the region as a potential economic resource. It did not even view its presence in the region as providing potential leverage to achieve accommodation with the United States. In general, there was never a unified doctrine to guide Soviet policy in the region.[2] On the contrary, there were a number of different stimuli that motivated Soviet policy toward Latin America.

Inertia was the most important of these. Bureaucratic inertia, coupled with an interest in appearance over action and the Soviet predisposition to "let things be as they are," had a most significant impact on policy.

A second motivation behind Soviet policy toward Latin America was ideology. Interested in doctrinal purity, the Soviet foreign policy apparatus prioritized the Latin American working class and Communist parties that were most loyal to the Communist party of the Soviet Union.

The Soviet Union also had what I call a "legitimization complex"—in other words, we used revolutionary triumphs as a confirmation that our system was the model for the future.

Political motivations for foreign policy decisions were much less important than ideological or bureaucratic motives, yet they also were present. In general, political factors were rhetorical "anti-Americanism" and rejection of the Monroe Doctrine accompanied, however, by extreme caution and a deep reluctance to get involved in the US sphere of influence. This approach rested on a realistic appraisal of the Soviet Union's direct state interests in the area (which were scarce) and of the real limits on Soviet possibilities in the region.

Another conditioning factor that shaped Soviet policy and acted as a counterweight to the inertia mentioned above was pressure from Latin American revolutionaries. Our innate passivity was balanced by the intensity of pressure from the Latin "machos," whose struggle was vital and urgent. They were fighting for life-and-death issues, for their people. On occasion, our aging leaders and solemn functionaries could not resist the youthful Latin enthusiasm, often reminiscent of our own past.

Temperament and personality also played a role in decisionmaking. Khrushchev's passion influenced policy as much as Brezhnev's apathy, and many of our octogenarians demonstrated obvious reluctance to get involved in the region at all.

In summary, our policies toward Latin America were based rarely on politics but more frequently on ideology and emotion. Our leaders were conscious of our historical affinity for Latin America in spite of its geographic distance, an affinity stemming from Khrushchev's involvement with Cuba and the long-term existence of a grass-roots youth solidarity movement with Latin America—the only informal semilegal political movement permitted during the pre-perestroika era.[3]

It should be emphasized that the various motivations behind Soviet policy rarely complemented one another. There was no coherent, homogenous, constructive regional policy. However, ideology was more important than the economic, political, or military dimensions of our policy.

Given our extreme caution in the region, one may wonder what was the basis of US accusations of "Moscow aggression," "Soviet beachheads," or "Kremlin's proxies." Only the missile crisis of 1962, and the US "proprietor's mentality," best expressed by the Monroe Doctrine, can explain such unsophisticated misperceptions. Once myths exist, they tend to perpetuate themselves.

The most striking example of US misperceptions propagating themselves is the way Soviet discussions of Latin American issues are analyzed in the United States. The obvious pluralism of ideas and the richness of debate about Latin America in the Soviet Union are viewed by some in the United States as proof of dangerous Soviet involvement today in the area. But those who truly understand the inner logic of Soviet perestroika will see this deepening of analysis and pluralism as irrefutable evidence of the absence of real Soviet interests in Latin America. Open discussions could not have taken place about areas such as Eastern or Western Europe where the Soviets had true national security interests.

Nowhere have Soviet interests been fewer than with regard to Central

America. The Soviet Union paid virtually no attention to this area until 1978. Even after the victory of the Sandinistas in Nicaragua in 1979, the Soviet government showed little interest.

Since the 1960s, the Latin American section in the Central Committee of the CPSU has not had a single official who "covered" Central America as a whole. The area has always been divided among four or five officials, and each of them has had other more pressing responsibilities.

In the early 1960s, Central America interested us primarily because we wanted to limit Chinese and Cuban expansion in the region. Soviet policy in the area was marked by extreme aversion to armed struggle (as in the case of Guatemala), support for peaceful solutions to regional problems, and improving relations with Costa Rica.

This remained so through the early 1970s. Although there was direct involvement in the strife within the Salvadoran Communist party, this contrasted with the Soviet Union's passivity toward the seizure and subsequent slaughter of the Guatemalan Communist party leadership.

The low profile of Soviet activity in the area was often attributed to the region's backwardness and to the concomitant lack of proper conditions for revolution. Soviet officials ignored predictions in the mid-1970s forecasting Central America's revolutionary potential, not because they did not believe the forecasts but because they had lost interest in revolution itself.

This helps explain why the Soviet Union maintained contact with the Nicaraguan Socialist party, and not the Sandinista revolutionaries. The Nicaraguan Socialists were considered "class relatives" of the CPSU, but the Sandinistas were viewed as "petty-bourgeois revolutionaries."

Furthermore, even after the Sandinista victory in 1979, there is significant evidence that although the Soviets recognized the FSLN as the "vanguard and leading force of the Nicaraguan revolution," they were still unwilling to respond to the FSLN's needs. The Soviet government's lack of response was based on several factors: a low-profile mentality, reluctance to become involved, scarcity of resources, and the priority of accommodation with the United States over yet-to-be-proven allies.[4]

Soviet policy toward Central America changed significantly in 1981 from a policy of benign neglect to a policy of engagement. Between 1981 and 1987 the Soviets increased economic and military assistance to the region, and Soviet political involvement increased commensurately. Pressure from old and new friends in the region as well as ideological factors contributed to the shift in policy. I believe that the impact of political factors played a much more important role then than in the past.

First, and most importantly, the new Reagan administration in Washington was pursuing a neoglobalist crusade. It is relevant to point out here that during the electoral campaign some crucial members of the

CPSU inner circle preferred a Reagan over a Carter administration in 1980, probably because of nostalgia for Nixon-era détente and outrage over the Carter administration's boycott of the Olympic games. After the election, however, Soviet officials became disillusioned. The cause was not so much the Reagan administration's blatant violation of the rule of law and its disdain for the sovereignty of the Central American and Caribbean region; the Soviet Union had some parallel experience in Eastern Europe. But unlike post-Khrushchevian Soviet foreign policy, the Reagan foreign policy was a globalist one, and it was aimed directly against the Soviet Union. Fred Halliday has pointed this out: "For all its vagueness and incoherence this [Reagan administration] attack on the Third World revolutionary states formed part of a much more comprehensive challenge to the USSR. The road to Moscow lay, it appeared, through Kabul, Pnom Penh, Adis Ababa, Luanda, St. George, and Managua."[5]

This aggressive policy provoked a natural reaction from the Soviet Union. In Central America above all, Soviet commitments were triggered not only by Reagan's crusade, but by the greater part of the world community's adverse reaction to it.

From the very beginning of the confrontation in Central America, the Soviet Union was far from being perceived as the "repugnant and isolated villain," as in the case of Afghanistan, or the "aggressor's accomplice," as in the Cambodia situation. On the contrary, it was seen as defending—without troops—the national sovereignty of a small, legitimate state (Nicaragua) against the aggression of a superpower. It was supporting the right of a small nation to choose its own way, and the majority of Western European public opinion backed Soviet involvement in the area or, at the very least, did not oppose it.[6]

Despite the fact that the Soviet Union wanted to avoid confrontation with the United States in its backyard, and the fact that Central America was of little importance to the Soviet Union, the Soviets did get involved in the region. Specific data on Soviet involvement in Nicaragua has been widely published elsewhere.

I personally believe that Soviet involvement in Central America was both morally correct and legal. The Soviet Union acted responsibly, in strict accordance with internationally recognized norms, and without seeking any unilateral economic or political benefits or military bases. Between 1981 and 1989, the Soviet Union never intervened in Nicaragua's internal problems, and always respected the choices and solutions chosen by the Nicaraguan government.

There were risks involved in these policies, however. The greatest risk was the possibility of direct superpower confrontation accompanied by US military intervention in Nicaragua itself. The situation was polarized from the start when former US secretary of state Alexander Haig said the

United States should "go to the source" (that is, take action against Cuba). Tensions were further heightened by the October 1983 US invasion of Grenada.

Soviet policy toward El Salvador was quite different from its policy toward Nicaragua. The Soviet Union viewed the Nicaraguan conflict as a case of aggression of the United States against a small sovereign country. The Salvadoran conflict, however, was seen as a civil conflict. Thus, the Soviets never became directly engaged in El Salvador because they believed the moral and legal aspects of intervention were far more dubious than in the Nicaraguan case.

Given the risks cited above, the Soviet Union, from the very beginning, strongly advocated a political solution to the regional conflict. In Nicaragua, the Soviet Union always advocated direct US-Nicaraguan negotiations, but never demanded participation in those talks. The Soviets gave complete backing and unconditional support to the Contadora process from the moment of its inception in 1983. When the Central American presidents initiated a dialogue in 1987–1988, the Soviet Union supported those efforts as well.

We have seen that the Soviet Union had no interest in, or plans for, military penetration or political domination of the region between 1983 and 1989. It supported all proposed negotiated settlements to the conflict, and insisted only on its right to assist Nicaragua and Cuba when they requested aid or arms to defend themselves against the United States. In 1987–88, the Soviets proposed the simultaneous termination of arms supply to the area on the part of both the United States and the Soviet Union.[7] The United States did not accept and continued the provision of arms, but the Soviet Union halted its supply anyway.

During the spring of 1989, there was a serious shift in US and Soviet policy toward the region. Since that time, the United States and the Soviet Union have been involved in intensive, confidential diplomacy in Central America. *Time* magazine documented in detail the eight months of negotiations between the two superpowers, aimed at solving the most difficult regional issues. Although the article is fairly comprehensive, it ignores several relevant issues including Soviet readiness to cooperate and new flexibility in Soviet policy in the area. This new flexibility was demonstrated in the Soviet Union's virtual renunciation of reciprocity and symmetry. Although the change was gradual, it did represent the end of the inertia that had characterized Soviet policy in the region in the past. From a policy based on ideology, the Soviets switched to a policy based on realpolitik. Under pressure from the United States, the Soviet political elite subordinated ideological interests and sometimes even moral considerations to its interest in resolving both global and national issues.

This turnaround in Soviet policy was based on several considerations:

1. The end of the Cold War was the first major contributing factor. The improvement of relations between the United States and the Soviet Union, and the Soviet desire to make the improvements "stick," further stimulated Soviet interest in a peaceful settlement to the regional conflict.

2. The change in Soviet policy was also the result of a structural crisis inside the Soviet Union born of twenty years of inefficiency and decay. The Soviet state's ability to "act and influence" began to dwindle in 1986.[8] In each subsequent year, it became more apparent that the Soviet state could not provide more, that its commitments exceeded its real political and economic potential.

3. The new political thinking in the Soviet Union constituted a third motive for the turnabout in the Soviet policy toward Central America. New thinking led to a long list of changes in Soviet decisionmaking and policy including de-ideologization of interstate relations; new weight and importance given to the Soviet Foreign Ministry over the CPSU, and over economic, military, and security institutions; the domestic implications of the Afghanistan problem; the upsurge of domestic political opposition that focused on the international arena, specifically Soviet aid to the Third World; and democratization, which opened channels for expression of mass discontent.

The cumulative effect of all of these factors led to a coherent outcome: the policy of disengagement. Active Soviet involvement in the Third World was relegated to the bottom of Soviet priorities. The deeper the Soviet Union plunged into its internal structural crisis, the more it embraced new solutions in Central America aimed at peaceful political settlements to the conflicts of the region.

In summary form, the policy of encouraging political settlements, initially a reaction to US interventionism in the region, was replaced by a joint US-Soviet policy designed to limit confrontation and bring peace (or at least to end bloodshed) in the area.

There is little doubt that Soviet efforts to promote a peaceful settlement in the region contributed to untying some of the knots of the Central American imbroglio. The United States has done far less to change its policy than has the Soviet Union.

Although the Central American regional conflict in the form it took during the 1980s has ended, the war, its bloodshed, and the acute instability it provokes, have not. The path from the present peaceful settlement in Nicaragua to a lasting peace in the area is long. Even in Nicaragua, there are still many unresolved issues. The Salvadoran conflict has not ended, nor has the Guatemalan, though there is now some cause for optimism in both cases.

My personal opinion is that the Soviet Union can do nothing more than it has already done. We have no trumps, nothing left to offer, nothing more to sacrifice for the sake of terminating the confrontation. We are virtually unable to influence the Salvadoran FMLN. Any pressure we put on the Salvadoran revolutionaries runs the risk of being counterproductive at this point. Even the Communist party of El Salvador, our historical brethren in that country, has gained a well-deserved reputation of being aggressively independent with a great sense of dignity and self-sufficiency. This is particularly true in its relations with the CPSU, with the Sandinistas, and with Cuba.

Thus, because the Soviet Union no longer wields influence in the area, the onus for resolving the Central American crisis now rests with the United States. Until now, I believe that the United States has been unwilling to sit down with all parties concerned and peacefully resolve the conflict. Rather, it has rejected direct Cuban participation in the solution. If, however, the United States is sincerely concerned over allegations that Cuba is shipping arms to Salvador, or over rumors of a new FMLN offensive, it should be willing to discuss the allegations and resolve the disagreements with the parties directly involved, and not with the Soviet Union.

Let there be no illusions. The Soviet Union is no longer involved in Central America. But Cuba, the Central American revolutionaries, the peoples of the isthmus, and their Latin neighbors do remain. No lasting peace, or enduring solution can be achieved without including all of the remaining parties.

Notes

1. There were two or three years during the Khrushchev era that the Soviet Union demonstrated some coherence of policy.

2. Stalin, however, did have an overall vision of the area: he believed that because it fell in the "US backyard," its governments would fill the role of Washington's "infantry" in the United Nations.

3. As a norm, our Latin America staff has been the most mediocre of all, with the possible exception of the Mexican embassy staff. However, because Latin America was of only marginal importance, some officials were given significant independence and personal autonomy never possible for officials involved with Europe or the Near East.

4. If there is any truth to the allegations of the "White Book" of 1981, published by the US government, that maintains that the Soviet Union shipped arms to the Salvadoran revolutionaries, I am certain that this action had far less to do with the state policy of assisting Central America than with a free-lance one initiated by an independent official.

5. Fred Halliday, *From Kabul to Managua: Soviet-American Relations in*

the 1980s (New York: Pantheon Books, 1989), p. 138. Robert Pastor also pointed this out: "The Reagan Administration looked beyond the long standing policy of containment to a more revolutionary strategy of seeing 'targets of opportunity' in vulnerable areas where US support for guerrilla movements could overthrow Marxist governments." Robert Pastor, *Condemned to Repetition: The United States and Nicaragua* (Princeton, N.J.: Princeton University Press, 1988), p. 243.

6. The Soviet stand on Central America constituted one of the most important links between the Soviet Union and the Third World in the mid-1980s.

7. The Central American Left, and the FMLN above all, did not accept this Soviet position with enthusiasm, to put it mildly.

8. The first realization of the structural crisis came in 1986. By 1987, it already had a direct impact on the area. In 1988–1989, the tendency was widely recognized.

Chapter 8 _____

New Challenges for Cuban Policy in Central America
_____ *Julio Carranza Valdes*

Since mid-1989 there has been a series of events at both the regional and global levels that has posed new challenges to Cuban policy in Central America.[1]

At the global level, the crisis of the Socialist camp in Europe is, of course, felt by the revolutionary movement in Central America and throughout the world. The international correlation of forces has suffered an abrupt change, giving the United States an unprecedented free hand to assert its interests in the global arena, as recent events in the Persian Gulf demonstrate. In fact, the revolutionary movement has been left without a powerful ally that could offer it support in time of war or an economic alternative in time of peace.

In addition, events in Eastern Europe have reduced the Socialist model's attractiveness to popular sectors in other countries. In Central America, the electoral defeat of the Sandinista National Liberation Front (FSLN) and subsequent events in Nicaragua have not only eliminated the only revolutionary government in the area, but also have cast doubt on the revolutionary movement's chances of overcoming the obstacles posed by the transitional process and the war of imperialist aggression. We can only wonder whether the Sandinistas' policy errors explain their electoral defeat, and what the prospects for their revolution would have been in the absence of those policy errors. But whatever the answers to those questions, it can be seen that the Sandinistas' electoral defeat led broad sectors of Central American society to question the viability of the revolutionary alternative.

In Guatemala, and particularly in El Salvador, the revolutionary movement has not been able to tip the scales of war in its favor, even though it continues to enjoy an indisputable military capability. The war has dragged on for more than ten years, with all the costs of war weariness that entails.

These realities have obliged the revolutionary movement to enter into a complex process of negotiations to advance even a minimalist program of transformation—a distinct come-down from what could have been accomplished had a revolutionary military victory been won.[2]

The dynamic of all these events, including the US invasion of Panama, has opened the way to a campaign on the part of the dominant local political and economic sectors, supported by the United States, to restructure the forms of domination. They propose the "modernization" of the political systems and changes in existing economic models along neoliberal lines. This fact, apart from its own limits and internal contradictions, presents a political scene that is even more complex for the revolutionary movement than the situation it faced halfway through the past decade.

Both the regional and international situations, together with the difficulties the Cuban economy has been facing since late 1989, have led to the perception among some Central American political actors that Cuba has lost its capacity for influence in the area.

All of these factors have affected Cuba's strategic interests and objectives in Central America:[3] the Sandinista revolution, far from consolidating itself, suffered an electoral defeat; in El Salvador and Guatemala, popular participation in power has not been achieved, and today the revolutionary movement in these countries confronts a complex process of dialogue and negotiation in which only a minimal program of transformation can be advanced; and US domination in the region, far from continuing to decline, has scored an obvious recovery. On the other hand, Cuba's role as an important actor in the area is now questioned by a number of regional actors.

Given all this, the challenge for Cuban policy in Central America has become one of sustaining its principles and promoting its interests within this more complex and hostile political context. What is called for, in our opinion, is the adjustment of Cuban objectives to meet this new challenge. Those revised objectives might be stated as follows:

1. To continue support for the negotiation process in El Salvador and in Guatemala so as to achieve social stability, with appropriate political space for the popular movements set out in the resulting agreements. In this context, UN mediation in El Salvador is seen as a most positive development.[4]

2. To promote diplomatic relations with those governments enjoying the greatest political legitimacy in the area with which Cuba does not maintain relations at present—namely, Honduras and Costa Rica. Toward this end, various contacts have been established with these countries, which could help to create a propitious climate for greater rapprochement.

3. To maintain diplomatic relations with the present government of Nicaragua on the basis of mutual interests. Thus, the Cuban government would continue its programs of civilian collaboration with Nicaragua.
4. To strengthen political relations with the broadest range of progressive sectors committed to the national interests of the region.
5. To retain its capacity to act as an important interlocutor for the political forces of the area.

Clearly one of the most important challenges faced by Cuban policy in these present circumstances is that of striking a coherent balance between Cuba's solidarity and political support for the revolutionary movement on the one hand, and its diplomatic relations with the established governments of the region on the other. Also, present circumstances require a more complex design for Cuban policy in the foreseeable eventuality of there being an upsurge of US aggressiveness in the wake of the recent results of the war in the Gulf.[5]

A more detailed examination of the region, however, suggests that the situation is far more complicated than the United States may believe and that the ultimate goals of US policy are far from being accomplished. From Cuba's point of view, there is room to continue the search for a negotiated solution that would take into account the interests of all parties.

Despite the problems faced by the revolutionary movement, and the relative advances scored by the United States in its campaign to rearticulate its domination of the area, the regional crisis has not been overcome, nor has it been possible to control the profound political confrontations affecting the area over the last few years.

Indeed, the structural causes that gave rise to the political crisis of the 1980s have not yet been resolved, nor have the revolutionary organizations struggling for change been defeated. Income distribution continues to be extremely polarized, and the great majority of the region's peoples are thus condemned to live under extremely depressed conditions. The economic crisis, which has not been resolved, only makes matters worse. In El Salvador and Guatemala, the land tenure system is essentially unchanged.

US policy, despite some relative successes, suffers from deep contradictions and offers no solutions to the underlying social and economic problems that, in the final analysis, are at the root of instability and tensions of the area. The neoliberal economic model called for by the political and corporatist forces of the so-called "new right" of Central America, and supported by US policy, cannot resolve the basic structural problems behind the region's social and political crisis. Nontraditional export promotion, the opening to foreign capital, and the operation of a free market system all presuppose a cheap labor force together with a very limited tax structure to keep the regional productivity competitive and to attract foreign capital. There is thus a fundamental contradiction between, on the one hand, the US objective of transnationalizing the Central American economy along the lines of a neoliberal policy, and, on the other, the possibility of lowering the social tensions in the area. US policy, in effect, places obstacles in the path of crisis solution. Furthermore, the economic stagnation and regression of recent years, now complicated even more by a considerable foreign debt, lead to a situation in which social tensions can only deepen.

After the 1984 Kissinger report, all parties, including the United States, have recognized the need for foreign financial assistance as an indispensable prerequisite for overcoming the region's problems. Yet, neither the United States nor any of the other advanced industrialized countries have delivered the minimal levels of financial assistance needed to alleviate the crisis and to establish a new economic accumulation model.

This point constitutes one of the central contradictions of the US Central America policy. Central America is regarded as an area of high strategic interest; it received great attention from the United States during the past decade, and consequently high levels of US assistance, especially of a military nature. But the relative success achieved by US policy—for example, the electoral defeat of the Sandinistas—has not been accompanied by even the minimal economic resources needed by the new Chamorro government to achieve a degree of stability. And this has been the pattern throughout the region. At the presidential summit in Antigua, Guatemala, the US secretary of state pledged only that the United States would be a part of and would coordinate a multinational group seeking economic aid for Central America.

It may be worthwhile to ask: Why is it that the United States, or at least the ruling elite in the United States, is not willing to commit even the bare minimum of financial assistance needed to obtain political stability in an area considered to be strategic? More than likely, the answer to that question is that the immediate revolutionary threat has faded and Central America no longer represents an area in which US hegemony is challenged by the other global power, particularly given the level of accord reached with the Soviet Union.

It would seem thus that the United States does not believe it necessary to pay the bill to achieve objectives it sees as already being assured. More than anything else, however, this may demonstrate how US policy has failed to grasp the essentially indigenous nature of the factors leading to the Central American crisis, and how these factors persist independently of changes in the international arena.[6]

This view is reinforced if one observes how US political contradictions go beyond the merely economic dimension. US rhetoric in favor of a negotiated solution for the region, particularly in the case of El Salvador, is not backed up by correspondingly strong policy action. This is true also of rhetoric calling for improvement in respect for human rights.

More than likely, the United States believes that, given the electoral defeat of the Sandinistas, the disintegration of the Socialist camp, and the difficulties through which Cuba is currently passing, the Central American revolutionary organizations will not be able to survive over the medium term. From this perspective, the negotiating process is seen simply as a means of wearing down the revolutionary movement until it finally can be defeated.

In fact, however, it is clear that despite the new difficulties they face, the revolutionary movements are still factors in the area. The movements are reorienting their strategy to bring it in line with the new challenges they are forced to confront. For example, in Nicaragua, despite their electoral defeat, the Sandinistas still have the best structured political party in the country, supported by 40 percent of the electorate. And they retain control of the army and the police.

In El Salvador, even though the FMLN has not been able to turn the war in its favor nor spark a massive popular insurrection, it still has the initiative, militarily on the battlefield and politically at the negotiating table.

Guatemala, despite the blows struck against the Revolutionary Union of Guatemala (UNRG) since 1982 by the Guatemalan army's counterinsurgency campaign, nevertheless has been able to reconstitute itself and remain a military and political factor that must be taken into account.

Furthermore, all of these societies are experiencing a resurgence of political activism on the part of social organizations, particularly the trade unions, who are making their demands with greater force than ever.

As we see then, Central America remains an unstable region in which the eruption of serious confrontations is still a distinct possibility. The internal dynamics, indeed, point toward this danger, particularly in the three countries that have long been the focal points of crisis: Nicaragua, El Salvador, and Guatemala.

Nicaragua has neither sufficient resources nor a sufficiently coherent policy to respond to the popular sector's demands. The government suffers from sharp internal discrepancies and is being pressured by counterrevolutionary forces, which still have not disbanded. In Guatemala, the violation of human rights has increased, and in El Salvador the war could again escalate if there is a stalemate in the negotiations.

All this confirms the Cuban thesis that without a solution to the fundamental structural problems in these countries, and without a negotiated solution that commits all parties and recognizes the political force of the popular movement in El Salvador, Guatemala, and Nicaragua, there can be no definitive solution to the region's crisis and thus no healthy, stable society.

In this complex situation, Cuban policy is one of using its influence[7] to encourage negotiated solutions that guarantee the mutual security of all the nations of the area, as well as that of its immediate neighbors, including Cuba and the United States. Cuba had, of course, hoped for more, but in fact its foreign policy objectives would be fulfilled by a Central America that was socially and politically stable and not hostile to Cuba. If the US goal is also to have a socially and politically stable region, there may be common ground between the two positions. The United States, however, should reflect upon the fact that such a region cannot exist until the chronic social and economic imbalances have been redressed. And Cuba is not the obstacle to that process.

Notes

1. Julio Carranza Valdes and Juan Valdes Paz, "Cuban Policy Toward Central America," and *Revista Cuadernos de Nuestra America*, No. 15, 1990. In this essay, written approximately one year prior to the present chapter, the authors laid out what they understood to be the principles, interests, actions, and perceptions of Cuban policy in Central America. The analysis in the present chapter is a continuation of that earlier work that especially stresses the recent evolution of the situation. A review of the previous article is recommended so that the reader may take into account elements that are not repeated here.

2. Julio Carranza Valdes, "The Conflict and Negotiation in El Salvador," *Revista Cuadernos de Nuestra America*, No. 14 (January–June 1990).

3. In "Cuban Policy Toward Central America" (see note 1), the following are defined as the strategic interests of Cuba in Central America: (a) the breaking of US domination in Central America; (b) the security of the nations linked to the region; (c) social change; and (d) the existence and development of diplomatic and economic relations with the Central American nations. This work also explains how, from the Cuban perception, the regional and international situations demanded a negotiated political solution which Cuban policy has tried to promote. In this sense specific Cuban objectives would include the following: (a) to prevent the United States from escalating from indirect intervention to direct; (b) to assure the survival of the Sandinista revolution; (c) to promote popular participation in the political process in El Salvador and Guatemala; (d) to encourage the remaining regional regimes to acquire greater autonomy from the United States; and (e) to support the conditions flowing from a negotiated solution for a program of social transformations as expressed in the Sandinista program of a mixed economy, political pluralism, and non-alignment. Cuba has promoted these objectives through a policy subject to international law.

4. Cuba has clearly supported all of the region's negotiating processes, from Contadora to the present, while expressing various reservations in each case. See

Carranza Valdes and Valdes Paz.

5. Cuban policy rejects any consideration whatsoever in favor of the geopolitics of borders and of security, spheres of influence, hegemonic area, and so on, but at the same time it follows the concept of mutual security and the search for negotiated solutions in which the legitimate security interests of all nations of the region are addressed. See Carranza Valdes and Valdes Paz.

6. The Cuban position is that any negotiated solution must be of an integrated character and offer political, military, security, and economic guarantees for all parties. Cuba defends the principle of the autonomy of the regional actors in the face of any agreement between the superpowers.

7. Cuba has rejected the proposition that codes of conduct can be imposed on the revolutionary movement; Cuba does not deny, however, the influence it could galvanize in support of a negotiated solution. It has maintained friendly relations with the revolutionary movement over a long period of time, has held a distinguished position in the Non-Aligned Movement, and at present exercises a position on the Security Council of the United Nations.

Chapter 9

The US Response to Soviet and Cuban Policies in Central America

Donna Rich-Kaplowitz

During the last five years, Mikhail Gorbachev's liberal reforms in the Soviet Union have literally turned the world around. Out of old "balance of power" paradigms, a post–Cold War dynamic is emerging, leaving little untouched. The Soviet Union has renounced the concept of world revolution, a basic tenet of its foreign policy for the past sixty years.[1] Some of the regional conflicts fueled by superpower confrontation have already been resolved. The way was opened to a peaceful solution in southern Africa, for example, when all involved parties signed accords in December 1988. In Central America, a peace accord signed by the five presidents of the region helped end Nicaragua's decade-long civil war by way of democratic elections. Furthermore, direct talks between rebels and government officials show promise of leading to peace agreements in El Salvador. Positive changes in Central America, however, have come about for the most part in spite of, not *because of*, US policy. In this fluid, changing world, the United States has not yet adapted to the new Soviet and Cuban policies in the region.

US policy toward Central America was long based on the premise that regional conflict was fomented by Soviet-Cuban intervention. According to this thesis, Cuba acted as a proxy for the Soviet Union, and the goal of both countries was to establish Marxist-Leninist governments in Central America.[2] This has never been an entirely accurate view. Regional conflicts erupted because of dismal internal conditions, not because they were engineered from Moscow or Havana. Indeed, although the Soviets and Cubans were to some extent actors in the drama, their roles were never as central as depicted by Washington; rather, they were more like bit players. As Kiva Maidanik points out in Chapter 7, Moscow paid virtually no attention to Central America until 1978, and even after that it failed to develop any coherent strategy or even clear objectives in the area. With the end of the Cold War, the administration's view of the Soviets and Cubans as the progenitors of regional turmoil has become not just an exaggeration, but an anachronism.

This chapter chronicles Soviet and Cuban policy toward Central America and the US response to it. Focusing primarily on the second half of the 1980s, when the Gorbachev reforms in the Soviet Union served as a catalyst for foreign policy changes around the world, it demonstrates how until the final year of the decade the United States failed to respond to the monumental Soviet policy shifts that helped move the Central American region toward conflict resolution. And it illustrates how, even then, the United States could not bring itself to engage Cuba in the process. Finally, the chapter concludes with suggestions for a more appropriate US response to the sweeping changes in Cuban and Soviet policies in Central America.

US Perceptions and Central American Reality

As indicated in the historical overview with which this book begins, Fidel Castro began to de-emphasize support for revolution in 1968. Both Cuba and the Soviet Union reconsidered prospects for armed struggle briefly in 1979 after the surprise Sandinista victory, but quickly reversed themselves after the failure of the FMLN offensive in El Salvador in January 1981. Both countries have stated time and again, publicly and privately, that they favor negotiated solutions, national reconciliation, and nonintervention. And both countries long ago gave up hopes of "communizing" the region, recognizing that the conditions for that simply do not obtain.

From the beginning of Ronald Reagan's presidency, however, the United States took the position that the crisis in Central America derived from Soviet and Cuban intervention. A 1980 report written by the Santa Fe Committee became the basis for the Reagan administration's policy toward the region. The Santa Fe report presented the Central American conflict strictly in East-West terms. According to this report, Cuba, acting as a surrogate for the Soviet Union, was instigating revolution in the region. Hence, it was said to be up to the United States to respond. The report emphasized military options such as strengthening regional security arrangements, revitalizing the Rio treaty, and stepping up military assistance.[3]

Even though the US government openly blamed the Soviet-Cuban connection for the conflict in the region, US government analysts did not always believe this was an accurate reflection of the situation. A confidential cable sent from the US Interests Section in Havana to the US State Department just prior to Somoza's ouster, for example, stated:

> We believe, however, that Cuba will be cautious about blatant involvement in the Nicaraguan crisis. Current Cuban Latin policy is to attempt to expand state-to-state relations with non-rightist regimes. Too obvious encourage-

ment of guerrilla action, or exercise of revolutionary firebrand role, particularly during time of high Cuban African involvement, detracts from
possibility of pursuing this policy.[4]

A recently declassified secret document from the Bureau of Intelligence and Research of the US Department of State, dating from the time
of the Nicaraguan revolution, concludes that the links between Cuban and
Central American guerrillas "are obscure." The document says that although Cuba "maintains some contact with major subversive movements
in Guatemala, Nicaragua—and probably El Salvador—[Cuba] does not
direct or coordinate their insurgent activity." The document concludes by
saying, "Cuba is unlikely to become much more active in Central
American insurgency in the near future."[5]

Despite secret documents such as these indicating doubts, the US
government publicly blamed Cuba and the Soviet Union for Central
American insurrections throughout most of the 1980s. In February 1981,
for example, a State Department spokesperson told the press that the
leftist guerrillas in El Salvador "did not represent a native insurgency,"
but were directed by Moscow. The infamous Department of State white
paper published that same month claimed the insurgency in El Salvador
had become a "textbook case of indirect armed aggression by Communist
powers through Cuba."[6] A joint State Department–Defense Department
publication in 1985 described "Soviet and Cuban military power and
intervention in Central America and the Caribbean . . . as much a part of
the region's crisis as the better known indigenous and historic factors."[7]

Apparently, the longer the Reagan administration was in office, the
less objective the Department of State's analysis. Thus, a recently declassified telegram sent by the US State Department in 1987 to US embassies
in Latin America stated: "A country-by-country examination of Cuba's
activities in Latin America and the Caribbean makes it clear that Cuba
has renewed its original campaign to promote armed revolution and install
pro-Cuban governments in the hemisphere." This document goes on to
emphasize the alleged Soviet-Cuban connection:

> Cuba's enormous investment of energy, money and agents in this campaign
> of violence would not be possible without Soviet help. . . . A major difference
> from the 1960s is that, instead of throwing up obstacles, the Soviet Union
> generally has backed Cuban efforts to incorporate non-doctrinaire groups
> into broad political-military fronts dedicated to armed struggle. Particularly
> in Central America, Soviet ties to local communist parties and bloc relation-
> ships have been used to favor insurrectionary violence. . . . Allowing Havana
> to take the lead in the hemisphere enables Moscow to maintain a low profile
> and cultivate state-to-state relations and valuable economic ties with major
> countries like Brazil and Argentina.[8]

This document shows that even two years after Gorbachev took office and initiated his reform program in the Soviet Union, the US State Department continued falsely to blame Central American insurgencies on Soviet-Cuban aggression. In response to this erroneous prognosis, the United States pursued a single-track strategy of military opposition. Although publicly avowing support for negotiated settlements, the United States in fact refused to pursue or seriously endorse any attempt at peaceful resolution in the region, and until 1989 rejected (or ignored) all overtures for negotiations made by Cuba and the Soviet Union. In 1989, the United States finally agreed to engage the Soviets—but not the Cubans—in a Central American dialogue.

What were the Soviets and Cubans really doing in the region? There is no doubt that the Sandinista victory in 1979 led Havana and Moscow to reevaluate the possibilities for revolution in the hemisphere. In the wake of the Nicaraguan revolution, the Communist parties in Guatemala and El Salvador endorsed armed struggle and began searching for assistance. In response to a 1980 request for aid from Salvadoran Communist party Secretary-General Shafik Handal, for example, Cuba and the Soviet Union provided some material assistance to the FMLN guerrillas in El Salvador.[9]

After the defeat of the Salvadoran rebel "final offensive" in 1981, the Soviets and Cubans retreated from advocating armed struggle. And although they may have provided some degree of material support for Salvadoran and Guatemalan revolutionaries afterward, they were also prepared to negotiate a settlement to the conflict. The Reagan administration, however, continued to portray Moscow and Havana as the aggressors and refused to meet them at the negotiating table. Until 1988, when the Gorbachev reforms were universally recognized and the Soviet Union cut off material assistance to Nicaragua, the United States regularly refused even to acknowledge Soviet and Cuban overtures toward a negotiated solution.

Cuban Interest in Negotiations

Despite consistent rebuffs from the US government, the Cubans and Soviets tried time and again to initiate a dialogue over the Central American conflict. A number of examples illustrating Cuban interest in negotiating and the US response—or lack thereof—follow.

In the late spring of 1981, the Nicaraguans, Hondurans, and Costa Ricans met to discuss border guarantees and reducing regional tensions. At that time, the Cubans stated their support for regional negotiations and mutual security guarantees. They went on to say that they would be willing to play a positive role in bringing such negotiations about. The US reaction to Cuba's apparently new moderate policy was an escalation of pressure against Cuba—tightening the embargo, establishing Radio Marti, allowing Cuban exiles to resume paramilitary training, and strongly threatening military action. The US actions were based on the fallacious assumption that pressuring and intimidating Castro would lead to his demise. Cuba predictably responded to increased US aggression by tightening its ties with Moscow, yielding results contrary to Washington's desires.[10]

A clear Cuban effort to pursue negotiations began with a confidential meeting between Secretary of State Alexander Haig and Cuban Vice-President Carlos Rafael Rodríguez in Mexico City in November 1981. The latter stressed that Cuba favored a peaceful settlement in Central America and was prepared to cooperate in that effort. But Haig said the United States wanted to see actions, not words. As a follow-up, General Vernon Walters visited Cuba in March 1982 and talked to Fidel Castro. As is now known, in that conversation Castro expressed the view that most bilateral problems between the United States and Cuba could be resolved quickly; issues such as Central America and Africa would be more complicated and would take longer to resolve. Castro did *not*, however, in any way indicate a refusal to negotiate those foreign policy issues, as the Reagan administration subsequently claimed. Quite the contrary, he was clearly signaling his readiness to discuss such issues. To his credit, General Walters himself did not repeat this misrepresentation on the part of the Reagan administration. Rather, he restricted himself to saying that in his judgment, the prospects for successful discussion of the foreign policy issues were "not bright." It was left to Assistant Secretary of State Thomas Enders to assert to the US Congress that Castro had *refused* to discuss Central America.[11] As were so many of the Reagan administration's assertions about its Central American policy, this statement was an outright lie. The truth was that in late 1981, as a follow-on to the Haig–Rafael Rodríguez conversation and in an effort to improve the atmosphere for dialogue, Cuba for a time suspended military shipments to Nicaragua. The United States ignored the gesture. Clearly, Cuba was seeking negotiations, and the United States was refusing them—the exact opposite of what the administration claimed.[12]

Beginning in the early 1980s and continuing until the electoral defeat of the Sandinistas in 1990, both the Reagan and Bush administrations attempted to portray Cuba as the radicalizing force behind the Nicaraguan revolution. In fact, quite the opposite was true. From the beginning of the Nicaraguan revolution, Castro privately counseled moderation to his Nicaraguan allies. He advised them to maintain a pluralist society and a mixed economy, to maintain good relations with the church, to encourage foreign investment, and to preserve good relations with the United States.[13]

In March 1982, Cuba endorsed a Mexican proposal for a negotiated settlement in El Salvador, a nonaggression pact between the United States and Nicaragua, and US-Cuban talks to reduce tensions. The United States flatly turned down the Mexican proposal.[14]

In July 1983, Castro stated his willingness to consider, in consultation with Nicaraguan officials, the removal of all Cuban military personnel from Nicaragua and an arms embargo applied to the Central American region, with the proviso that the United States withdraw militarily and respect the embargo. Although that particular formula was unacceptable to the Reagan administration, instead of using it as a starting point for negotiations, the United States never explored the issue with the Cubans.[15]

In 1984, Castro expressed regret that the United States did not follow up on his proposal. In an interview with Wayne S. Smith, Castro said that he believed grounds for accommodation still existed. "The grounds for an accommodation acceptable to all are there. . . . If there is ever any seriousness of purpose on the [US] side, Cuba is prepared to cooperate in the search for peaceful solutions in Central America."[16]

Again in 1985, Castro told US Congressmen Bill Alexander, Jim Leach, and Mickey Leland that he supported the Contadora peace process in Central America and that he was prepared to cooperate actively in finding a peaceful solution, including the withdrawal of his military personnel, halting arms shipments to the area, and accepting verification procedures. The US State Department responded by expressing skepticism about Castro's motives and refusing to test them.

Examples of Cuban overtures to promote dialogue over the Central American crisis abound. In November 1987, Vice Minister Jose R. Viera of Cuba told a visiting US delegation that conditions for socialism simply did not exist in any Latin American country [other than Cuba], but that conditions did exist for the establishment of democracy.[17] Viera also told the delegation that Cuba wanted a regional agreement that would peacefully end local conflicts, allow Central America to develop economically, and move from partial to full democracy. The vice minister concluded by saying that Cuba was willing to respect the Arias peace plan:

> We have on several occasions indicated our support for the Arias peace plan. We are prepared to respect its provisions, so long as other extra-regional powers respect them as well. We cannot formally commit ourselves to adhere to the plan, however, unless the United States is equally committed.[18]

This was typical of the Cuban position at that time. Cuba was willing to withdraw from the region as long as the United States also respected the terms of any agreements reached. Rather than using the Cuban offer as a point of departure for negotiations, however, the United States simply ignored the Cuban overtures.

Another example of Castro's willingness to assist his neighbors in resolving the conflict occurred in 1988. President Oscar Arias of Costa Rica approached Fidel Castro during the inauguration of President Rodrigo Borja of Ecuador. Aides to President Arias said that the Costa Rican president asked Castro to exert his influence on the Sandinistas as well as on the FMLN in El Salvador. They said Castro responded by saying that his leverage in the region was "relative," but that he would do his best to help revive the peace process.[19]

When the Soviet Union suspended all military shipments to Nicaragua in 1988, Cuba promised that no Soviet weapons would be transshipped to irregular forces in Central America. Again, at that time Havana indicated to Washington that it was willing to discuss the whole arms-supply issue in a bilateral or multilateral format. And again the Bush administration ignored the Cuban offer.[20]

In 1988, on instructions, the Cuban delegation to the peace discussions for the resolution of the southern Africa conflict indicated its government's willingness to negotiate all issues in disagreement between the two countries. They expressed the hope that the satisfactory results of the southern Africa negotiations could be carried forward in resolving other issues of concern to the United States and Cuba. Central America, of course, headed the list. As usual, the United States did not respond.[21]

Cuban interest in promoting dialogue and peace in Central America is not altruistic. It is based on the fact that a negotiated solution supports Cuba's best interests in the region. Cuba no longer believes that the right conditions exist for armed struggle in Central America or anywhere else. Cuba's promotion of stability is pragmatic. It does not want to expend its scarce resources in support of a cause it does not believe it can win.

Soviet Support for Negotiations

Similarly, the Soviets have also supported negotiated solutions to the Central American conflict. From the early days of the Sandinista government, the Reagan and later the Bush administrations attempted to portray Sandinista Nicaragua as a valuable "advance base" for the Soviet Union. However, the Soviet Union refused to provide Nicaragua with requested economic assistance for its ailing economy, and Soviet petroleum to Nicaragua began to dwindle in 1987. The Soviets never had combat aircraft, submarines, missiles, or offensive weapon systems of any kind in Nicaragua. Had Moscow viewed Nicaragua as its advance base in the region, it could have been expected to provide the necessary aid to keep the country afloat. It did not. Further, the Soviet Union did not even consider Sandinista Nicaragua to be a member of the Socialist family of nations, as then Soviet ambassador to Nicaragua, Valery Nikolayenko, stated categorically in 1988. He also said that Moscow did not have any interest in drawing Nicaragua closer to the Socialist bloc. Instead, the Soviets encouraged and helped bring about pluralism and elections.[22]

The Soviet Union has also supported regional attempts at a peaceful resolution to the crisis. An official Soviet statement in August 1987 welcomed the accords signed by the five Central American presidents and emphasized the Soviet government's "determination to respect the decision approved by the five presidents."[23] During the 1987 summit between Soviet secretary-general Mikhail Gorbachev and US president Ronald Reagan, Gorbachev indicated that Moscow would halt all military aid to Central America if the United States would do the same. Gorbachev was particularly interested in establishing a Central American demilitarized zone.[24] Rather than responding with a counteroffer, the Reagan administration simply did not respond to the proposals posited by the Soviets.

Over a year later, in 1988, the Soviet Union unilaterally suspended all military shipments to Nicaragua. Previously, they had terminated all assistance to the guerrillas in El Salvador. During his April 1989 visit to Cuba, Gorbachev told the Cuban National Assembly:

> We favor a Latin American solution to the conflict, a solution based on a balance of the interests of all parties concerned, without any outside inter-ference and with the guaranteed right of each nation to independent develop-ment. . . . Fidel and I have discussed this question and we are firmly convinced that it can only be resolved by political means.[25]

This came at a time when US officials were saying that "Soviet officials have not yet even begun to show any signs of their so-called 'new-thinking' in Central America."[26]

Once again, in August 1989, the Soviet Union indicated its support for a political solution in Central America. In the peace accords signed in Tela, Honduras, the Central American presidents agreed to stop outside aid to insurgencies in the region, and the Soviet Union welcomed the agreement.[27]

By the fall of 1989, public announcements of the end of world revolu-tion were emanating so clearly from Moscow that Washington was hard pressed to continue blaming the Soviet Union for the crises in Central America. In September 1989, a new line emerged in Washington. The United States expressed its readiness to open discussions with Moscow, but not with Cuba. US Secretary of State James A. Baker said at a press conference that "the US government does not challenge the Soviet Union's claim, first expressed in a confidential letter from Soviet President Mikhail Gorbachev to President Bush, that Moscow has stopped its shipments of weapons to Nicaragua."

Baker, however, went on to say that the United States was concerned about an increase in Eastern Bloc weapons from other sources, moving through Cuba and Nicaragua to Central America. "We would like to see the Soviet Union do as much as it possibly could with Cuba to stop that flow," Baker said.[28]

Since then, Cuba has become Washington's sole demon. Ironically, rather than accusing Cuba of being a proxy for Soviet expansionism in the hemisphere, as Washington did for three decades, Washington's new twist has been to plead with Moscow to moderate its headstrong ally. Moscow's "new thinking," however, specifically prohibits the Soviet Union from dictating to anyone, smaller allies included.

The Reluctant US Response

Why was the United States so reluctant to enter into negotiations with Cuba and the Soviet Union over Central America? One reason given was that Castro would not abide by any agreements reached. Therefore, the argument went, there was no point in entering discussions. But it is not a valid argument. The United States had no way of judging Cuba's sincerity without testing it. And in Central America this was never done. In southern Africa, on the other hand, where Cuban sincerity was tested, it proved to be solid. Cuba negotiated in good faith, signed the peace accords, and scrupulously abided by them. In fact, all Cuban troops left Luanda by May 1991, ahead of schedule. The record shows that when they were engaged, the Cubans were serious and honest negotiating partners.

US officials also claimed that US-Cuban negotiations might confuse or dishearten our allies in the region. But this also was an empty argument. If both sides of the Salvadoran conflict are able to sit at a negotiating table together, surely they could understand US motives for direct talks with Cuba over related issues. A willingness to talk doesn't imply weakness; rather, it demonstrates a desire to achieve stated goals through diplomacy, if possible.

Finally, the Bush administration has indicated that its reluctance to talk with Havana specifically rests on its expectations that Castro is about to fall. Why, Washington asks, should the United States begin a dialogue with Castro, thereby legitimating him, at a time when his regime is about to collapse?

Although his popularity on the island may have waned in recent years as economic problems beset Cuba, it is unlikely that Castro is in immediate danger of being replaced. Bush administration officials are fond of comparing Castro's Cuba to Eastern Europe; however, such comparisons only mask reality. Eastern European leaders were imposed on their countrymen by Soviet tanks. Castro came to power through a popular revolution. Moreover, Castro's charisma and popularity have never been equaled in the Socialist camp.[29]

The conflict in Central America stems from internal conditions—from economic underdevelopment and social injustice—far more than from global politics. A handful of wealthy elites have ruled a poor majority in far from democratic conditions for nearly as long as those countries have existed. Poverty and political repression have led men and women in the region to attempt to change their social conditions both through force of arms and around the negotiating table. The Soviet Union and Cuba are actors in the Central American crisis, although they did not create the problems. Neither country wishes to perpetuate the situation, as Washington has charged. Violent revolution to bring about socialism was dismissed by pragmatic Soviet analysts almost half a century ago. The Cubans de-emphasized armed struggle in 1968. And although Cuba and the Soviet Union may have provided some material support to the Salvadoran and Guatemalan guerrillas, both countries have also encouraged the idea of a negotiated solution to the Central American conflict time and again. The United States refused to respond to the bargaining offers posited by both countries until 1989, when it finally began speaking with the Soviets but continued to ignore the Cubans.

The United States would do well finally to engage Cuba in dialogue about a constructive resolution to the conflict, as it has with the Soviets. To a large extent, the crisis in Central America has been reduced from its boiling point in the mid-1980s to a low simmer today. The Nicaraguan conflict was resolved in favor of democracy (elections were held there on February 26, 1990), proving that peaceful negotiations could work after a decade of military struggle failed to solve anything.

It now appears that a compromise may be reached in El Salvador. A peace treaty signed between the FMLN and Salvadoran government officials in April 1991 under UN mediation yields the most hope for peace that that war-torn country has seen in over a decade.[30] There is even some hope of ending the violence in Guatemala. At this time of new thinking in Moscow and repeated Cuban expressions of interest in dialogue, Washington would profit from finally agreeing to engage Havana in the peace process. Because Havana does pull some weight with the scattered revolutionary forces in the region, any peace arrangements put in place would have a better chance of succeeding and enduring if they counted with Havana's firm commitment to respect them. It behooves Washington not simply to complain of Cuba's residual support for revolution in these countries, but to engage Cuba in the diplomatic process so as to change that conduct.

Lessons from southern African peace negotiations, in which all parties to the conflict sat down together and resolved the issues,[31] could serve the Central American purposes well. When the United States brokered the peace negotiations with Angola, Angola was an avowed Socialist country fully aligned with the Soviet Union and Cuba. Today, two years after the successful completion of negotiations, Luanda has opted for political pluralism and a mixed economy, and it recently signed a peace treaty with US-backed UNITA rebels.[32] This does not imply that negotiations between the United States and Cuba would automatically lead Cuba to abandon Marxism, but it does suggest that negotiations can lead to more than resolution of the conflict at hand. If the United States and Cuba could resolve their differences over the Central American conflict, the way might be opened for dialogue over a number of issues that have troubled the two countries for the last thirty years. These include human rights, the Guantanamo Naval Base, and migration issues, to name just a few.

If lessons from Nicaragua and Angola teach us anything, it is that diplomacy has worked where years of military conflict have failed. Is it not time fully to apply those lessons to remaining conflicts in Central America—and even to US-Cuban relations?

And, finally, as Julio Carranza Valdes points out in Chapter 8, the basic causes of instability in Central America are economic underdevelopment and social injustice. With peace returning to the region, at least for the moment, does it not behoove the United States to cooperate in mounting a concerted and large-scale economic development program? In the final analysis, that is the only way to assure political stability and peace in Central America. So far, however, US economic assistance to the region has been piddling. Even in Panama and Nicaragua, US efforts have been so limited and ineffective as to raise serious doubts about the Bush administration's seriousness of purpose. It is time to put those doubts to rest with a major effort.

Notes

1. See Chapter 1 in this volume, by Georgi Mirsky.
2. Department of State and Department of Defense, "The Soviet-Cuban Connection in Central America and the Caribbean," March 1985, Washington, D.C.
3. *A New Inter-American Policy for the Eighties* (Washington, D.C.: The Council for Inter-American Security, 1980). See also Wayne S. Smith, "Misperceptions and Missed Opportunities: U.S. Overreaction to Cuban Policy in Central America," paper presented at the Latin American Studies Association Conference in Albuquerque, New Mexico, April 20, 1985.
4. A cable from the US Interests Section in Havana to the US State Department, February 2, 1978, confidential (declassified February 28, 1991).

5. "Does Cuba Orchestrate Central American Insurgency?" secret report of Bureau of Intelligence and Research, US Department of State, July 27, 1978 (declassified February 28, 1991).

6. *The New York Times*, December 4, 1980, p. 1.

7. "The Soviet-Cuban Connection in Central America and the Caribbean," State Department–Defense Department, 1985, Washington, D.C., p. 1. The booklet goes on to say that "Soviet-backed guerrilla movements attempting to seize power... [in order to] ...establish regimes similar to those of their patrons—one party communist dictatorships" (p. 41).

8. "Cuban Covert Activities in Latin America," Department of State telegram, December 27, 1987, confidential (declassified), pp. 1, 3.

9. Wayne Smith, "The Soviet Union and Cuba in Central America," *Dialogue*, Fall 1989, p. 49.

10. For excellent details on this, see Wayne Smith, "Dateline Havana: Myopic Diplomacy," *Foreign Policy*, Fall 1982, pp. 162–163.

11. Smith, "Misperceptions and Missed Opportunities," pp. 10–11.

12. Wayne Smith, *The Closest of Enemies* (New York: W.W. Norton, 1987), pp. 254–255.

13. *The New York Times*, July 9, 1980, p. A10; see also Smith, *The Closest of Enemies*, p. 181.

14. Smith, *The Closest of Enemies*, p. 255.

15. Smith, "Misperceptions and Missed Opportunities," p. 14.

16. Wayne S. Smith, "Cuba: Time for a Thaw," *New York Times Magazine*, July 29, 1984.

17. Wayne S. Smith, "Havana and Washington," in *World Policy Journal*, Summer 1990, p. 562.

18. Wayne S. Smith interview with Viera in "Guardians Against Democracy," unpublished paper, 1989, p. 28.

19. *Miami Herald*, August 12, 1988, p. 17A.

20. Smith, "Havana and Washington," p. 571.

21. According to a source close to the negotiating team, who wishes to remain anonymous.

22. *The Washington Post*, November 6, 1988; for good detail on this, see Wayne Smith, "The Soviet Union and Cuba in Central America."

23. Soviet embassy press release, August 12, 1987.

24. Smith, "Guardians Against Democracy," p. 30.

25. "Gorbachev's Speech in Havana," *Times of the Americas*, April 5, 1989, p. 10.

26. *The New York Times*, March 30, 1989, p. A1.

27. *The Washington Post*, September 28, 1989, p. A44.

28. Ibid. This new line from Washington emerged only in late 1989. When President Gorbachev visited Cuba in March of that year, administration officials were still saying that "Soviet officials have not yet even begun to show any of their so-called 'new thinking' in Central America" (*The New York Times*, March 30, 1989, p. A1).

29. US Congress Western Hemisphere Subcommittee, hearings on Cuba and the Soviet Union, April 30, 1991; see also Smith, "Havana and Washington," p. 567.

30. *The Washington Post*, April 29, 1991, p. A3; *Wall Street Journal*, May 6, 1991, p. A12.

31. The parties involved were Angola, South Africa, and Cuba. The United States and the Soviet Union served as observers. The agreement, signed Decem-

ber 23, 1988, provided for the independence of South African–ruled Namibia by April 1990, and the UN-supervised, phased withdrawal of all 50,000 Cuban troops stationed in Angola by July 1991. See *The Washington Post*, December 23, 1988, p. A1; *The New York Times*, January 8, 1989, p. A5; *The New York Times*, January 11, 1989, p. A10.

32. Negotiators representing the Angolan government and the US-backed UNITA rebels reached an agreement on May 1, 1991, setting terms for a cease-fire and multiparty elections in Angola. *The Washington Post*, May 2, 1991, p. A31; *The New York Times*, May 2, 1991, p. A1; *Miami Herald*, May 2, 1991, p. 11A.

Part 4

The Soviet Union and Cuba

Chapter 10

The Future of the Soviet-Cuban Relationship

——————————— Sergo Mikoyan

Why has the question of the future of Soviet-Cuban relations become such an intriguing one, and one so persistently asked? For several years now, and especially since the economic difficulties of the Soviet Union became such a matter of public knowledge (but painstakingly concealed in the past by official Soviet statistics), foreign analysts and even some Soviet citizens have been asking a common question: Given the strains in Soviet-Cuban relations, when will the former stop providing the latter with huge subsidies amounting to $5–8 billion per year?

In fact, this is not a difficult question to answer. First of all, the alleged $5–8 billion subsidy was in fact (as we shall see below) nothing more than an invention of the CIA produced by deliberately using a fictitious exchange rate. True, Soviet-Cuban trade has run in Cuba's favor and has involved what could be described as Soviet subsidies, but the amount involved has not been large, even on paper. And by and large that is where the cost remained—on paper. The Soviet Union did not pay Cuba in hard currency; rather, until 1991, trade was on a barter basis, with accounts kept in rubles.

Second, political relations between the two have *not* been strained— or at least, have not been nearly so strained as portrayed in the US media. The two have different approaches to their problems and may not always agree, but such differences are easily accommodated within the parameters of a relationship in which respect for one another's sovereign prerogatives has long been embedded.

The very fact that the question is asked reflects a lack of comprehension on the part of the questioners as to the true motives underlying Soviet-Cuban cooperation and amicable relations. Such comprehension, it can be said, never existed in the United States, and in the Soviet Union it has recently been almost lost, along with many other values of the past, both good and bad.

Soviet Domestic Approach

Even before the events of August 1991, changes inside the Soviet Union and in its foreign policy came so rapidly that they resembled an avalanche. Questions related to Soviet-Cuban relations were now motivated not simply by considerations of economic balance or imbalance, but by serious political factors. New political thinking has evolved from theoretical concept to the point of practical implementation in various areas of foreign affairs.

Cuba was perhaps the last country of the Third World and of the Socialist system to become the subject of hot debate in the Soviet media, the Supreme Soviet, and in the Soviet society at large. This debate has not always been based on facts, or even involved serious arguments. Often the latter have been frivolous and in some cases have resulted from the automatic and emotional rejection of "old truths"—that is, the idea that anything said to have been true in the past must, by definition, be considered untrue today.

General Political Considerations

The process of democratization in the Soviet Union gave birth to new views of and approaches to Socialist regimes in other countries. This began with Mikhail Gorbachev's visits to various fraternal countries during which, with great care not to interfere in their internal affairs, he conveyed the message that change was inevitable and that "he who is late is the loser." His visits themselves became inspirations for change. The people of these countries knew their leaders did not like Gorbachev's speeches; in the German Democratic Republic, in Czechoslovakia, and in Romania, the circulation of texts was often restricted so that they could not be widely read.

When in the fall of 1989 the Eastern European countries began their rapid transformation toward more democratic regimes, it was celebrated not only in Eastern Europe but in the Soviet Union itself. Since the "Czech spring" of 1968, progressive forces in the Soviet Union had nurtured the hope that changes in their own country toward democracy—toward socialism with a more human face—would begin with changes in Eastern Europe. Those hopes were frustrated by the Brezhnev doctrine, and when change came its origins were reversed. It flowed from the Soviet Union itself into Eastern Europe, not the other way around. All the Eastern European regimes were fatally shaken by Soviet perestroika and by Gorbachev's categorical repudiation of the Brezhnev doctrine.

As a consequence of the vast changes in Eastern Europe, Socialist countries that were unmoved by these events, such as North Korea and Cuba, came to be seen as oddities and became the center of attention. In the Soviet Union, both North Korea and Cuba were known by the names of their leaders. Often, little more than that *was* known about them by those who entered the debate, but the more identifiable the name, the greater the tendency to see the whole question in terms of Stalinism—this tendency still being very strong in the Soviet Union.

Kim Il Sung has rarely been mentioned in the mass media over the years, but Fidel Castro is a well-known figure, and thus became the victim of the tendency to identify him with Stalinism as well as the belief that anything that was considered "good" in the past was now "bad."

That is why even some parliamentarians who should know better have assailed Fidel Castro in their speeches, and why journalists have found it stylish to criticize him and the country he leads, often without any real knowledge of either. For instance, in the text of one of his speeches last year (prepared for a parliamentary session but not delivered because of the limited time for the discussion of foreign policy issues), Vitali Ginsburg, a specialist in theoretical physics and a member of the Congress of the People's Deputies, sharply attacked Cuba, referred to Fidel Castro as "the last Stalinist," and demanded that Soviet subsidies be halted. As to the magnitude of those subsidies, Ginsburg simply accepted the kind of figures put forward by the CIA.[1]

The fact that Fidel Castro has resisted Soviet influence and leadership toward change irritated many. This irritation, however, is only partly inspired by preference for democratic reforms. One can easily discover the same messianic mentality—a mentality characteristic of Russia for centuries and only strengthened by the "proletarian messianism" of the Soviet period—all through the course of Soviet history.

There has been an immense interest in developments within the Soviet Union on the part of all the peoples of the Western Hemisphere. For Cuba, however, those developments have had a special importance. Fidel Castro and other members of the Cuban leadership were unhappy with what they saw as deviations from Socialist solidarity and internationalism, and often they did not try to conceal their irritation. This strengthened the hopes of US officials and some other foreign observers that Soviet-Cuban relations were deteriorating and might be near a breakdown that could even bring the termination of economic ties. This, in turn, raised expectations concerning economic chaos in Cuba leading to political collapse and the removal of Fidel Castro. As the then US ambassador to the United Nations, General Vernon A. Walters, put it bluntly in January 1988: "If the Soviets are willing to throw Najibullah overboard, there may be some hope that they are willing to throw Castro overboard. Three billion dollars a year is a lot of money in anybody's counting, even in rubles."[2]

Economic Issues

The amount of Soviet aid to Cuba has been distorted not only by the CIA but, in the past, by Soviet sources as well. One of the vices of the Soviet propaganda system in years past was to exaggerate the significance and amount of Soviet aid to other Socialist countries and, since the Khrushchev period, to the Third World as well. Sometimes only area specialists with inside information knew that these Third World countries in fact received incomparably more aid from the West than from the Soviet Union. True, the conditions attached to Soviet aid might be more favorable: the interest on loans was lower, the terms longer, and there were no special political or economic conditions such as might be put forward by the World Bank or in bilateral agreements with Western governments or private banks. Nonetheless, the amount of economic assistance provided by the West was usually considerably greater than that provided by the Soviet Union.

This was not necessarily true when it came to Cuba, but the tendency to overblow the magnitude of Soviet aid was certainly prevalent. True, Soviet journalists were sometimes asked at Central Committee briefings, or at those given by the Foreign Ministry, not to forget about the *mutual* advantages of Soviet-Cuban trade (it was feared the Cuban side might be displeased by a patronizing tone in Soviet press reports). But short comments concerning mutual benefits usually came only at the end of the much longer passages having to do with the importance of Soviet assistance. And it was the latter that stuck with Soviet readers, who often knew little of what the Soviet Union received in exchange from Cuba. Not even Cuban grapefruits and juices in the supermarkets changed that much. In short, the main thrust of Soviet propaganda was to emphasize Soviet generosity toward Cuba. The Soviet people accepted the message and believed their country was sending huge quantities of money and resources to the faraway island in the Caribbean.

In fact, Soviet-Cuban economic relations began to change dramatically in the 1980s. Gone were the ruble gifts of the 1960s and the significant subsidies of the 1970s.

Even during those earlier decades, however, long-term agreements on prices for sugar, nickel, and oil often resulted in situations in which Cuba found itself at a disadvantage, at least in terms of the contractual price. There were years, for example, when the Soviet Union paid Cuba less than the world market price for nickel. In 1968, for example, it paid only three-quarters of the market price.[3]

According to the data provided in a recent book edited by Eusebio Mujal-Leon[4] based partly on CIA reports and analyses, during the period 1960–1984, Soviet subsidies in oil totaled $8,088 million and subsidies in sugar totaled $19,528 million. At the same time, wheat and corn deducted $255 million from the Soviet subsidies. Thus, according to these figures, the total sum of Soviet subsidies to Cuba in these main commodities over a twenty-four–year period was more than $21 billion dollars. Total Soviet economic aid, according to these same calculations, reached $36–38 billion.

These figures, of course, stand in stark contrast to those mentioned earlier, also provided by the CIA, which place Soviet aid to Cuba at some $5–8 billion per annum. And even the more realistic estimates ignore a number of other factors and considerations. All major developed countries that import sugar, for example, have long paid special preferential prices to their steady suppliers. The quite understandable special treatment accorded by COMECON countries to their less-developed fellow members such as Cuba, Mongolia, and Vietnam is no different, for example, than the special treatment established years ago by the Andean Group for Ecuador and Bolivia.

Another consideration is that the services offered in Cuban ports to Soviet ships in the Atlantic have been invaluable. Some of those services would have cost the Soviet Union substantial sums in US dollars had they been rendered elsewhere. Others could not have been provided at all had it not been for Cuba.

Still another factor to be taken into account is that almost all Soviet goods supplied to Cuba (with the exception of petroleum and armaments) were of decidedly inferior quality. If calculated in US dollars, their prices should be evaluated at perhaps five times less than those fixed by Soviet indexes.

When all these things are factored into the picture, one begins to wonder: Who was paying a subsidy to whom? The element that has most distorted the picture, however, and that renders even the more reasonable figures in the Mujal-Leon book untenable, is the exchange rate used by the CIA in calculating Soviet-Cuban economic activity. During most of the thirty-year period under consideration, the official rate of exchange was 0.62 rubles to the dollar, but this was entirely artificial. Had CIA analysts been asked to use it for any other purpose, they would have replied that they preferred not to deal in fantasies. But applying it to Soviet-Cuban trade, they were able to present a fantasy that suited the interests of the US government—one that portrayed Cuba as dependent on massive annual subsidies from the Soviet Union.

How was this done? By using the artificial exchange rate, for example, to transform, say, the 0.26 rubles per pound the Soviet Union was paying (on paper) for sugar at a given moment to forty-two cents per pound. As the world market price would be only somewhere around eight cents, the CIA would thus report that the Soviet Union was paying a subsidy of thirty-four cents per pound. If one multiplies thirty-four cents per pound by the four to five million tons of sugar Cuba sold annually to the Soviet Union, one comes up with a huge dollar amount. Never mind that on international markets the rubles in which trade accounts were kept were literally worthless.

A more meaningful figure has recently become easily calculable. In 1990, the Soviet government introduced a tourist rate of exchange: 6.2 rubles to the dollar. Even this inflated the value of the ruble. When, in 1991, it was decided to base the official rate of exchange on the open market rate, the exchange immediately fell to 27.5 rubles to the dollar. Even if we use the earlier tourist rate as a base for calculations, however, we see that if the Soviet Union was paying 0.26 rubles for a pound of sugar, it was in effect paying no more than five cents per pound, well under the world market price. The fact of the matter has been that there was no subsidy—except in the CIA's calculations.

Be that as it may, and whatever the balance on paper, Soviet-Cuban trade has long been advantageous for both countries. Cuba needed Soviet petroleum and various other products, but the Soviet Union also needed Cuban sugar, nickel, and citrus products. Had the Soviet Union had to acquire sugar and nickel, for example, on the world market, it would have had to pay a much higher price, probably in dollars. As it was, it acquired a steady supply on a barter arrangement, without any outlay of hard currency.

In any event, the old system of trade has been discarded. Dramatic changes in economic conditions inside the Soviet Union combined with new export opportunities for Cuba have resulted in a realignment of their trading relationship. In December 1990, a new agreement was signed under which the two have begun to change over to an exchange of goods on a commercial basis, with the accounts kept in dollars rather than rubles. Subsidies are no longer a part of the scheme, even on paper. Importantly also, the agreement covers only a one-year period, rather than, as in the past, five years. This is because the two are feeling their way toward a new kind of arrangement during a period of great change in both countries; projecting terms of trade five years into the future is simply no longer possible.

Despite the new trade agreement, which for all practical purposes eliminates even the concept of subsidies, US analysts and the media continue to discuss Soviet-Cuban trade as though nothing had changed. An editorial in *The Washington Post* on June 2, 1991, for example, urged the Bush administration to demand the termination of the billions of dollars in Soviet trade concessions to Cuba as a condition for US economic assistance to the Soviet Union. But how can one terminate that which does not exist, even if, in theory, one were willing to accept so humiliating a condition?

Military Issues

With the end of the Cuban military operations in Africa, Soviet military assistance to Cuba has been reduced dramatically. Further reductions may be registered in the future, but, in my opinion, not until the United States reviews its own policy toward Cuba and halts its efforts to isolate and intimidate the island. Until then, Cuba must take seriously the need to defend itself against attack. US hostility toward Cuba is such that Cuban leaders cannot, in prudence, count on indefinite adherence to the 1962 US pledge not to invade. Much less can they do so in the wake of the US invasions of Grenada and Panama, the latter having violated the United Nations Charter, the Charter of the Organization of American States, and international law generally.

Even the war in the Gulf—although fought to turn back an act of open aggression and thus to be praised—was at the same time read by many as signaling a greater disposition on the part of US leaders to use military actions elsewhere in the world against regimes the United States simply regards as unpalatable. That, of course, would include Cuba.

So long as such tensions obtain in US-Cuban relations, Cuba will be concerned with assuring its defense capabilities, and the Soviet Union will probably feel obliged to help in that endeavor. Soviet military assistance to Cuba, then, may remain an irritant in US-Soviet relations, in the absence of some change on Washington's part.

US observers claim that one source of irritation has to do with the quantity and sophistication of the weapons supplied by Moscow. They point out that by 1990 Cuba had 262 MiG combat aircraft, 122 Mi helicopters, and more than 200 surface-to-air missile launchers. Subsequently, in May 1991 a squadron of MiG-29s was delivered, in accordance with previously signed agreements.

Jaime Suchlicki, a professor at the University of Miami, put a sinister interpretation on such assistance. He wrote: "If the U.S. were to launch an invasion of Cuba, certainly no amount of weapons the Cubans could amass would deter or defeat an all-out American attack on the island. Cuban weapons then are aimed at intimidating and controlling the Cuban people."[5]

But reasonable people will find it difficult to follow the logic of such an argument. First of all, although no one would argue that Cuba could "defeat" an all-out US attack (and obviously the Kremlin would no longer think of pushing any fatal buttons in response to such an attack), deterrence is something else again. Calculations of potential losses are always an important consideration—sometimes the most important one—in decisions to launch or not to launch a military action. The prospect of unacceptable damage, relative to the goals of the action, will sometimes deter a stronger country from attacking a weaker one. Hence, the Cuban objective is to make it clear that it could inflict serious losses and that an invasion of Cuba would not be a quick, easy affair, as was the invasion of Panama. It is hoped that this will cause the hawks in the United States to think twice about launching any such adventure.

And how can we imagine MiG-29s and surface-to-air missiles being used against the Cuban people? This is an absurd proposition in itself, but it is rendered even more so by the fact that after the invasions of Grenada and Panama, practically the entire adult population of Cuba was armed by the government. Small arms supplied by the Soviet Union, in other words, far from being intended for use *against* the Cuban people, have actually been placed in their hands. Evidently, the Cuban government had little fear of any popular insurrection. What it did fear, and still does, is a US attack.

Subversive Activity

If one judges by books such as Maurice Halperin's *The Rise and Decline of Fidel Castro*, one would think Cuba was responsible for more military interventions in Latin America than the United States. Ironically, Halperin's list of interventions begins with Panama, Guatemala, and the Dominican Republic.[6]

Halperin is, of course, correct that the actions he calls "subversive" have a two-century–old tradition in the history of Latin America. This tradition of "export of revolution" began when Simón Bolivar of Venezuela fought for the liberation not only of his country but of Colombia, Peru, Ecuador, and Bolivia (in those times called "Alto Perú") and put forward the idea of the Panama Congress. It began when General San Martín marched from his native Argentina across the Andes into Chile, and then to Peru and Ecuador. Under their banners, people from all over the world fought for independence. There were even a few from the distant and unknown Russia. And this came only a few decades after George Washington had attracted to his banners Europeans such as Lafayette, and Kościuszko.

The spectacular victory of the Cuban revolution inexorably began a new tide of guerrilla wars of liberation, and gave rise to a whole new series of movements eager to duplicate the experience of Castro's 26th of July movement. It is difficult indeed to imagine Castro turning his back on those movements; rather, to be sure, Cuba did provide training, advice, and even some arms to its sympathizers in Venezuela, Colombia, Peru, and elsewhere. The zenith—and the beginning of the end—of that sort of activity was the unsuccessful attempt of Che Guevara to create "another

Vietnam" in the heartland of South America.

And what was the Soviet Union's relationship to this kind of activity? In the United States, there seemed to be only two answers to that question: Either the Soviet Union had at least made it possible for Cuba to implement such a subversive policy, or it was manipulating Castro's "plans for world conquest" to serve its own purposes.

I have spent countless hours trying to convince people from the United States that this was not true. First of all, Fidel Castro himself is simply not of such a character as to be anyone's puppet. Second, the guerrillas themselves were fighting for their own causes, not to serve the interests of anyone else.

The Cuban decision to send troops to Angola to save the Popular Movement for Angolan Liberation (MPLA) from defeat at the hands of the invading South Africans (Operation Carlotta, 1975) was a good example. Few in the United States had any comprehension of the motives behind that decision or believed that it was one taken by the Cubans themselves without consulting, or even notifying, Moscow. Not until Arkady Shevchenko, the defector from the Soviet Foreign Ministry, reported in 1982 that this had been the case did US analysts begin to give some credence to the idea that the Cuban intervention in Angola was entirely Cuba's initiative—although subsequently, of course, the Soviet Union provided some logistical support to the effort.

Why this tendency to believe that everything Castro did was instigated by Moscow? Perhaps the best answer to that was provided by W. Raymond Duncan:

> Fidel Castro is nobody's puppet, but so heavy has his dependence on the Soviet Union become for economic and military support that the presumption of subservience to the Kremlin's wishes runs strongly through many analyses. Even those who are uncomfortable with such assessments seem not to come to grips with the elusive reasons for the anomaly of a dependent Castro nonetheless pursuing an often independent foreign policy line or a policy that advanced his ambitions far more than it resulted in discernible benefits for the Soviet Union.[7]

Whether anomaly or in the natural order of things, the Soviet Union was never able, and in fact never really hoped, to exercise a deciding influence in Cuba. Influence was measured by the ability to persuade, to explain, and to convince. The pattern of the smaller country, the receiver of aid, inducing the larger partner to take a greater role in regional conflicts than it would otherwise have wished or than its immediate interests dictated, may not be an anomaly; it may be the norm. In any event, being the hostage of the smaller partner was not a role that fell only to the Soviet Union. One need only examine US relations with Israel to understand that it was one played by both superpowers.

And, strangely, it was South Africa that dragged the United States into absolutely counterproductive behavior in Angola. Noting that the CIA even urged Savimbi not to participate in efforts to bring about a negotiated settlement, Richard Payne concluded that:

> U.S. policy toward Angola was characterized by confusion, inconsistency and expediency. . . . Not only was U.S. credibility shattered further and its position as a global power seriously eroded, but indecisiveness and an awkward approach in Angola paved the way for increased Soviet-Cuban involvement in Ethiopia.[8]

But let us return to the purpose of Soviet weapons supplied to Cuba. Suchlicki holds that a second reason for their acquisition may relate to the projection of Castro's power abroad. As recently as March 1991, Suchlicki wrote that:

> With the protective umbrella of the Soviet Union, Castro continues to play a major role in Africa, Latin America and the Middle East, supports revolution on three continents, and plays a major leadership role in the non-aligned movement—a role totally out of proportion to Cuba's size and resources—all at the expense of the Cuban people.[9]

Here we have a generalization, which while perhaps effective in influencing those who are not acquainted with the facts of the matter, can hardly be accepted as a serious argument. By March 1991, almost all Cuban troops had been withdrawn from Africa. (The last, in fact, departed Angola in May 1991, two months ahead of schedule.) Suchlicki suggests Castro is stirring up violent revolution in Africa and the Middle East. One can only ask: Where? And what role would M-72 tanks and MiG-29 aircraft play in that process?

What role, indeed, would such weapons play in Latin America? Here, the Soviet Union has made a clear distinction between weapons that are necessary for Cuba's defense and those that might be intended for guerrilla forces. It supplies the first, but by no means the second. True, a few rifles and other small arms of Soviet manufacture have turned up in Central America in recent years, but that has certainly not been by Soviet design. Further, such items as the Kalashnikov rifle have become international commodities, produced in several countries and until recently sold widely even in "guns and ammo" stores in the United States. Their use by a few of the guerrillas in Central America over recent years hardly constitutes evidence of Soviet support for such groups.

And what of Cuban policy? Has Castro really been supporting revolution throughout Latin America in recent years? Quite the contrary, even as of 1982 Cuba had come around to saying that conditions for armed revolution existed in only two countries: El Salvador and Guatemala. In no other country has there been any recent evidence of Cuban support for national liberation groups, and even in El Salvador and Guatemala, Cuba has since at least 1985 expressed its full support for negotiated solutions. It has also consistently offered to discuss the question of outside arms supply with the United States—offers the United States has just as consistently rebuffed.

In sum, the vision of Cuba stirring up revolution around the globe with weaponry supplied by the Soviet Union is simply false. There may have been a time years ago when it had somewhat more relevance, but in 1991 it has none.

Double Standards

When in 1989 a small plane that had taken off in Nicaragua came down in El Salvador with a number of surface-to-air missiles aboard, the United States expressed outrage. The facts of the case were confused, but it was eventually established that the missiles had been supplied by Nicaraguan army officers (supposedly without authorization). Neither Cuba nor the Soviet Union had anything to do with the case. It was, nonetheless, a violation of international norms and it was encouraging to note that the matter was thrashed out between El Salvador and Nicaragua and resulted in corrective measures.

This was by no means the first time that surface-to-air missiles had been supplied to guerrilla forces. The United States had been supplying them for years to the mujahidin in Afghanistan, who had used them not only to shoot down Soviet helicopters, but Afghan passenger planes as well, with a great loss of civilian lives. Strangely, that caused no indignation at all in the West.

Similarly, there was great consternation over the tragic downing of the South Korean airliner by Soviet forces back in 1983, even though the plane was over Soviet territory, but none over the downing of an Iranian passenger plane by the US Navy over the Gulf, although that plane was over international waters. These episodes simply prove that double standards exist and must be eliminated if we are really to move toward a new world order.

That tendency to think in terms of double standards certainly damaged US stature in the world during the recent war in Central America. The United States persisted in describing Soviet and Cuban military aid to the Sandinista government in Nicaragua as evil and part of a sinister expansionist strategy, while referring to its own aid to the Contras as highly moral and above reproach. Aid to the Contras indeed took on some of the aspects of a holy crusade, with President Reagan describing them as the moral equivalents of the Founding Fathers of the American Republic!

This double-standard mind-set has always impaired understanding and reasonable reactions on both sides. Both the United States and the Soviet Union have been guilty of it. That is one of the reasons that the path to reconciliation and to the peaceful resolution of conflicts was so lengthy and so difficult.

The Soviet Union helped the people of Nicaragua to defend themselves, supported the Vietnamese liberation of Cambodia from the genocidal Pol Pot regime, protested against the invasion of Cuba at the Bay of Pigs and against US interventions in the Dominican Republic, in Grenada and, yes, in Vietnam. But, on the other hand, the Soviet Union fought fiercely against the people of Afghanistan, violently crushed the will of the peoples of Hungary and Czechoslovakia, and in Ethiopia supported what amounted to a new emperor more bloodthirsty than Haile Selassie.

The conflict in Central America, where both Cuba and the Soviet Union were indirect participants, began to wind down when the US Congress suspended military aid to the Contras. This bold action created real conditions for a peaceful resolution of the long and destructive war in Nicaragua. The president of Costa Rica, Oscar Arias, won the Nobel Peace Prize, but in my opinion it really belonged to the US Congress. After that, the Soviet Union, and even Cuba, brought their massive military aid to Managua to an end. And, finally, the February 1990 elections showed conclusively that a policy of national reconciliation can be more effective than a military approach, which serves only to aggravate problems whose roots lie in economic underdevelopment and social injustice. Such military approaches had been supported by the superpowers because they viewed regional conflicts through the prism of their own global strategic rivalry.

Cuba's acquiescence to the settlement in Nicaragua, and its full cooperation in bringing about accords in Angola and Ethiopia, surprisingly had no positive impact at all on US policy toward its "closest of enemies," to use the title of Wayne Smith's book on US-Cuba relations.[10] Neither did a more constructive US approach elsewhere spill over into some areas such as Afghanistan, where the United States and Pakistan practically ignored the articles of the Geneva agreement. It would be foolish of the Soviet Union to bring back the concept of linkage, but still the absence of reciprocity has been disappointing.

The New US Demands

Now that the regional conflicts that used to be at the epicenter of the controversy have wound down, what are the new US objectives with respect to the Soviet-Cuban relationship?

We have heard a number of US pundits complain that Cuba's economic links to the Soviet Union have enabled it to survive US efforts to strangle it. Did such pundits expect the Soviet Union to participate in strangling Cuba? It would almost seem so, for there are voices everywhere in the United States, in both official and unofficial quarters, suggesting that the Soviet Union should utilize its economic leverage to force Cuba to hold free and fair elections.

Such demands enter a new dimension. They go far beyond the old demands related to Angola, Ethiopia, and Central America, and even beyond any limits of respect for international law. Nor are they consistent with the cordial relationship the United States itself enjoys with countries such as Saudi Arabia, which has never held an open election, and with various others whose human rights practices make Cuba look innocent in comparison. (In this regard, I cannot forget a newspaper report some years ago about the execution of a young couple from the huge Saudi royal family for their unsuccessful attempt to leave the country in order to marry.)

Strangely, also, the new US demands that the Soviet Union intervene in Cuba's internal affairs came just at the time that the United Nations was painstakingly looking for a formula that would make it possible to save the lives of millions of Kurdish men, women, and children from Saddam Hussein's genocidal campaign against them, yet at the same time not blatantly intervene in the internal affairs of Iraq, even though it is governed by one of the cruelest, most bloodthirsty and cynical dictators of modern times.

And yet, despite the nature of the regime and the fact that it had twice used chemical weapons against the Kurds, no one, including the Soviet government, considered that it had placed itself beyond the framework or beyond the protection of international law.

President Bush was wisely inclined not to try to isolate China following the Tiananmen Square massacre. He was correct in saying that trying to isolate a country is not the best way to influence it.[11] He would do well, however, to apply the same reasoning to Cuba.

Probably the Heritage Foundation is the one US institution that sympathizes most strongly with the ultraconservative Cuban-American National Foundation in Miami, whose leaders are anxious to install in Cuba the same version of democracy they try to implement in Miami (in other words, anyone who disagrees risks being blown up). That is why the Heritage Foundation[12] and even some members of the US government are ready to attach a whole spectrum of conditions related to Cuba to the development of Soviet-Cuban relations. The realization that the Soviet Union had economic difficulties (without any understanding of the potential consequences to the outside world of aggravating those difficulties) brought forth in 1990 and 1991 a series of demands in the sphere of economic cooperation that resembled an ultimatum.[13] Indeed, they read more like the conditions for a cease-fire put forward to a defeated Saddam Hussein than an economic program to be negotiated with the other superpower,[14] whose view and policies are still key to world security.

Again, the New Demands

These new demands, irrespective of their exact wording, are that the Soviet Union join, or make more effective and ruinous for Cuba, the embargo policy. The only visible goal is to bring the Castro regime to its knees (which I personally can never imagine) and possibly to get the Miami exiles, mostly extremists, back to Cuba as its new rulers. Let us not be deceived by words about bringing democracy to Cuba: democratic reforms on the island would not be welcomed in the "corridors of power" in the United States (and even less so in Miami). It seems clear that those who have long advocated such a policy of bringing Cuba to its knees and now would like to drive or seduce the Soviet Union to join it, are not much concerned with international law[15] and even less with common sense. No one asks why Saddam Hussein merits the protection of international law but Fidel Castro does not.

Why do observers in Washington and Miami think the Soviet Union would join their efforts against Cuba? They give two reasons: (1) Because Fidel Castro has refused to accept perestroika and thus is no longer an obedient puppet of Moscow (which these same observers believe him to have been earlier); or (2) because of economic and political difficulties in the Soviet Union itself, which have resulted in its retreat from the Third World.

The first point has already been discussed. I will simply add here that although reforms are indeed being contemplated in Cuba, their scope, nature, and ultimate direction must be and will be determined entirely by those who live on the island. Cuban reforms may follow a path very different from perestroika, but that is the sovereign right of Cubans to decide.

As to the second argument: Although it is true that Mikhail Gorbachev's new thinking has been the basis for a policy of reconciliation and the peaceful settlement of conflicts in the Third World, that is not to say that the Soviet Union is prepared to abandon long-term friends like Cuba to the designs of the United States. Demanding that Moscow join the efforts of Washington and Miami to strangle Cuba is really too much to ask.

There will be those in the United States who will ask, "Why should you place strains on your relationship with the United States, whose cooperation you need, for the sake of a small country so distant and of declining interest and value to you?"

I cannot presume to provide a definitive answer for the Soviet government—or governments. Views abound in our country, and I can offer only my own. But with this reservation, I can think of several reasons to continue the relationship with Cuba on as normal a basis as possible.

1. A great country cannot gladly accept isolation and humiliation. No matter how important US-Soviet ties may be, a complete loss of face in the Third World, and a tarnished image elsewhere, including Western Europe, would be too high a price to pay for the questionable honor of becoming an accomplice to Washington's abnormal obsession with Cuba.

2. Countries, like ordinary human beings, have (or should have) such elementary characteristics as dignity, faithfulness to long-term friendships, distaste for submission under pressure, and the realization that selling out one's friends is simply wrong, even if—or especially if—the betrayal may bring good profits.

3. The Castro regime cannot be compared to those of Ceausescu, or even of Honecker. Neither should it be measured by the standards of Austria, Finland, or Holland; it should be measured by those of Guatemala, Honduras, Haiti, or the Dominican Republic. And announcements in Washington about the triumphs of democracy in those countries convince no one who knows their reality. Whatever its faults, Castro's Cuba offers its people the best health care and education in Latin America. And it is free. There are no homeless and no one is starving. You will not see packs of impoverished, hopeless children in the streets of Havana stealing from passersby or killing; rather, in Cuba you will see them attending school and being cared for. And is not the way children are cared for, irrespective of the kind of society, the most important criterion for judging its sickness or its health?

4. To be sure, Cuba needs a mixed economy and democratic reforms. Rigid state ownership and full control over the economy have proved to be obstacles to economic and technological development. A paternalistic approach to leadership of any society can be a positive factor only for certain and brief periods of time. Pluralism of opinion, including the opinions of those who disagree with the leadership, is essential for normal political development; it is essential that people be assured that they can influence the decisions that affect their lives and that they can feel pride in the achievements of the society and a certain responsibility for its mistakes and failures. All this is true, but how can the Soviet Union insist that Cuba accept perestroika as the only path to reform when in fact our

great country, while boldly striving for the best, has managed to accumulate perhaps the greatest assortment of acute and pressing problems perhaps ever faced by a single society? Can we really say with a straight face that we are the example that other countries should follow?

The Soviet-Cuban relationship and the absence of a normal US-Cuban relationship have become tightly entwined. There are those in the United States who seem to believe that international developments such as the collapse of socialism in Eastern Europe and the growing problems of the Soviet Union "have weakened the argument for normalization of relations and that the issue now is whether to maintain the current policy [that is, the current US policy toward Cuba] or to toughen it."[16]

Short of an invasion, one can only wonder how the policy could be toughened. The author of the above passage speculates that Castro might be murdered by disgruntled Cuban army officers, but at least she does not urge the CIA to give them a hand; at least we have not gone back to that.[17]

In conclusion, rather than adjusting its Cuba policy to the post-Cold War era we have now begun—an era we had hoped would be characterized by the end of global confrontation, by the peaceful settlement of regional conflicts, and by a conciliatory spirit and rule of law in the international community—the United States continues its confrontational policy toward Cuba and is even considering ways to increase the pressures. It is a policy that obviously flows from the worst kind of Cold War mind-set and causes one to wonder whether we have really entered a new era at all. It is an approach unworthy of the United States, especially at what should be the most hopeful juncture in world history. And certainly it is too much to expect that the Soviet Union would join in such a Cold War approach. Quite the contrary, to answer the question with which I began this chapter, Soviet-Cuban relations do have a future, albeit one within a reduced framework devoid of outdated strategic considerations. If the United States persists in efforts to disrupt this perfectly normal, nonthreatening relationship, it will mean that the new world order President Bush speaks of so much is one based more on the mind-sets of the past than of the bright new future for which we had all hoped.

Notes

1. *Moskovski Komsomolets*, July 18, 1990.
2. Vernon A. Walters, "Reflections on Gorbachev's Policies and East-South Relations," University of Miami Graduate School of International Relations, Occasional Papers Series, Vol. 2, No. 4, January 1988, p. 15.
3. Eusebio Mujal-Leon, ed., *The U.S.S.R. and Latin America: A Developing Relationship* (Boston, Unwin Hyman, 1989).

4. Ibid.

5. From a paper presented to a seminar, organized by the Institute for Soviet and East European Studies of the University of Miami on March 18, 1991.

6. Maurice Halperin, *The Rise and Decline of Fidel Castro* (Berkeley: University of California Press, 1989), Chapter 28.

7. W. Raymond Duncan, *The Soviet Union and Cuba* (New York: Praeger, 1985).

8. Richard J. Payne, *Opportunities and Dangers of Soviet-Cuban Expansion* (New York: State University of New York Press, 1988), pp. 166–167.

9. Jaime Suchlicki, see note 5.

10. Wayne S. Smith, *The Closest of Enemies* (New York: W.W. Norton, 1987).

11. *The Washington Post*, May 29, 1991.

12. The Heritage Foundation, Backgrounder 768, May 14, 1990.

13. See the article by Thomas L. Friedman in *The New York Times*, May 31, 1991.

14. Foreseeing doubts as to the applicability of the term "superpower" to today's Soviet Union, I believe I should focus on the original meaning of that term. Despite all its economic, political, and ethnic difficulties the Soviet Union (or finally, perhaps, Russia proper) is still a superpower. If it were simply the rate of economic development that determined that title, Japan or Germany could challenge the United States; and if the criteria were the absence of ethnic or racial problems, again, the United States could be challenged by many. Unfortunately, our present imperfect world makes superpowers only of those who can destroy each other and the whole globe. That doubtful honor belongs so far only to the United States and the Soviet Union (or to that future country, the capital of which will be Moscow).

15. Says Senator Daniel P. Moynihan:

> The president has cited international law as the basis on which America was proceeding. There was one press conference in late August [1990] in which the president used the term "international law" six times in fifteen minutes. That's as much as his predecessors had done in the last thirty years. Something happened ... I don't know whether we turned to international law procedures as a form of convenience, or whether, in a new setting, this seemed a reasonable and appropriate approach to the management of world conflict. . . . Either we can move into a kind of *PAX AMERICANA*, where we perhaps use these standards for reasons that really are of convenience rather than conviction, or we can move into a world where we are more genuinely attached to these norms, feel they are in our interest, and pursue them accordingly. (Woodrow Wilson Center Report, March 1991, Vol. 2, No. 5, p. 9)

16. Susan Kaufman Purcell, "Cuba's Cloudy Future," *Foreign Affairs*, Summer 1990, p. 128.

17. Ibid.

Chapter 11

The Cuban Perspective on Cuban-Soviet Relations

Estervino Montesino Segui

In speaking of relations between the Soviet Union and Cuba, it should be kept in mind that their history is one of linkage between two autochthonous revolutions (the great Socialist revolution of October 1917 and the Cuban revolution of 1959). The two have their similarities, but they also have their own peculiarities, given the specific historic conditions from which each emerged and in which each developed. The two are, and always have been, distinct. We see clear evidence of this today. Since the mid-1980s, the Soviet Union has entered into a restructuring of its entire society and Cuba has begun a process of rectification of errors and negative tendencies. These processes of change are occurring simultaneously—and in each case in a Socialist country—yet they are different. Each responds to the particular internal conditions.

Soviet-Cuban ties were forged during the tensest years of the Cold War and were shaped by the unrelieved hostility of the United States toward Cuba. It is now accepted wisdom that the Cold War is over. Perhaps it is, but not all of the attitudes that fed it have been overcome. There are many examples to illustrate this, but it is enough to take note of the various economic and bilateral US-Soviet summit conferences at which the United States has taken the position that the Soviet Union must sever its ties with Cuba, and that failure to do so will impede an improved climate between the United States and the Soviet Union. Clearly, although US policy toward the Soviet Union and Eastern Europe has changed, a Cold War paradigm persists when it comes to US-Cuban relations and, by extension, to US attitudes toward Soviet-Cuban relations.

Worth noting are the remarks of Yan Burliay, the deputy director for Latin America in the Soviet Foreign Ministry, who described US policy toward Cuba as being clearly locked in the Cold War past. He proposed a dialogue between Cuba and the United States so as to lower tensions between the two countries, and to move toward resolution of the problems between them. Furthermore, he warned, "the United States cannot expect any change in Havana so long as it pursues a policy consisting of military pressure, an economic blockade and cultural aggression."[1]

At present, the US government looks upon the international climate as being very favorable to its interests; there is no longer a Socialist bloc to challenge those interests. Not surprisingly, then, it continues to pursue a policy precisely such as that described above. At the same time, the Cuban government continues to place a high priority on and give special attention to relations with the Soviet Union because that is the country that has provided Cuba with constant political support and that has offered Cuba an invaluable military supply line, allowing it to guarantee its national defense and maintain a satisfactory level of economic relations. This support, which in many spheres is of vital importance for Cuba's economic well-being and national security, has continued despite the internal difficulties of the Soviet Union.

Political Realities

Current Soviet-Cuban relations take place within the framework of the Treaty of Friendship and Cooperation, signed on April 4, 1989. This treaty specifies the political principle that ought to govern relations between the two countries:

> Based on the premise of relations of fraternal and indestructible friendship and solidarity, on the community of ideology, the doctrine of marxism-leninism and internationalism, and the common objectives of constructing socialism and communism; ... the high contracting parties ratify their determination to continue developing and enriching their fraternal, bilateral relations on the basis of the traditional principles of non-intervention, mutual respect and equality as an effective contribution to the prosperity of their peoples and the strengthening of peace.[2]

This statement of principle in no way contradicts the UN Charter. Quite the contrary, it invigorates the charter, and is harmonious with the new political attitudes in the Soviet Union and with the rectification process in Cuba. Furthermore, Article 12 explicitly states that this treaty "is not directed against third countries."[3]

Therefore, bilateral relations between Cuba and the Soviet Union ought not to be interpreted as implying a security threat to any Caribbean, Latin American, or other hemispheric country.

In the same manner, President Gorbachev, in a speech before the Cuban National Assembly of People's Power in 1989, stated "The USSR does not have, nor does it intend to have, naval, air or missile bases, or intend to place nuclear arms or any other weapons of mass destruction there." He then added, "We call upon the other powers to follow a similar approach so as to contribute to the transformation of Latin America into a region of peace, security, and stability."[4] The Soviet leader also noted, "The Soviet Union and Cuba have had a common approach to the key problems of international life."[5]

There is, in fact, abundant evidence to affirm that last statement. A vote analysis of Cuban and Soviet positions on all resolutions taken up in the UN general assemblies from 1985 to 1989, for example, reveals a high degree of identity. On 93.7 to 96 percent of the resolutions, the two countries cast identical votes. The areas of relatively greater divergence concerned disarmament and budgetary and finance issues.

On May 8, 1990, the foreign ministers of Cuba and the Soviet Union exchanged messages of congratulation on the thirtieth anniversary of the re-establishment of diplomatic relations between their two countries. Both messages stressed the importance of the Treaty of Friendship and Cooperation of 1989.[6]

At the anniversary ceremony in Havana, José Machado Ventura, a member of the Political Bureau and Secretary of the Central Committee of the Cuban Communist party said:

> Cuban-Soviet collaboration over these 30 years has been a determining factor in the creation of the material and technical base of socialism in Cuba. It affects nearly all of the facets of the national economy. So it is fitting to stress on a day like today, as has been done, how Soviet-Cuban relations, due to their moral content, transcend the material level, and constitute a lasting example of fraternity, respect and loyalty.[7]

Links between the governments and the peoples of the two countries have taken on new dimensions over the last few years. For its part, for example, the Cuban government has been particularly interested in making certain its rectification process is better understood by the Soviet people and that it is able to counter whatever perceptions, interpretations, or comparisons certain sectors in the Soviet Union may make between the outcome of the Socialist processes in Eastern Europe and the revolutionary process in Cuba. Similarly, Cuba has sought different means to counter certain nongovernmental attitudes in the Soviet Union. These exhort the Soviet Union to follow a hyperpragmatic approach, abandoning its policy of proletarian internationalism. In this effort, Cuba is striving to neutralize any internal tendencies in the Soviet Union that might harm not just Cuba's interests, but those of the Third World in general. Further attesting to continuing good relations between Moscow and Havana have been a number of visits to Cuba over the past two years by the highest level Soviet leaders. Among these were the visits of the Soviet foreign minister, the chairman of the Joint Chiefs of the Soviet Armed Forces, and the vice president of the Council of Ministers, Leonid Abalkin. Abalkin heads the Inter-governmental Soviet-Cuban Commission on economic and scientific-technical collaboration.

Choice of Different Paths is Not Unusual

In sum, Soviet-Cuban relations remain quite normal and there is nothing to suggest the two governments do not wish to keep them that way. Differences between the two, to the extent that they exist, are not found in the stated goals of the processes of change being carried out in each country, but rather in the different paths they have taken to achieve those goals. As the two processes respond to different conditions and circumstances, it is not surprising that their methods of implementation also differ. The Soviet government, for example, believes that a market economy and a pluralist political system are the best instruments for restructuring Soviet society. The Cuban government, however, believes that under present conditions there is no need to introduce such mechanisms in its rectification program.

This difference in methods has not provoked any confrontation between Cuba and the Soviet Union. On the contrary, the two maintain a strict sense of mutual respect for the independence of their respective criteria of choice.

In the West, there has been some effort to portray the two processes as locked in battle and beset by contradictions. But such a portrayal overlooks the fact that while the Soviet-Cuban treaty of 1989 stresses their shared values and identity of objectives, it implies no obligation to apply the same mechanisms to reach those common goals.

Furthermore, both the Soviet Union and Cuba have stated that practical measures must be evaluated, above all else, on the basis of how they affect the population, and of what might be their social and ideological consequences. Such an evaluation clearly implies a variety of possible choices.

On the external level, some Soviet and Cuban assessments concerning the current and foreseeable international situation are not the same. Cuba has expressed its concern over the conclusion of certain Soviet politicians that we are living in a more secure world. This seems to be a generalization coming from the arms limitation and reduction agreements. But it overlooks or underestimates the US government's interpretation of international security on the regional level, which is to the detriment of the juridical equality of nations under international law. The current US perception takes into account the crumbling of the European pillar of the worldwide Socialist camp, the serious socioeconomic crisis in the Soviet

Union, and other factors limiting the Soviet Union's influence and placing it in a disadvantaged negotiating position before its Western counterparts.

Economic Relations: Mutually Beneficial

In the economic sphere, Soviet-Cuban linkages are characterized by a general commitment to develop and perfect "by all means, the economic and technical-scientific collaboration and trade relations;" and further-more, "the parties will continue to coordinate their economic plans, looking for the most efficient ways and direction of bilateral inter-action so as to keep improving the material and cultural quality of life for the peoples of both countries."[8]

Before the so-called "peaceful revolution" of 1989 in Eastern Europe, Cuba's foreign trade with the Soviet Union represented 70 percent of its total foreign trade. According to a protocol agreement signed in April 1990, the results for 1990 were expected to show more than an 8 percent increase over 1989. They were, in fact, expected to reach 9.2 billion rubles, their highest level ever.[9] This positive perspective was encouraging, despite Cuban awareness of the complex situation in the Soviet Union.

In an interview in Havana with the *Pravda* correspondent, published on April 20, 1990, Abalkin said there were great perspectives for col-laboration between the Soviet Union and Cuba, specifying three direc-tions in which that collaboration would develop. The first direction is that of consolidation, involving the stabilization of relations based on mutual and real complementarity of the respective economies. The second direc-tion is the development of new forms of cooperation, including nontradi-tional areas of cooperation, including, especially, pharmaceuticals, medical equipment, and the utilization of scientific advances and biotech-nology. The third is in seeking a flexible mechanism adequate to the conditions of the world market.[10]

In another interview, in this case with the newspaper *Sovyetskaya Rossya*, Abalkin referred to the importance of exchange with Cuba, stating:

> The supply of Cuban sugar satisfies up to 30% of the Soviet domestic demand; 20% of the cobalt produced in the USSR is derived from [Cuban] nickel-cobalt concentrate. Without the supply of Cuban nickel, the factories in the Urals would not be able to produce high quality steel. [Cuban] shipments of citric fruits represent the base 40% of our national market. If we did not have these levels of [Cuban] supplies, it must be understood that we would feel quite differently, for we would have to pay capitalist countries between $1.5 to $2. billion dollars for the same production.

Similarly, the Cuban economy would not be able to survive without the supply of Soviet petroleum."[11]

Clearly, the Soviet government has recognized, and continues to recognize, that a high degree of interdependence exists between the two countries as the result of their history of collaborative relations.

At the same time, Abalkin stated:

> In 1990 [Soviet] exports to Cuba will increase by 5.9%, while [Cuban] sales to the Soviet Union will increase by 7.5% over the previous year. Over the three decades of its development, Cuba has amassed a considerable and quite good scientific capacity, and has had considerable success in the development of medicine and in developing a tourist industry.[12]

For Yuri Petrov, former Soviet ambassador to Cuba, the key elements in Soviet relations with Cuba are not so much what has been achieved already, but the great potential presently opening up.[13] This can be seen in the Collaborative Protocol between Cuba and the Russian Federation, signed in September 1990, which covers the areas of public health and medical sciences. It foresees the creation of joint ventures to produce various technical medical materials, pharmaceutical formulae, exchange of specialists in different branches of medicine such as mothers' health care, the campaign against infant mortality, and protection of the environment.

Nikolai Karkishenko, deputy minister of health in the Russian Federation, praised Cuba's Ultra Micro Analytical System (SUMA). SUMA uses high-sensitivity, automated systems to diagnose various infectious diseases, such as AIDS, hepatitis, and leprosy, among others.[14]

Humanitarian Ties

In addition to promoting an active exchange of high-level visits with the Soviet Union, the Cuban government also shows its proletarian internationalism toward the Soviet Union on a more humanitarian level. A moving illustration of this was the Cuban decision to accept, beginning on June 2, 1990, up to 100,000 children affected by the Chernobyl accident for rest and treatment in Cuban hospitals. Ambassador Petrov expressed great appreciation for this friendly gesture.

Cuba also provided all the necessary conditions for the rehabilitation of an undetermined number of people physically handicapped from the war in Afghanistan. And Cuba was one of the first countries in the world to offer aid to the victims of the earthquake in Armenia (in December 1988), supplying blood, plasma, and a medical brigade of more than a hundred people, plus food and a field hospital. In addition, there was a major mobilization of the Cuban population to collect voluntary donations of blood.

The Cuban government and people assumed a similar attitude in the case of the catastrophe in the Soviet region of Ufa, providing those people with nearly all of Cuba's reserves of blood, as well as donating a Cuban-produced medication for burn treatment known as epidermic growth factor (EGF).

The Soviet Union, on more than one occasion, has acted in the same way toward Cuba. This has occurred with food aid, with the Soviet scientist Fiodorov's contribution to the development of optical microsurgery, with military supplies for defensive purposes, and, among other examples, with the training of skilled personnel in various technical-scientific disciplines.

Problems in the Soviet Union: A Special Period in Cuba

Since mid-1990 the domestic situation in the Soviet Union has deteriorated rapidly. For Cuba, this meant serious delays in the shipment of various products of high priority for the Cuban economy and growing uncertainty about the continued feasibility of various projects then under way.[15]

A review of Soviet data clearly shows that at the end of the summer and beginning of the fall of 1990, the Soviet energy problem had become extremely critical. The newspaper *Pravda* revealed that the Soviet energy industry was suffering from inadequate usage of natural resources, insufficient security in the electronuclear plants, and inadequate transport of gas and petroleum. It warned that various Soviet regions are facing a shortage of electrical energy, and that the problem could grow worse. A solution to the Soviet food problem will take until at least 2003. The housing problem will continue until between 2007 and 2010, approximately ten years later than the forecast.[16]

The complexity of the situation was such that at the end of September the Soviet chemical and petroleum minister, Nicolai Lemayev, resigned. According to Lemayev, neither the minister nor the ministry were left with much authority after the new laws were passed. They no longer were able to administer the approximately seven hundred enterprises in their sector. Prices are set in such a way that what is good for the enterprise is not good for society. And the situation could not be changed by an order or a state request.

Former minister Lemayev found that in some cases local authorities would not follow the instructions of the central authority, whereas in others suppliers demanded payment in articles rather than in devalued currency, adding to deficits.

Lemayev recently stated:

> In a meeting of the presidium of the Council of Ministers we examined the problem of the gasoline shortage in the USSR. This gasoline shortage has aggravated the problem of gathering the harvest. The situation is paradoxical. Producing more petroleum than any other country in the world, we have had to purchase gasoline abroad at $400 per ton.[17]

These circumstances had the effect of slowly replacing a certain sense of optimism felt at the beginning of 1990 with deep uncertainty by the end of the year. No one knew at what level Cuba could expect further collaboration from the Soviet Union. This forced the Cuban leadership to adopt a series of restrictions such as general curbs on domestic energy use and internal shifts in both the sale and distribution systems of food and industrial products, among other things.

As a result, Cuba entered the first stage of the "special period in a time of peace."[18] At the same time, the Cuban government put major emphasis on accelerating its Food Production Program.

After various agreements signed with the Soviet Union, Cuba had reached a petroleum consumption level of 13 million tons, imported from the Soviet Union in different quantities each trimester. Despite these agreements, by 1990 the backlog in petroleum deliveries had reached 1,894,000 metric tons.[19]

Other difficulties for Cuba came in addition to these problems. The crisis in the Gulf as of August 2, 1990, raised the price of a barrel of petroleum from $14 at approximately mid-year to $40 per barrel by the end of September. This significantly reduced the chance of Cuba obtaining petroleum from sources other than the Soviet Union.

On September 28, 1990, President Fidel Castro characterized the present situation through which Cuba is passing thusly:

> At this moment we do not know what the level of our trade with the USSR will be next year. Right now no one knows how much they are going to pay us for our sugar, for our exports, or how much they are going to charge us for the products they supply us, or how much fuel we are going to receive. No one knows anything about this right now despite the fact that there are only three months left before the end of the year.
>
> Before, we struck five year agreements which were drawn up a long time in advance; we concluded these agreements almost a year in advance, or at least with a lot of lead time. Under the old system, by now almost all of the merchandise would have been agreed upon; but in fact there is very little agreed upon, and we're only three months from the beginning of 1991.[20]

Despite these circumstances, the Cuban government has explicitly stated, time and again, that it does not interpret the difficulties that have arisen as being the result of bad faith on the part of the Soviet government;[21] rather, Cuba believes the problems in its trade relation with the Soviet Union are beyond the control of the Soviet government. Thus, for Cuba, the present uncertainty does not mean any lack of trust in the governmental institutions of the Soviet Union. It simply means facing up to the realities of the existing situation. That remains the case even after the events of August 1991.

Military Relations

The military factor has been an important element in Cuba's bilateral relationship with the Soviet Union for many years. Currently, it is the cause of contentious and possibly dangerous speculation in the United States. Certain US columnists, for example, have even spoken recently of the delivery of Soviet missiles to Cuba. This is so ridiculous as to be amusing were it not for the possibly provocative intent behind such allegations. Are they designed to provide a pretext for some move against Cuba? Cubans hope not, but must expect the worst.

Despite the fact that there is no military treaty between the Soviet Union and Cuba, there has been a general sense of satisfaction regarding the level of the current relationship, a level that makes it possible for Cuba to count on a modern defensive military potential. In fact, for years the Soviet Union maintained treaties of friendship, cooperation, and mutual assistance with various underdeveloped countries, but not with Cuba.

On many occasions the Cuban government has reiterated its appreciation for Soviet aid rendered at the most difficult moments of the revolution. As an example, in an October 1962 letter to Nikita Khrushchev, Castro said: "I want to let you know, once again, of the infinite gratitude and the recognition by our people of how generous and fraternal the Soviet people have been with us."[22]

Soviet-Cuban relations in the military sphere have been based on the principles outlined in the 1989 Treaty of Friendship and Cooperation. On February 5, 1990, Mikhail Gorbachev stated: "The military threat has not disappeared; the United States and NATO maintain offensive doctrines and concepts. At the same time they are maintaining their armies and military budgets; that is why we need an army which is well prepared and well equipped."[23]

It is not difficult to imagine that if such a military threat is perceived by the Soviet Union, Cuba, being geographically much closer to the United States, feels more directly threatened and thus must rely on its traditional defense links with the Soviet Union. In fact the United States has maintained a military base on Cuban soil for many years, while the Soviet Union does not have any such base in Cuba.

In May 1990, the US State Department confirmed reports of three different types of military maneuvers around Cuba or close to its shores. These operations were dubbed "Ocean Venture 90, Global Shield, and Defex."[24]

The US government has characterized these military exercises as "routine," but nevertheless, from the Cuban government's point of view, they can only be considered provocative, leading Cuba to respond with Operation Cuban Shield. Such actions by the United States do not contribute to the resolution of differences between the two countries. Further, it is difficult to understand why they were carried out at a time when Cuban military personnel had returned from Ethiopia, when other Cuban troops were withdrawing from Angola, when the Sandinista government was no longer in office in Nicaragua, when Noriega had been deposed, and when the Warsaw Pact had become inoperative. All of these previous conditions had been used by the United States as arguments to justify earlier acts of aggression against Cuba. Apparently, the acts of aggression will continue, with or without a pretext.

Another important element to keep in mind when discussing Cuba's military situation is its preparations for its own self-defense, such as the training of the civilian population to repulse an invasion with or without assistance from the Soviet Union. Cuba is well aware of the US military exercise "Ocean Venture," which was carried out in the Atlantic with the purpose of testing the capabilities of US forces in blocking Soviet assistance to Cuba by sea in case of war.

In referring to preparation of the Cuban population for self-defense during the 1980s, the aggressive rhetoric and outright threats of the Reagan administration against Cuba should be kept in mind. Cuba's preparations were not in response to an imaginary problem. Secretary of State Alexander Haig's vow to "take it to the source" gave substance to the threat.

Further, the idea of Cuban defense preparedness is not new; it dates from the beginning of the 1960s and the missile crisis. In a 1962 letter to Khrushchev, for example, Fidel Castro stated, "Perhaps now more than ever, our people need to trust in themselves."[25]

For all these reasons the Cuban government, at the beginning of the 1980s, decided to reinforce and update its capabilities for self-defense. An extensive defense program was drawn up and put in place. The principal results have been:

- The theoretical formulation of a new military doctrine called "War of All the People"[26]

- Plan for the application of this theory
- The creation of a new civil-military structure, based principally on the Territorial Militias, and the Production and Defense Brigades. During the 1980s, 1,400 defense zones were set up in Cuba's 14 provinces and 169 municipalities.[27]

The defense zone is considered to be the basic component of the territorial defense system. Each defense zone has its own Defense Council, which is the command and control center for activities during periods of peace and war. The Cuban high command is not preparing the country only for conventional warfare, but also for the eventuality of a total or partial occupation of the country. Cuba may be overrun, but it will not be conquered. Arms in Cuba, as part of this new defense strategy, are located in more than a thousand places. This will allow easy and rapid distribution of arms to the people. Cuba hopes that never becomes necessary, but if it should, the Cubans are prepared.[28]

In review of the current status of Soviet-Cuban relations, the following can be said: politically, interstate relations are stable; economically, there is a great deal of uncertainty as to the future; militarily, Soviet support has made possible the preparation and equipment of Cuba's armed forces—but, again, the future is uncertain, especially in the light of Soviet decision in September 1991 to begin a gradual withdrawal of its military personnel from Cuba.

Future of the Relationship

A number of uncertainties have arisen in Soviet-Cuban relations and must be overcome if the relationship is to continue on the same harmonious, mutually beneficial basis as it has in the past. The principal uncertainty, without any question, is in the field of economic relations; this stems from a number of problems and factors, among them:

- The difficulties the Soviets are having in reconciling their budgetary criteria and the guidelines for the 1991 plan
- The disorderly transitional process of introducing market mechanisms into the Soviet economy
- The changes in terms of the agreements governing bilateral trade, especially the reduction of the time span from five years to only one, and the dispersal of the contractual process

Contracts are no longer signed just with the Soviet state, but also with countless Soviet firms involved in production, transportation, and various other aspects of the process. In sum, bilateral trade and economic collaboration now require infinitely more complex procedures.

In addition to these specific problems, there is an overriding uncertainty that cannot be ignored: The different methods chosen by the two countries to improve their Socialist societies could end up altering their very essence, and thus alter the framework and the content of the relationship—a relationship in which understanding, mutual assistance, and proletarian internationalism have been such key factors.

In the particular case of the Soviet Union, the greatest danger lies in the unforeseeable outcomes that may be produced by reforms in the political and economic systems and in the military sector. These could be very different from what the government intended as it started along the road of perestroika.

The present juncture in the Soviet Union is a special one. The existing economic system cannot rescue the country from its present stagnation, but, in our view, neither can the market mechanisms now being adopted. At the same time, there is a growing lack of trust in the government itself to a degree never seen before. Following the abortive coup of August 1991, this crisis of confidence has resulted in demands for the resignation of the senior leaders of the country.

Another area of uncertainty that impacts directly on the bilateral relationship has to do with the continuity of the Soviet Union as a multinational state—that is, of the continued unity of its republics and the avoidance of a civil war. The breakup of the present union of republics will force Cuba to reorder its ties and to come up with new ways of relating to the fragmented entity or entities that would result.

Of great significance also for the future of the Soviet-Cuban relationship is the new level of interaction between the executive power and the Parliament in the Soviet Union. In this new situation, the executive may have the best intentions of maintaining excellent relations with Cuba, but then encounter opposition from within the Parliament that would make that difficult. Should such a situation develop, it would put all the persuasive powers of the executive to the test.

There is also the risk that a coalition, or a new government, could emerge in the Soviet Union. The correlation of forces within such a governing entity is difficult to predict, but it would be likely to include at least elements of a non-Socialist persuasion, and these could seek to halt the Soviet Union's political and military support for Cuba.

Uncertainties arise, too, out of the more diversified role of the mass media in the Soviet Union. The media now disseminates not only governmental positions, but ideas directly counter to those of the government. Soviet-Cuban relations could be adversely affected by a proliferation of unobjective judgments concerning the nature and scope of bilateral collaboration. No general tendency in the Soviet media to distort that relationship has yet become evident, but there are some clear signs that such a tendency could develop. The negative impact of such an eventuality would be most unfortunate. If presented with the facts of the matter and given the opportunity to reach an objective judgment, most Soviet citizens would understand that Soviet-Cuban collaboration benefits both peoples.

Cuba must, of course, make certain that Soviet collaboration is utilized in the most effective ways possible. That is an obligation that Cuba recognizes and is honoring.

Finally, but no less important, are the effects on Soviet-Cuban relations of international developments and pressures. In particular, the United States can be expected to exert every effort so that the Soviet Union not honor its commitments to Cuba and that it instead abandon a fraternal relationship of more than thirty years' standing.

Conclusions

The future of the Soviet-Cuban relationship, then, will depend upon the dynamic of change now taking place in the Soviet Union, in Cuba, and in the international system, and on how Cuba and the Soviet Union respond to the challenges resulting from the deep transformations taking place in all three. Given that there is a high degree of interdependence in the multiple ties between the two countries, there is no reason to think that, despite all the uncertainties described above, those ties will not endure, even if they must develop under the influence of the new market economy in the Soviet Union.

Notes

1. Spanish News Agency (EFE), Panama, August 30, 1990. For more information on the Soviet rejection of US pressures toward Cuba, see *Granma*, July 10, 1990; and *Trabajadores* (official publication of the CTC), July 12, 1990, and August 14, 1990. The official position of the Cuban government regarding US pressures has been and continues to be that Cuba will never link the improvement of relations with some other country to the introduction of internal changes in Cuba. (See the statements of Carlos Aldana, member of the secretariat of the PCC in Lima, Peru, as reported in *Trabajadores*, July 3, 1990, p. 11.)
2. Fidel Castro and Mikhail Gorbachev, "An Unbreakable Friendship," *Editora Politica*, Havana, 1989, pp. 32–33. This pamphlet contains the complete text of the Treaty of Friendship and Cooperation of 1989.
3. Ibid., p. 36.
4. *Granma*, April 5, 1989, p. 6.
5. Ibid., p. 5.
6. *Tass*, Moscow, May 7, 1990, taken from *Boletín Diario*, Havana, APN, May 7, 1990.

7. *Granma*, May 10, 1990, p. 4. Also see the speech delivered by Carlos Lage, alternate member of the Political Bureau of the PCC, on the commemoration of the seventy-third anniversary of the October (Russian) revolution, published in *Granma*, November 8, 1990, p. 5.

8. Castro and Gorbachev, p. 33.

9. See statements of Leonid Abalkin, vice president of the Soviet Council of Ministers, as reported in Moscow, April 20, 1990, in "The Soviet Press Writes About Cuba," *Tass*, taken from *Boletin Diario*, APN, Havana, No. 77, April 20, 1990.

10. *Pravda*, Moscow, April 20, 1990.

11. The complete text of the interview appears in *Granma*, May 7, 1990. It should also be kept in mind that Cuba receives more than 700 products from the Soviet Union, and practically satisfies its needs in sheet metal, machine tools, wood and similar commodities. Trade with the Soviet Union constitutes 70 percent of Cuba's total foreign trade. Cuba is in sixth place among the Soviet Union's trade partners. See *Granma*, May 8, 1990, p. 4.

12. *Granma*, May 7, 1990.

13. *Granma*, May 8, 1990, p. 4.

14. *Granma*, September 18, 1990.

15. For more information, see the speech of President Fidel Castro in the Commemoration of the 30th anniversary of the Committees for the Defense of the Revolution (CDR), as reported in *Granma*, October 1, 1990, p. 3.

16. *Pravda*, September 17, 1990.

17. *Isvestia*, October 1, 1990; *Tass*, October 1, 1990.

18. *Granma*, August 29, September 24, and September 26, 1990.

19. *Granma*, September 12 and October 1, 1990. Felix Pita Astudillo's article in the September 12 issue of *Granma* responds to two articles that had appeared in the Soviet press distorting data on bilateral trade between Cuba and the Soviet Union in 1990.

20. *Granma*, October 1, 1990, p. 3.

21. Ibid.

22. *Granma*, November 23, 1990, p. 5.

23. Special Bulletin, Agencia de Prensa Nacional. Mikhail Gorbachev, Secretary General of the Communist party of the Soviet Union, PCUS, and President of the Supreme Soviet of the USSR report to the Central Committee of the PCUS, February 5, 1990 concerning the Central Committee's platform for the 18th PCUS (Party) Congress. Complete text, February 6, 1990, p. 13.

24. *Tass*, May 4, 1990, reporting statements of the US Department of State on military exercises off the coast of Cuba, Washington, D.C. See also *Bastion*, May 25, 1989, notes from the Cuban Armed Forces Ministry; and *Granma*, April 29 and 30, 1990.

25. *Granma*, November 23, 1990, p. 5.

26. *Para Evitar la Guerra (To Avoid War)*, MINFAR (Ministry of the Revolutionary Armed Forces) Authors Collective (Havana: Far Press, 1988), pp. 99–117. Also see *Military Terminology Dictionary*, First Edition (Ministry of the Revolutionary Armed Forces, Republic of Cuba, 1987), p. 200. See the speech of General Raul Castro, minister, FAR, in "Domingo Universitario de la Defensa," *Granma*, November 19, 1990, p. 2.

27. *Para Evitar la Guerra*, p. 100.

28. Ibid, p. 104.

Chapter 12

Comments on the Soviet and Cuban Perspectives
Wayne S. Smith

Cuba and the Soviet Union were brought together in the first place by US reaction to the Cuban revolution. This is not to accept the rather hackneyed view that the United States refused to accept revolutionary reforms, denied economic assistance to Fidel Castro, and thus drove him into the arms of the Soviet Union. Quite the contrary, even the Eisenhower administration initially brought itself to accept the revolutionary reforms Castro had called for (contrary to popular belief, it did not reject the agrarian reform; it only voiced concern that affected US citizens be adequately compensated), and during Castro's visit to the United States in April 1959, US officials raised the possibility of economic assistance, an overture to which the Cuban government never responded. But it would have been surprising if it had, for if Castro's objective was to break free of US hegemony, how then could he accept its largess? Indeed, the question points up the fact that the central dynamic of the goals behind the Cuban revolution carried Cuba and the United States inexorably toward an adversarial relationship. It was not that the United States gratuitously pushed a passive and static Castro toward the Soviet embrace. Rather, it was that Castro's policies and objectives, and US reaction to them, carried him there.

And what was it, principally, to which the United States was reacting? Why, to the very messianic nature of the Cuban revolution. Castro's overarching objective was not simply to free Cuba of its ties of dependency on the United States, but beyond that to encourage other Latin American revolutionaries to follow the Cuban example. As Castro told one adviser just before his 1959 visit to the United States, he believed his destiny was to complete the work of Simón Bolívar. Bolívar, he said, had freed Latin America of Spanish political control. Now, a century-and-a-half later, he intended to free it of US economic control.[1] Castro did not say so, but clearly the first step in that process was the overthrow of what Castro often referred to as the "vendepatria" Latin American governments—that is, governments such as Batista's that had sold out to the United States and that protected US interests in their own countries.

Castro's objective, then, was hemispheric in scope, and was well summed up by the slogan: "We will turn the Andes into the Sierra Maestra of South America."

Now, the Cubans argue that, in fact, they did not at first undertake active efforts to overthrow the other governments; rather, from 1959 until Cuba was expelled from the OAS at the Punta del Este Conference in January 1962, they put their faith in the example of the Cuban revolution—that is, that it would of itself spark other revolutions. Only after the Punta del Este Conference, at which, as the Cubans saw it, the other governments lined up with the United States against them, did they begin to give active support to guerrillas and other subversive groups in neighboring states.

This—the Cuban view—is, of course, subject to debate. But even if one accepts its principal thesis as true, even if there were few *active* efforts before 1962, there was an unending flow of rhetoric touting the Cuban example as the portent of things to come in the rest of the hemisphere, and enough in the way of actions on Cuba's part to help the process along (such as the "unofficial" expeditions launched from Cuba against Panama and the Dominican Republic in 1959) to suggest to the US government that it had real cause for concern. Further, Castro's inflammatory rhetoric against US imperialism, although perfectly understandable from the standpoint of the Latin American nationalist that Castro was, was not received with good humor by the United States. Seeing that Castro meant to reduce US presence and influence in Latin America, the United States, in turn, began to gear up to contain Castroism.

Castro was thus left with two options: (1) he could abandon his hemispheric goals; or (2) he could turn to a more powerful patron for a shield behind which he might continue to pursue those goals. He took the latter course and began to turn to the Soviet Union. In the final analysis, then, he turned to the Soviets for protection against the United States— protection that would enable Cuba to break free of its hegemonic hold and Castro to pursue his Bolivarian dreams for the hemisphere.

Needless to say, Castro's turn to the Soviets simply confirmed all of Washington's worst fears and sharpened its determination to get rid of him. It also resulted in increased Cuban tensions with Latin American governments, which, as mentioned above, joined with the United States in 1962 in voting to suspend Cuba's membership in the OAS on grounds that Cuba was a threat to the other members.

Cuba turned to Moscow for protection. Moscow, although initially suspicious of Castro, eventually responded because in its zero-sum game with the United States, removing Cuba from the Western camp and adding it to the Eastern implied a clear gain. Having a foothold in the Western Hemisphere, an advance base for Soviet forces, and what Moscow had hoped would become a showcase of Socialist economic success in Washington's own backyard were all simply frosting on the cake.

As Estervino Montesino Seguí puts it in Chapter 11: "Soviet-Cuban ties were forged during the tensest years of the Cold War and were shaped by the unrelieved hostility of the United States toward Cuba."

If it was US reaction that brought Cuba and the Soviet Union together, that was also the main glue that bound them closely together over the next thirty years. Not that the two did not have their own disagreements and divergences of tactics and objectives. These are discussed in the Introduction of this book. Suffice it here to say that the factors that held them together were stronger than those that divided them, and over time the two worked out a rather harmonious, mutually beneficial relationship.[2] Cuba benefited at home from Soviet economic support and advice, and abroad from its logistical backstopping for such sorties as the intervention in Angola. Beyond those concrete benefits, the fact was that as the active military ally of one of the superpowers, Cuba counted for more on the world stage than it would have otherwise. At times, thanks to Soviet underpinning, it seemed almost to play a role once reserved for great powers.

The Soviet Union, although prevented by the Kennedy-Khrushchev understandings of 1962 (see Chapter 13) from positioning offensive weapons systems in Cuba, found it convenient to use the island as a port of call for Soviet naval exercises; to deploy naval reconnaissance aircraft to the island; to maintain a major electronic eavesdropping facility at Lourdes, just to the east of Havana; and to portray Cuba as the forerunner of a Socialist tomorrow in the hemisphere. Further, under the Cold War rules of the game, anything that made the United States uneasy had to be good for the Soviet Union.

But as the preceding chapters have indicated, all that has changed. The Cold War is over, and with it the zero-sum game of the past. Moscow is no longer seeking ways to make the United States uneasy; neither does it have any continuing interest in maintaining a foothold in this hemisphere with a view to facilitating Socialist revolution. The Soviet Union is not in a position to pay for or benefit from any more Socialist states in Latin America, even if there seemed to be some prospect of that. Neither does it any longer have a need to deploy naval reconnaissance aircraft or even to hold naval exercises in the Caribbean. The electronic listening station at Lourdes is important for the moment as a means of verifying US compliance with arms reduction treaties, but that, too, will pass. Cuba, in short, is of diminishing strategic value to the Soviet Union. Soon it may be of no such value at all. Trade with Cuba benefits the Soviet Union as well as Cuba, but is not vital. Keeping open trade routes to a nation ten thousand miles away, moreover, becomes ever more difficult for a nation in turmoil, as the Soviet Union certainly is.

For its part, Cuba at this point still needs its economic ties to the Soviet Union, but, as suggested in Chapter 11, it is perfectly aware that conditions in the Soviet Union are in such a state of flux that the outcome cannot possibly be predicted. Thus, Cuba must begin to prepare for a life without the Soviet Union. It is doing so, inviting in private foreign capital, moving to diversify its exports and trading partners, and dramatically expanding its tourist industry. Within another few years (if it has that long), Cuba may be in a position to get along without preferential trade with the Soviet Union.

Certainly Cuba's alliance with the Soviet Union is of little avail anymore in terms of Cuba's position in the world at large. With the end of the world revolution, the Soviet Union has no further interest in underwriting foreign adventures such as the 1975 intervention in Angola. Cuba is in no position to carry them out on its own, and in any event realizes that the time for that has passed. As some have put it, the age of the romantic revolutionary, which opened with Castro's triumph in 1959, ended with the electoral defeat of the Sandinistas in Nicaragua in 1990. For all practical purposes, there are no more guerrilla fronts in Latin America for Cuba to support, except in El Salvador and Guatemala, and even there Cuba supports negotiated settlements.

Certainly Cuba's international image is little enhanced any more by being the ally of the Soviet Union. Rather than placing Cuba on the leading edge of a Socialist tomorrow, that now associates it with failure. The sense of disillusionment and bewilderment that must accompany that realization is reflected in Chapter 11, which seems to say, "We followed their lead, and then they abandoned the struggle and told us we were wrong to have followed them. Today we are alone."

As mentioned above, and as pointed out in greater length in Chapter 10, Soviet-Cuban trade continues to have benefits for both countries. Further, there are sentimental ties that hold the two together. Thousands of Soviets have served in Cuba over the years, and thousands of Cubans have been trained in the Soviet Union. Hundreds have intermarried. In international relations, however, sentimental ties have never been sufficient glue to hold two partners together. That is true also of Soviet-Cuban relations. The principal binding agent, now as in years past, is neither trade nor nostalgia; rather, it is the continuing hostility of the United States toward Cuba. As Ambassador Valery Nikolayenko states clearly in Chapter 4, the only reason the Soviet Union continues its military assistance to Cuba is because of the external threat faced by that country from the United States. Whether that assistance is increased or terminated, he suggests, depends upon whether the United States begins to normalize relations with Cuba.

Given that the Cold War is over, one can see no objective reason why the United States should *not* begin to do just that, especially if by doing so it could bring about the termination of Soviet military assistance from the island. In fact, however, the United States has done the opposite; it has raised tensions with Cuba to their highest level since the 1960s.

US concern over the Soviet-Cuban military relationship during the Cold War years was inevitable. It was not simply that the United States had to constantly worry that the Soviets might decide to ignore the Kennedy-Khrushchev understanding and reintroduce nuclear weapons; rather, the Soviet connection colored Washington's reaction to everything Cuba did. The presence of Cuban troops in Africa might have been viewed as an unimportant distraction had it not been for Cuba's ties with Moscow. And had it not been for those same ties, the United States might have interpreted Cuban activities in Central America somewhat differently. But as it was, Washington assessed all Cuban foreign policy moves in the context of its global competition with Moscow. Such assessments, however, have now become irrelevant. Indeed, the old view that a potential threat to US security was part of the very warp and woof of the Soviet-Cuban relationship has become obsolete. If the Soviets have respected the 1962 Kennedy-Khrushchev understanding all these years, certainly they will continue to do so now. In fact, they have already gone well beyond the provisions of that understanding. It does not, for example, cover support to revolutionary groups in the hemisphere, but as part of its retreat from the whole concept of world revolution, all such support has long since been terminated.

Nor should there be any compelling concerns over Cuba's own foreign policy actions. Those once of concern to the United States by and large have been resolved. All Cuban troops are out of Africa, the Cuban role in Central America is of no further significance, and fear of a Soviet threat mounted from Cuba has been overtaken by events.

The Bush administration seems to have realized that recitation of these issues no longer provides a convincing rationale for its policy. It began by citing them as the impediments to improved relations,[3] but soon began to shift its ground as they became increasingly irrelevant. By March 1990, President Bush had moved the goal posts; he had dropped the standard foreign policy conditions that Cuba remove its troops from Africa, reduce its military relationship with the Soviets, and stop fueling the conflict in Central America. Now he put forward new conditions. Before there could be any improvement in relations, he declared, Cuba must first have a market economy, hold internationally supervised elections and reduce its armed forces.[4]

Why the shift? Essentially because the Bush administration came to believe that it might now be possible to achieve what all along had been the optimum US goal—but one which until recently had been considered to be just beyond the edge of the possible—the end of socialism and of the Castro regime in Cuba. The United States has never been prepared to negotiate seriously with Cuba, and certainly not on the basis of equal respect for sovereignty. It has not, in short, been willing even to consider an accommodation acceptable to both sides. Perhaps Cuba is too emotional an issue for that to have been feasible. The controlling image for most US political leaders has been of a tiny nation that used to be our protectorate but that for thirty years has defied us and gotten away with it. Nothing is more likely to induce irrationality in a superpower than that.

In addition, the Bush administration is under the strong influence of the most ultraconservative elements in the Cuban-American community and must worry about the reactions of the hard-liners in the Republican party, whose favorite President Bush is not. The very thought of negotiating with Castro is anathema to both these groups, and that counts heavily with the Bush administration.

Still, some years back the United States might have been prepared to accept a Castro who could be viewed as "tamed." It was not enough that he be willing to negotiate the question of arms supply in Central America, for example; rather, he would have been required to halt any activities of his own without any corresponding moves on the US side. And that would have been true across the board. Only a Castro who had retired behind the barricades of his own island—a Castro who had in effect given up his foreign policy, his so-called "internationalism"—might have been acceptable. Now, not even that is enough. With the fall of Communist governments in Eastern Europe, the defeat of the Sandinistas at the polls in Nicaragua, and the collapse of the Marxist/Leninist system in the Soviet Union itself, the United States has been encouraged to think Cuba may be the next domino to fall. Issues related to Cuba's foreign policy and to human rights have thus been put aside in favor of the end of socialism itself.

Is even this a serious negotiating position? Assuming that Cuba moved in the direction of a market economy and agreed to hold fully democratic elections, would the Bush administration then favor a thaw with the Castro government, assuming for a moment that Castro won those elections? At this point, probably not. Inclusion of the condition having to do with the reduction of Cuba's armed forces *before* there can be any accommodation with the United States strongly suggests that these conditions also were designed as nonstarters. It is, after all, totally unrealistic to ask Cuba to reduce its defenses without some assurances that the United States will not take advantage of that reduction—assurances that the Bush administration obviously has not the slightest intention of giving, at least not just yet. The latest Bush package then would seem to be in keeping with the time-worn practice of putting forward impossible conditions for negotiations. In fact, because of domestic political considerations, the United States does not wish to negotiate with Cuba anyway. It simply wants what would amount to Cuba's capitulation. And, as Sergo Mikoyan complains in Chapter 10, the United States wants to force the Soviet Union to acquiesce to, if not indeed to collaborate in, forcing this capitulation.

Such an approach on Washington's part could have unfortunate consequences. It could easily have a seriously adverse effect on what should be our hopeful new relationship with the Soviet Union. And a Castro who is given no way out, who is backed into a corner, could be a very dangerous Castro indeed. This is not Romania. Although popular disgruntlement has grown in Cuba as the economic situation has deteriorated, a significant percentage of the population continues to support Castro. Should internal pressures reach a moment of critical mass at some point in the future, it would be with a deeply polarized society. And with the armed forces also divided, one would have all the ingredients for a bloodbath. That would most certainly not be in the interests of the United States. What it should wish to see is a process of reform, as smooth and as peaceful a transitional process as possible. As of mid-1991, however, US policy seems designed to impede such a process and to *raise* the chances of bloody confrontation.

Will US policy always be so inflexible, so counterproductive even in terms of the interests of the United States itself? Not necessarily. In politics, nothing is immutable, and in the United States, the edge of the political horizon can be no more than four years in the future. In this case, it is even closer. Assuming that the Cuban revolution survives, albeit in a modified form, and is showing signs of revitalization as it moves toward a mixed economy and a more open political system, the Bush administration, or some other administration, may at some point in the future conclude that as the Cuban revolution is not going to simply go away, and that as, after all, the United States could influence its direction more by dealing with it than by ignoring it, it at long last behooves us to begin to discuss our differences with Cuba and to normalize relations. That is to be eminently desired, for it is high time to put this last remnant of the Cold War, our Cuba policy, behind us.

Ironically, when that time comes, the basic raison d'être of the Soviet-Cuban relationship will quickly dissipate. Sergo Mikoyan is prophetic when he writes in Chapter 10 of a relationship "within a reduced framework devoid of outdated strategic considerations." Without the need to help Cuba defend itself against the United States, Moscow's relations with the island might within a decade or two be little different from its relations with Mexico or Brazil. And thus, Estervino Montesino Seguí will also have been proved right in suggesting in Chapter 11 that should the Soviet Union move away from socialism, as in the wake of the abortive August coup it most certainly is doing, the nature of the relationship would change. Change, yes, but ties would endure, "even if they must develop under the influence of the new market economy in the Soviet Union."

Notes

1. See Wayne S. Smith, *Castro's Cuba: Soviet Partner or Nonaligned?* (Washington, D.C.: The Woodrow Wilson International Center for Scholars, 1984), p. 6.

2. Ibid., pp. 22–30.

3. Hearings before the US Congress, House Western Subcommittee, August 2, 1989. Administration witnesses insisted that Cuban export of revolution and other policies objectionable to us continued unabated.

4. Gil Klein, "Bush Lays Down his Conditions for Normal Relations with Cuba," *Washington Times*, March 20, 1990.

Havana Ground Rules: The Missile Crisis, Then and Now

James G. Blight
Aaron Belkin
_____ *David Lewis*

Q: Is there anything that Castro can do, other than abdicate, that would lead to a different US attitude towards him, do you think?
The President: Well, . . . free and fair elections and a recognition of the democratic changes that are taking place, and a shifting from a highly militarized island to something that would be more helpful to his own people . . . would all be helpful steps. . . . But instead . . . he's digging in. He's going against the tide. He's alone.
Exchange between President George Bush and a reporter, March 1990[1]

The more enemies socialism has, the more it is endangered, the more I love socialism.
President Fidel Castro, July 26, 1990[2]

The manager of the home team . . . shall establish any ground rules.
Rule 3.13, *Official Baseball Rules*[3]

The Beginning: The Cuban Revolution, 1959

The Cuban revolution triumphed on January 1, 1959, during the waning days of the Eisenhower administration. But it was during the Kennedy administration that US animosity toward Fidel Castro's regime reached its zenith. A US-sponsored invasion of Cuba by Cuban exiles occurred in April 1961, less than three months after Kennedy took office. "Operation Mongoose," a large-scale effort to destabilize the Castro regime by means of covert operations, was put in place during the Kennedy years. And in October 1962, during the Cuban missile crisis, the island was the theater of operations for the most tense and dangerous confrontation of the Cold War.

Anyone having the opportunity to peruse the stacks of declassified material in the John F. Kennedy Library in Boston will encounter a powerful, objective index of the extent to which Castro's Cuba was once almost an obsession of the US government. Of the 140-odd large boxes of declassified material in the Kennedy Library labeled "National Security Files," nearly *one-third* have "Cuba" embossed on their spines; one-third of the security-related paper flow in the US government in the early 1960s was generated by US attention to Cuba.

After drifting into the background of the Cold War for decades—excepting a few episodes having mainly to do with US concern for Soviet military presence in Cuba—Cuba is once again closer to the center of attention of those who make US foreign policy. However, Cuba's return to prominence is for the very opposite reason than that which accounted for the US obsession with Cuba in the early 1960s. At that time, Cuba was regarded by the United States and Soviet Union alike as a testing ground for the thesis that communism was the wave of the future, a wave so powerful that, in Cuba, it could successfully invade Washington's Caribbean "backyard." The recent attention given to Cuba, however, is a result of Cuba's estrangement from what the playwright, former prisoner of conscience, and now president of Czechoslovakia Vaclav Havel has called the "velvet revolution" in the former Communist empire of Eastern Europe. Since 1989, nascently democratic, free-market–oriented regimes have swept to power throughout the region. Cuba, thought of in the United States as an integral part of the Eastern European Communist empire of the Soviet Union in all but geography, has almost overnight become another kind of anomaly: not the wave of the future but, as it is seen in Washington, an ossified remnant of a way of life and governance that is now thoroughly discredited.

The net result of this unexpected development has been something resembling a "feeding frenzy" on the part of many people in the United States with a vested interest in Cuba. Cuban exiles in Miami, for example, have begun registering their rights to land they once owned in Cuba. Scholars and journalists speak commonly of Cuba as the "next domino to fall," the next remnant of the Soviet empire to collapse. The Bush administration has gotten into the act as well. Whereas for decades, stretching back to the Eisenhower administration, the main problem with Cuba had been untoward Soviet influence and presence in this hemisphere, the new pressure on Cuba—the new "requirement" placed on it by the United States—is that it must become *more* like the Soviets, embracing perestroika as a means of fostering democracy and a market economy.

Having "won" the Cold War in Europe and in this hemisphere, the United States is poised, so it seems, to go for a total victory: the elimination, at long last, of the Castro regime and socialism in Cuba. The most important tactic in the US strategy to isolate, irritate, and eventually eliminate the Castro regime is to pressure the Soviets to radically reduce their military assistance and trade subsidy to Cuba. Beginning at the Malta summit between Bush and Gorbachev in December 1989, US officials have continually tried to convince the Soviets to begin in a serious way to cut their ties with Cuba. The feeling in Washington is this: Because Cuba relies on the Soviet Union for about 85 percent of its material goods, the Soviets hold the key to turning the screw on Castro. At every subsequent summit, ministerial, and at meetings of mid-level Soviet and US officials, the United States has turned up the heat with regard to Cuba. In July 1990, President Bush publicly made the Soviet dumping of Cuba one of three conditions for granting direct financial assistance to the Soviet Union (the others being significant movement toward a market economy and deep cuts in Soviet military programs). This is the most important feature of the US strategy to bring Cuba eventually into line with the requirements of the velvet revolution: pressure the Soviets to pressure the Cubans to get rid of their leader and of "backward" socialism.

The Model: Removing Missiles From Cuba, 1962

The origins of the US strategy for dealing with Cuba via pressure exerted on the Soviets goes back to the Cuban missile crisis. This is not the place to rehearse even in broad outline the events of the missile crisis, but we ought to note certain features of it if we are to understand the origins of US policy toward Cuba now and evaluate its probable outcome. By 1961, the Cubans felt sufficiently threatened by the United States to request massive Soviet military assistance. This they received to an unexpected extent. Soviet leader Nikita Khrushchev proposed, in May 1962, that Cuba become the site for the first-ever positioning of Soviet nuclear missiles outside the country. However, Khrushchev's scheme was discovered in midcourse by the United States, and a grave crisis ensued between the United States and Soviet Union. The crisis was resolved, with the United States pledging not to invade Cuba and the Soviet Union pledging to remove its nuclear missiles from Cuba. The important and overriding point to the Cubans was that they believed the Soviets had abandoned them in a moment of crisis, leaving them vulnerable to US military action. This is precisely the situation many Cubans believe they face today: threat from the north and abandonment from the east. Furthermore, they believe that Soviet abandonment, if it does come, may be the result of US pressure on the Soviets. In 1962 it was military pressure. This time it would be economic pressure, with the Soviets in effect "selling" Cuba for US economic assistance.

Cuba as such mattered hardly at all to the United States trying to manage its way through the missile crisis. It wisely limited its goal to the removal of the Soviet missiles and correctly assumed that the Cubans were not in charge of the nuclear missile operations on the island. Any decision to remove them would thus be a Soviet decision. Even so, it is useful, we believe, to try to understand the Cuban perception of those momentous events for the lessons they yield about the present situation, when the Cubans—largely the same Cubans, including their leader, Castro—see such parallels between 1962 and the present. We will not enter here into the larger question of whether, or how much, the Cuban government influenced decisions in Washington or Moscow during the missile crisis. Instead, we wish to point out the remarkable extent to which what we will call "Washington hypotheses" differed in the event from "Havana rules": During the missile crisis, Washington hypothesized that the Soviets held the answer to the US problem with Cuba. At the same time, Cuban rules emphasized Cuban sovereignty and the US threat to the island and to the revolution, and they deeply resented being left out of the US-Soviet deal that resolved the crisis.

We have outlined the incommensurability between Washington and Havana in Table 13.1. To Washington, the Soviets were the threat; to the Cubans, the Soviets were the answer to the US threat. To Washington, Cuba was a veritable "parking lot" on which were located a few dozen Soviet nuclear missiles; the crisis would be resolved only when the Soviets "unparked" their missiles and carted them away. In Havana, the feeling was that the moment of total destruction, the moment they had feared since the Bay of Pigs invasion the year before, had arrived. To Washington, Castro, while a nuisance, was regarded as having nothing significant to do with the presence or the eventual removal of the missiles, and thus he was ignored. In Havana, however, Fidel Castro (along with

Table 13.1 Getting the Missiles out of Cuba, 1962

	Soviets	Cuba	Castro	Policy
Washington hypotheses	Offensive Soviet threat	"Parking lot" for missiles	Irrelevant to missiles	Overt and covert "squeeze" on Soviets
Havana rules	Defensive request from Cubans	Threatened with total destruction	Missiles to be used for defense of Cuba	Cuban buildup "on a war footing"

other members of the Cuban leadership) believed that the nuclear missiles were to be used by the Soviets in the event of a US attack on the island. Finally, the policy advocated eventually by the Kennedy administration, the "quarantine" or partial naval blockade of the island, was designed to "squeeze" the missiles out of Cuba, and no more. But in Havana, the naval encirclement of the island was perceived as an act of war, causing the entire island to go "on a war footing," as it was referred to on the island.

Although Castro was utterly ignored in Washington during the missile crisis, this was not because he was hesitant to express his opinion regarding the evolution of events. Immediately upon hearing of the Kennedy-Khrushchev accord, Castro sent a letter to the acting secretary-general of the United Nations U Thant. In that letter of October 28, 1962, the Cuban leader said that the Kennedy-Khrushchev agreement would be inoperative unless the United States also agreed to give up its naval base at Guantanamo Bay (on the eastern tip of Cuba), cease overflights of the island, and adhere to several other stipulations that were politically impossible for Kennedy to accept.

But it is Castro's letter to U Thant on November 15, when he was under very heavy pressure from Khrushchev's envoy Anastas Mikoyan to agree to the Kennedy-Khrushchev terms, that is most instructive for the present situation. In that passionate letter, Castro claimed, not without justice, that Cuba had gotten nothing in the deal. He concluded his letter by saying:

> Our right to live is something which cannot be discussed by anyone. But if our right to live is made conditional upon an obligation to fall to our knees, our reply once again is that we will not accept it. We believe in the right to defend the liberty, the sovereignty and the dignity of this country, and we shall continue to exercise that right to the last man, woman or child capable of holding a weapon in this territory.[4]

This is almost exactly what the Cuban leader now says when he speaks of the possibility that the United States will somehow cause the Soviets to abandon Cuba. "If destiny assigns us the role of one day being among the last defenders of socialism," Castro said in December 1989, "...we will know how to defend this bulwark to the last drop of blood."[5]

Havana Rules, 1962: Cuban Reality in the Missile Crisis

Recently, Fidel Castro and other Cuban officials have begun to speak in detail about their views of the missile crisis, particularly the threat they felt from the United States, and their fear of abandonment by the Soviets. New Cuban willingness to discuss their perceptions of the United States and Soviets first surfaced at a January 1989 conference in Moscow, attended by senior delegates from the period from the United States, Soviet Union, and Cuba. The Cuban delegation was stimulated by the opening remarks of former secretary of defense Robert S. McNamara: "If I were a Cuban," he said, "and read the evidence of covert American action against their government, I would be quite ready to believe that the U.S. intended to mount an invasion."[6] But McNamara, supported by all his former colleagues from the Kennedy administration, went on to say that, however compelling the evidence may have appeared to the Cubans (and Soviets), an invasion of Cuba was out of the question. Believing otherwise, he said, although understandable, was nevertheless to fall victim to a serious misperception because in his view contingency plans for a US invasion of the island would never have been enacted.

At a subsequent triangular conference held in Antigua in January 1991, Cuban Interior Ministry official General Fabian Escalante rejected McNamara's "misperception" theory. Citing information drawn from Cuban intelligence sources, Escalante set out to document "not that planning for an attack was merely a contingency, a result of military routine," but rather that "it was based on objective facts that constituted irrefutable proof that such a plan was in the works."[7] Escalante concluded his presentation thus:

> War is not only combat with tanks, aircraft, machine guns, cannon and missiles; war is the placing of bombs, war is generalized terrorism, war is indiscriminate murder—war is all of this. War is armed groups, war is people being trained in the U.S. How many Cubans did the CIA have at its base in Miami? Documents say over 3,000 Cubans were agents, collaborators at the CIA operations base in Miami. Well, if this is not a war, ladies and gentlemen, may God judge us.[8]

This much seems clear: Cubans believed uniformly in the inevitability of a frontal assault by US forces on the island. After they defeated the US-backed invasion at the Bay of Pigs in April 1961, Cuban leaders turned desperately to the Soviets for assistance. Of course, they never thought to ask for nuclear missiles because the Soviets had never deployed such weapons anywhere outside Soviet territory. Nevertheless, when offered, they were gratefully received by Cuba, as the feeling grew on the island that the ultimate deterrent to the US invasion was about to arrive and become operational.

Yet the secret, deceptive deployment had hardly begun when the Cubans began to suspect that the Soviet gambit was not well thought out. Che Guevara and Emilio Aragonés, two members of the ruling, six-man secretariat, were sent to Moscow in late August to urge the Soviets to go public with the deployment, lest the United States discover it in midcourse and use their presence on the island as an excuse to attack and invade Cuba. At the Moscow conference on the crisis, Aragonés said that

> we maintained that we had to sign a pact and announce that both countries, by sovereign decision, had put the missiles in Cuba and that this was absolutely moral and legal. . . . Khrushchev said no. He wanted to buy time; he said . . . that it would not be discovered . . . [and] that in case that happened, he would send the Baltic Fleet to Cuba and that he would still defend us."[9]

From the moment of receiving Khrushchev's dubious assurance regarding the Baltic Fleet, the Cubans appear to have felt increasingly uneasy about having placed their fate (as they believed) in the hands of the Soviets.

We are only now coming to appreciate the fear and anger in Castro's Cuba that accompanied Khrushchev's agreement to remove the missiles in return for a public pledge from Kennedy not to invade the island and a private assurance that "analogous" Turkish missiles belonging to NATO on the Soviet southern border would be removed within a few months. The deal seemed to Castro to have placed Cuba in imminent danger, and he was furious in any case at the Soviets for having struck such a deal without consulting Cuba. He told Lee Lockwood in 1965 that it had never occurred to him, when the Soviets began to deploy the nuclear missiles, that they might be withdrawn. But he did not say then, nor later, as has recently been revealed by the declassification of his crisis correspondence with Khrushchev, that he had become sufficiently desperate to make a contingent request to the Soviets that they launch their nuclear missiles at the United States should an invasion take place. Castro cabled Khrushchev on October 26, 1962: "If they manage to carry out an invasion of Cuba . . . then that would be the moment to eliminate this danger forever, in an act of the most legitimate self-defense. However harsh and terrible the solution, there would be no other."[10] Khrushchev, horrified by what he took to be a request for nuclear preemption, together with other information indicating that the United States was indeed preparing to invade the island, immediately agreed to Kennedy's terms and thereby ended the intense phase of the superpower crisis.

Soviet abandonment of Cuba in the missile crisis and its refusal to consult with Cuba over the terms of the resolution still rankle Cuban officials nearly thirty years later. Cuban Political Bureau member Jorge Risquet recalls the Cuban position this way:

> If Nikita's message to Kennedy said, "We are willing to withdraw the missiles from Cuba, provided that Cuba's security is guaranteed, *in Cuba's view* . . . and there would be no negotiations about Cuba without Cuba" . . . that problem . . . would have been resolved.[11]
> We always told our Soviet friends that we disagreed with Cuba's

exclusion from the negotiations. They said that this was a matter of time, or lack thereof; but ... Khrushchev's response to Kennedy ... had to be resolved in a conference where Cuba was present. Had he added five more words to his message ... the problems between Cuba and the U.S. that led to the crisis in the first place would also have been discussed."[12]

Cuban security analyst Rafael Hernandez recently summed up the connection between Cuba's experience of the missile crisis and Cuban deterrence as follows: "As a result of the crisis, one lesson for Cuba was that, in the future, Cuba would have to be able to defend itself by its own means, on its own territory. Therefore, the consolidation of its own defensive capacity would thenceforth be the principal means of deterring the external threat."[13] This has resulted, according to US scholar Jorge Dominguez, in a "Cuban style of deterrence," characterized chiefly by the capacity to inflict unacceptable damage on any would-be aggressor, by cultivating a reputation for high-risk irrationality, and by the establishment of close relationships betwen Cuba and other Third World countries on whom it feels it can depend in the court of world opinion, especially in the United Nations.[14]

One of the most interesting documents declassified so far by the Cubans and Soviets regarding the missile crisis contains the notes of Ambassador Alexander Alexeev from conversations between Castro and Anastas Mikoyan, November 3, 1962, just after Mikoyan arrived in Cuba as Khrushchev's special envoy. Mikoyan's task was to convince Castro that giving up the missiles was necessary. Castro's reaction, as recorded by Alexeev, shows the depth and the object of Cuban concern. According to Castro:

> Our people were not psychologically prepared. They felt deep disappointment, bitterness, pain. As though we were being deprived not of missiles, but of the very symbol of solidarity. Our people thought the news about the withdrawal of the missiles was a lie.... For some forty-eight hours this feeling of bitterness spread among the whole people.... We were very worried by the sharp fall in the people's moral spirit. It affected their fighting spirit as well.... All this was badly demoralizing. These feelings could have been used by the counter-revolution to incite anti-Soviet moods.... I myself am to blame for the situation that has been created.... Cuba cannot be conquered, it can only be destroyed.[15]

From these poignant passages, and from recent Soviet-Cuban recollections of the crisis, three important messages for US officials are suggested: first, Cuba would never have relinquished the missiles had it had any say in their final deployment; second, the Cubans will try very hard never to be caught unprepared in this manner again; and third, any important US initiative with respect to Cuba would have a better chance of succeeding fully if it involved the Cubans in discussions as well as the Soviets.

The Pattern: The Thirty-Year Disconnect Between Washington and Havana

Although Cuba receded from the forefront of US consciousness after the missile crisis (with periodic exceptions), attitudes developed in Washington and Havana that are as remarkable for their divergence as for the nearly uniform assent they are given in each capitol. It would be unwise to attribute all aspects of this divergence to the outcome of the missile crisis. Many factors have entered into what has become, by now, the received wisdom in Washington regarding Havana, and vice versa. But the essential fact is that these views are polar opposites of each other and that features of the current US position are consistent with that held during the missile crisis. We choose to call the attitudes in Washington "hypotheses," not because there is any widespread doubt there regarding their validity, or because there is any wish to test them, as one would customarily test hypotheses. Rather, we wish to emphasize that if they had been treated as hypotheses, they would long ago have been refuted and replaced with hypotheses more consistent with the Cuban reality they are alleged to represent. This approach may, we hope, assist us in our search for a US policy toward Cuba that is less mechanistically derived from the kind of approach that worked in October 1962, but has not worked since.

We must recall the historical context in which the disconnect between Washington hypotheses and Havana rules evolved. Nikita Khrushchev was widely cited in the West as having said that he and his Soviet colleagues, perhaps in league with "Red" China, would "bury" the West. In addition, Fidel Castro had said not long after the missile crisis that he and his Cuban colleagues, with Soviet assistance, would "transform the Andes into the Sierra Maestra of Latin America," the latter being a reference to the mountains in eastern Cuba from which he and his 26th of July movement had launched their revolution in the mid-1950s.[16] The Cubans, moreover, did more than talk. Cuba actively tried to foment revolution in a number of Latin American countries, an initiative that ended symbolically with the death of Ché Guevara in Bolivia in 1967.[17] This was the particularly galling aspect of the "Cuban problem" for successive administrations in the United States: not only did the Cubans represent heavy Soviet influence, thought to be a violation of the Monroe Doctrine, but they did not disguise their admiration for any and all in Latin America devoted to armed struggle against established governments, and for the establishment of Socialist regimes. That they were unsuccessful in this regard was less important than that they tried.

After a period in the late 1960s and early 1970s, in which Cuban "internationalism" (as it is called) was distinctly less visible, it returned in force in 1975. With "Operation Carlotta," Cuba moved tens of thousands of its troops to southern Africa to defend Angola's newly independent government from the South Africans. A few years later, Cuba came to the aid of a Marxist government in Ethiopia. In both instances, Cubans and Soviets were involved together. The return of Cuban and Soviet activity on behalf of Marxism-Leninism in the Third World was, in fact, influential in Ronald Reagan being elected president in 1980. He pledged to roll back Communism everywhere it had taken root, and he was particularly insistent on rolling it back in regions where the Cubans were heavily involved, such as southern Africa and Central America—especially Nicaragua, where the Sandinistas had come to power in 1979 and were soon embraced by Castro's Cuba.

Table 13.2 summarizes the deep divide between Washington and Havana during this period of antagonism. Washington never seems to have doubted that the Soviets were, in most important respects, directing the Cubans to do their bidding in Third World conflicts. It was during this period that the present US policy settled firmly into place. Because Cuba was in fact so heavily armed and dangerous, as Washington saw it, a direct military attack on the island was hardly feasible. And so the "embargo," what the Cubans call the economic "blockade," was tightened, and every attempt was made to isolate Cuba, to hurt it economically—in theory to make it more difficult for Cuba to afford to engage in international adventurism on behalf of communism. Pressure, it was thought and hoped,

Table 13.2 The Thirty-Year Disconnect Between Washington and Havana

	Soviets	Cuba	Castro	Policy
Washington hypotheses	Always in charge	International Communist threat	Ruthless dictator	Pressure will squeeze Castro regime out
Havana rules	Often in tow	Small country under siege	Charismatic popular leader	Pressure unifies Cuban people behind Castro

would eventually bring down the regime.

That this strategy has failed in its objective for nearly three decades suggests that the hypotheses upon which it is based are faulty. In fact, if we try to get inside the evolving situation as experienced by the Cubans, we notice that the rules by which they play the game are often the *inverse* of those attributed to them by the United States. The Soviets, far from controlling the Cubans, have often seemed to the Cubans to be reticent in just that endeavor that has so concerned US policymakers throughout the years—Soviet-Cuban collaboration in Third World countries. For example, it has become increasingly clear in retrospect that the massive air- and sealift of Cuban soldiers to Angola in 1975 was a *Cuban* initiative, and that the Soviets entered the picture only after the Cubans had thrown themselves into the fray. Even a cursory reading of official Cuban documents from the period, especially Castro's speeches, will indicate a host of motives for responding positively to the request for assistance that are intrinsically Cuban. For example, the very name of the initiative, "Operation Carlotta," serves to commemorate a Cuban black woman who was enslaved and brought to Cuba from an area not far from the point at which the Cuban forces disembarked, as they saw it, to liberate black people from the threat of annihilation at the hands of racist South Africa.[18] Soviets can only have looked on this sort of motivation from afar if, indeed, the leadership of Leonid Brezhnev could make any sense of it at all.

In other respects, too, the rules of the game as the Cubans play it are the inverse of those attributed to them in the US hypotheses. Regarded in Washington as an international Communist threat, the Cubans tend to regard themselves as a small, poor, country under siege from the United States. This is not to say the Cubans do not enjoy being citizens of a country that matters on the world scene. They clearly do. But they also feel vulnerable, economically and militarily, and seldom more so than recently, because of uncertainties regarding the Soviets' ability to keep their commitments to them.

Fidel Castro, portrayed unrelentingly in Washington as a ruthless dictator and a Soviet tool, is in fact regarded by the majority of Cubans as a charismatic, popular leader. And, as the Cubans like to point out, Castro is held in high regard in many countries of the Third World. The disconnect between Washington and Havana regarding Castro himself is related to the odd fact that the persistent US policy of isolation and intimidation, in the hope of the elimination of Castro and Communism from Cuba, has the opposite effect of that intended. Nothing, it seems, so unifies the Cuban people, nothing provides Castro with so useful a platform from which to exhort his people to circle their wagons and dig in with gusto, than US attempts to squeeze him and his revolution from the island. In early March 1990, Castro had this to say to the Fifth Congress of the

Federation of Cuban Women:

> Once again the United States underestimates us; all the time there has been underestimation. Underestimation at the time of the counterrevolutionary bands, with the blockade, when they wanted to destroy us economically, at the Bay of Pigs and during the missile crisis. They're always underestimating us. . . . They want the Soviet Union to help them with this. Just imagine![19]

It was in this speech that Castro exhorted the Cubans to expect a severe belt-tightening in a "special period" caused by the velvet revolution and the breakup of the Eastern bloc, with which Cuba had traded almost exclusively. On May 1, 1990, hundreds of thousands of Cubans turned out for the annual May Day festivities, when throughout the former Socialist bloc the day was ignored or noted only ironically. For now, it seems, Cubans are responding favorably to Castro. Now, as in the past, his "ace-in-the-hole" is overt US hostility.

The Initiative: Removing Castro and Communism from Cuba Now

Twice in the long and bitter US-Cuban relationship during the Castro era, radical elements in the Miami community of Cuban exiles have seen Castro's fall as imminent. The first such period was during the missile crisis, when the Cuban revolution seemed vulnerable to military intervention. In fact, during the missile crisis, brigades of Cuban exiles were training in special units at Fort Knox, Kentucky and elsewhere, ostensibly (as they seemed to have believed) to ready themselves for the final assault on the Castro regime. This, they believed, was to be a full invasion of the island by US regular forces, not just a small band of adventurers such as were humiliated at the Bay of Pigs. In President Kennedy's speech of October 22, 1962, in which he announced the presence of nuclear missiles on the island and the US intention to "squeeze" them out by means of a "quarantine" of the island, he made oblique reference to the hopes and dreams of the Cuban exiles. Beginning his speech with a reference to missile sites on "that imprisoned island" of Cuba, he concluded with "a few words for the captive people of Cuba," indicating that the missiles had made them a target and that they should hold their leader responsible.[20] The exiles believed they would have a chance to remove Castro after Kennedy's blockade removed the missiles. But the chance never came. The exiles had misread the Kennedy administration's intentions, which were strictly limited to removing the missiles in that crisis.

The second such period of Godot-like "waiting for Fidel" to fall began in the summer of 1989 and continues unabated, both in Miami and in

Washington. By the summer of 1989, cracks were beginning to appear in the Eastern Bloc—cracks that would split and finally destroy it in the velvet revolution of the following autumn. Encouraged by the Miami community, the Bush administration appeared to change course from what had been initially regarded by the Cubans as a welcome and pragmatic relief from the ideologically charged Reagan years. On August 2, 1989, Michael G. Kozak, deputy assistant secretary of state for interamerican affairs, concluded testimony to Congress as follows:

> [Castro] understands better than anyone else exactly what kind of threat we pose. We threaten Castro because the United States represents what people can achieve, including the Cuban community in the United States, given freedom and opportunity. In contrast, the Cuban revolution has impoverished and imprisoned the Cuban people.[21]

After a hiatus of almost three decades, the feeling in Miami was, by the late summer of 1989, that Castro's days were numbered. And this feeling was not lost on Washington. Once again, Cuba was being portrayed as an island of prisoners about to be liberated by pressure from the north.

By the winter of 1989–1990, the Soviet bloc had collapsed almost entirely and the Soviet Union itself seemed increasingly in need of cutting its ties with unproductive clients, such as Cuba was believed by Washington to be. On February 11, 1990, Secretary of State James A. Baker, in a speech before the Soviet Parliament, urged the Soviets to cut off Cuba, save the money, put the Socialist mistake behind them, and, in the process, improve US-Soviet relations.[22] Although he got a cold response, and several counterattacks regarding the US invasion of Panama (on December 20, 1989), this speech set the tone for current US Cuba policy. Washington urges the Soviets at every opportunity to give up Cuba; it characterizes the Castro regime as an embarrassment to the Soviets and an anachronism in the age of the velvet revolution.

And Washington has turned up the heat on Cuba. TV Marti, an anti-Castro television station beamed to Cuba, began operating in the early spring of 1990. Also in 1990, the Mack Amendment, prohibiting not only US-based firms from doing business with Cuba, but also their foreign subsidiaries, was passed in Congress. President Bush vetoed it on grounds that it caused unnecessary friction with large trading partners such as Canada, but it was reintroduced in 1991, and may yet become law. The Bush administration has also increased the pressure on Latin American governments not to expand their relations with Cuba. Washington hypotheses underlying these various initiatives are summarized, along with the Havana rules opposing them, in Table 13.3.

The Havana rules, in the present case as well as in the missile crisis and in the intervening years of the US-Cuban relationship, represent the

Table 13.3 Getting Castro and Communism Out of Cuba

	Soviets	Cuba	Castro	Policy
Washington hypotheses	Should/must cut off Cubans	Anachronistic totalitarian fossil	About to fall soon	Increase pressure/ squeeze to speed the inevitable
Havana rules	Soviet–Cuban relations mutually beneficial	Last bastion of revolutionary socialism	Robust, in charge, and defiant	Pressure unifies and raises level of defiance

inverse of the Washington hypotheses. Cubans (and many Soviets too) regard the Soviet-Cuban relationship as mutually beneficial, both as to trade and military cooperation. Although both Cuba and the Soviet Union expect this relationship to change, perhaps drastically, in the next several years, even the Soviets believe that change will be retarded, not expedited, by US pressure to foment it. Moreover, the constant drumbeat from the north to the effect that Cuba represents fossilized, discredited socialism, has been turned to advantage by Castro. He now characterizes Cuba as perhaps the last bastion of true socialism and, although it is difficult to judge accurately the feelings of the Cuban people, Castro's appeals have not been without their effect. It may be, as one Cuba-watcher has said, that "socialism on one island" suits Castro just fine.[23] No one can say, of course, whether such a phenomenon as this can long survive. But what does seem clear is that nothing the United States has done in the wake of the velvet revolution seems to have hurried Castro's demise. Quite the contrary.

Havana Rules Now: The Game After the Cold War

If the construction of US foreign policy were a science, the Washington hypotheses concerning its Cuba policy would long ago have been refuted. The policy of squeezing Cuba via an economic embargo, lately augmented by the attempt to insist that the Soviets join in the application of pressure, has failed for almost three decades. Fidel Castro came to power when Dwight Eisenhower was president. Castro is still in power, and he is

younger than George Bush. Politics is not a science, yet it still is difficult
to escape the impression that the US government, urged on at every turn
by radical elements in the Cuban exile community in the United States,
has figuratively been banging its head against a brick wall, getting
nowhere, but banging away all the same.

This is not exactly news, of course. But we believe it is high time for
reexamining US Cuba policy now, at the virtual, but not quite literal end
of the Cold War. In the past, the Washington hypotheses were saturated
by Cold War assumptions made not only by politicians but by the US
people too. Now that the Cold War is passing into history, we would do
well to examine the extent to which US policy, in addition to being
unsuccessful, is also utterly inconsistent with the requirements of post–
Cold War collaboration with the Soviet Union. In almost all other areas
of former conflict and disputation, we are moving from a zero sum
approach to a positive sum approach. We are seeking solutions, in other
words, in which both sides win and neither side loses. It is therefore
instructive to dwell on the very oddness of present US policy toward Cuba,
especially the tactic of pressuring the Soviets to dump Cuba, because it is
a bald request to the Soviets to throw in the towel and admit that they
have "lost" Cuba to us, the "winners." In short, US Cuba policy is still
based, as before, on false principles; but it is also notably out of line with
the fundamental assumptions of the velvet revolution we seek to promote.

What might happen if Washington began playing this triangular game
by Havana rules? That is, what if policymakers in the United States tried
to begin their process not with slogans left over from the Cold War, and
not with sound bites from Miami lobbyists, but with the sense of the game
as it is experienced by the Cubans? This would require, first of all, granting
what is factually obvious: that the Soviet-Cuban relationship is complex;
that Cuba is the source of Cuban actions, by and large; that Castro is
popular, in his way, among his people; and that pressure from the United
States is perhaps the Cuban leader's most formidable psychological
weapon as he attempts to urge Cubans to make still more sacrifices for
socialism. If US policymakers begin where the Cubans begin, in our
view—thus playing the game of US-Cuban relations by "local rules,"
instead of foreign fantasies—the resulting Washington hypotheses would
stand a greater chance of providing a base for successful policy, no matter
what the preferred policy might be.

A sequence of events consistent with a positive sum, post–Cold War
approach to US-Cuban relations might be as follows:

1. In a temporally coordinated fashion, the United States begins to
    normalize relations with Cuba, allowing the Soviet Union a face-
    saving opportunity to begin disengagement from Cuba.

2. The United States and Soviet Union issue a public affirmation of the 1962 understanding that resolved the missile crisis, broadening it to include joint pledges to allow Cuba to go its own way.

3. Cuba is brought in as a full signatory in this process; in so doing, the United States and Soviet Union agree to consider the Cuban points of disagreement with the final 1962 agreement. This becomes the US-Soviet-Cuban analogue to the accords by which Germany has been unified, thus ending World War II for good. Such a move would finally resolve the Cuban missile crisis for all *three* participants.

4. Cuban political developments are allowed to take their own course. Washington learns to ignore those aspects of "Miami advice" that require US intervention in Cuban affairs.

5. Political, cultural, and economic change occurs in Cuba as a function of normalization of relations with the United States and Soviet Union.

6. The outcome, whatever it might be, is a *Cuban* outcome. The Soviets get what they want, which is disengagement from Cuba without the pressure to do so; the United States gets what it wants, which is an opening and constructive engagement with Cuba; and the Cubans, not excluding the Cuban-Americans, get what they decide they want.

This positive sum strategy should appeal to the left, right, and center of the US Cuba question: To the left, Cuban sovereignty is respected. To the right, there is every reason to believe that Cuba will change in a more democratic direction, as it is opened to the north, Castro having been deprived in this fashion of both the Soviet security guarantee and US hostility. This is the logic behind former Nicaraguan Contra leader Arturo Cruz's argument that now is the time to "kill Castro and Castroism with kindness."[24] Finally, to those in the center of the ideological spectrum, this would be seen as a marvelous precedent for great power, positive sum collaboration in a world that has moved beyond the Cold War.

We return, finally, to the Cuban missile crisis of 1962. It was played out to its conclusion by both superpowers almost as if the Cubans did not exist. From the US point of view, pressure on the Soviets resulted in their agreeing to remove their missiles from the island. The flaw in the current Washington hypothesis that this strategy can still be adapted to Cuba as such, however, is this: the nuclear missiles were probably the only items ever to appear on the island of Cuba that were completely controlled by the Soviets. Castro is not. Cuba is not. The misapplication of the missile crisis, therefore, lay at the conceptual root of much that is wrong with US

Cuba policy: it is out of touch with the Havana rules that dictate how the game is played.

Yet, oddly, the missile crisis provides the clue to the direction US policy toward Cuba should take at the end of the Cold War. The missile crisis shocked and deeply frightened people the world over, President Kennedy among them. In an address several months after the crisis, sobered even in the depths of the Cold War by the possibility of nuclear catastrophe, Kennedy embraced a positive sum solution to US-Soviet tension that was startling at the time:

> And if we cannot end now our differences, at least we can help make the world safe for diversity. . . . Let us reexamine our attitude toward the Cold War, remembering that we are not engaged in a debate, seeking to pile up debating points. We are not here distributing blame or pointing the finger of judgment. We must deal with the world as it is, and not as it might have been.[25]

That portion of the "world" at issue here is the world of the Cubans, the way *they* understand who they are in relation to the United States and Soviet Union. If the United States takes Kennedy's good and hard-earned advice and begins our discussions with this world *as it is*, we believe several things could be accomplished at once: the rationalization of US Cuba policy, an honorable end to the Cold War in this hemisphere, and the meaningful integration of the darkest moment of the Cold War onto the ground floor of the positive sum edifice we ought to be trying to construct in a post–Cold War world.

Notes

1. George Bush, "The President on Cuba," US Department of State release, March 1990.

2. Fidel Castro, speech in Havana, Cuba, July 26, 1990; see *Miami Herald*, July 27, 1990.

3. *Official Baseball Rules*, 1988 edition (New York: The Sporting News, 1988), pp. 27–28.

4. Fidel Castro, letter to U Thant, November 15, 1962, quoted in David Larson, ed., *The Cuban Crisis of 1962* (Lanham, Md.: University Press of America, 1986), p. 211.

5. Fidel Castro, speech in Havana, Cuba, in honor of veterans of the African campaigns, December 8, 1989, reported in *The New York Times*, December 9, 1989, p. 9.

6. Robert S. McNamara, remarks in Bruce J. Allyn, James G. Blight, and David A. Welch, eds. *Back to the Brink: The Moscow Conference on the Cuban Missile Crisis* (Lanham, Md.: UPA, 1991). See also James G. Blight and David A. Welch, eds. *On the Brink: Americans and Soviets Reexamine the Cuban Missile Crisis*, 2nd ed. (New York: Farrar, Straus & Giroux, 1990), p. 329.

7. General Fabian Escalante, remarks in James G. Blight, David Lewis, and

David A. Welch, eds. "Cuba Between the Superpowers," transcript of a conference in Antigua, January 3–7, 1991, p. 1.

8. Ibid., p. 22.

9. Emilio Aragonés, remarks in Allyn et al., *Back to the Brink*, pp. 40-41.

10. Fidel Castro, letter to Nikita Khrushchev, October 26, 1962, quoted in *Granma Weekly Review*, December 2, 1990, p. 4.

11. Jorge Risquet, remarks in Allyn et al., *Back to the Brink*, p. 60.

12. Jorge Risquet, remarks in Blight et al., "Cuba Between the Superpowers," p. 167.

13. Rafael Hernandez, remarks in ibid., p. 181.

14. Jorge Dominguez, "Pipsqueak Power: The Centrality and Anomaly of Cuba in US-Soviet Relations," in Thomas G. Weiss and James G. Blight, eds., *The Suffering Grass: Superpowers and Regional Conflict in Southern Africa and the Caribbean Basin* (Boulder, Colo.: Lynne Reinner, 1992).

15. Fidel Castro, remarks to Anastas Mikoyan, recorded by Alexander Alexeev, November 3, 1962 (translated from the Russian by Stephen D. Shenfield). Available from the Director of Archival Administration, Soviet Foreign Ministry, Moscow.

16. This slogan, attributed to Che Guevara and used often by Fidel Castro, became an early rallying cry of the revolution. See Wayne S. Smith, *The Closest of Enemies* (New York: Norton, 1987), chapter 3.

17. Maurice Halperin, *The Rise and Decline of Fidel Castro* (Berkeley: University of California Press, 1972), chapters 28-29.

18. See Gabriel Garcia Marquez, "Operation Carlotta," in David Deutschmann, ed., *Changing the History of Africa* (Melbourne: Ocean Press, 1989), pp. 41–61.

19. Fidel Castro, speech at the Fifth Congress of the Federation of Cuban Women. Reported in *Cuba Update*, Summer 1990, pp. 20–21.

20. John F. Kennedy, "Radio and Television Report to the American People on the Soviet Arms Buildup in Cuba," in *Public Papers of the Presidents* (Washington, D.C.: US Government Printing Office, 1963), p. 809.

21. Michael G. Kozak, "Cuba: A Threat to Peace and Security in Our Hemisphere." US Department of State, Current Policy Paper No. 1204, August 2, 1989, p. 4.

22. *The New York Times*, February 12, 1990, p. 1.

23. Saul Landau, "Socialism on One Island?" *The Progressive*, June 1990, pp. 18–20.

24. Arturo Cruz, Jr., and Consuelo Cruz Sequeira, "The Autumn of the Caudillo," *The New Republic*, April 22, 1991, pp. 32–38.

25. John F. Kennedy, "Commencement Address to the American University in Washington," June 10, 1963. In *Public Papers of the Presidents*, Washington, D.C.: US Government Printing Office, 1964, p. 462.

Part 5
Conclusions

Chapter 14

Confronting New Challenges
Wayne S. Smith

There will be those who will ask: If the world revolution is over, and the Soviet Union is going through a period of severe economic difficulties and such intense political turmoil as to raise the specter of its disintegration, why should US analysts any longer be concerned with, or even interested in, its foreign policy? So long as our countries faced one another with fingers constantly on the trigger, and so long as the Soviet Union represented an antithetical ideological system holding that the world was not big enough for the two of us, the United States _had_ to pay close attention to Soviet views and policies. But neither of those two conditions obtain any longer. Can we not, then, simply settle back comfortably and watch our former rivals stew in their own juice, or, even better, ignore them altogether?

The answer, of course, is that we cannot. The Cold War is over, yes, and so is the world revolution. As is made abundantly clear in this book, the Soviet Union is no longer determined to spread socialism throughout the globe and it has come to regard even the prospect of nuclear war as intolerable. In the wake of the failed hard-line coup of August 2, 1991, it is moving quickly away from socialism. And so, the sort of bipolar world of intense superpower confrontation in which we have lived for almost the past half century is now behind us. It may be, as Sergo Mikoyan insists in Chapter 10, that the Soviet Union must still be defined as a superpower if only because it—along with the United States—still has the nuclear might to destroy the world. But however its role is defined, the fact is that it has changed. The Soviet Union may still be a military superpower, but it is no longer one determined to dominate the world. Quite the contrary, it now says that it intends to conduct its foreign policy within the parameters of international law and the UN Charter, and with full respect for the sovereignty of all other countries.

The Soviet Union still is, nonetheless, a great power. It is having economic difficulties to be sure, but it has tremendous resources and space and an intelligent work force. It would be myopic to assume that its economic engine, much adjusted, will not in time not only be running again, but running far more effectively than before. And although a number of the ethnic republics will break away, or at least become virtually autonomous, that will certainly not mean the end of Russia as a great power. Even if it comes down to the loss of all the ethnic republics, the Russian Republic alone (in terms of territory) would still be the largest country in the world. Despite all its present difficulties, the Soviet Union has not become, and will not become, the Duchy of Fenwick. Whether as Russia or as the Soviet Union, it remains one of the world's major powers, a country that others must even now take into account as they pick their way through the mine fields of international politics. Indeed, to a very large degree, the shape of the post–Cold War world will be determined by how the two superpowers (or former superpowers) structure their relationships with one another. Is it to be a constructive, cooperative relationship? Will joint efforts to resolve regional conflicts become an established pattern? Can the two giants work together in coming to grips with the challenges that *really* threaten the future of humankind—curbing nuclear proliferation, protecting the environment, ending the scourge of illegal drugs, redressing the dangerous North-South economic imbalance, and establishing a new world order? Indeed, will either of them even take advantage of the vast new possibilities opened by the end of the Cold War to focus on those challenges?

If the United States and the Soviet Union can turn their attentions and resources from the wasteful and essentially sterile nuclear arms race to the task of confronting these new challenges, and where possible to cooperate in efforts to resolve them, then the end of the Cold War may indeed be remembered by future historians as one of the most dramatic and hopeful turning points in the odyssey of humankind. If, on the other hand, the two do *not* take the lead in charting a more constructive course for humankind, if they simply revert to policies based on narrowly defined self-interest, writing off serious efforts to protect the environment, redress the North-South imbalance, and establish a new international order based on rule of law as "too expensive," and/or "quixotic"—then the end of the Cold War may prove to have been a matter of simply trading one sword of Damocles for another. In short, the question is: How will the great powers of the world, led by the United States and the Soviet Union, react to the end of the Cold War? Will they take full advantage of it and turn to building a better world, or, now released from the tensions and disciplines of the East-West conflict, will they fall back to petty squabbling and policies aimed at self-aggrandizement?

Latin America is probably not the best region in which to glimpse an answer to that question. Because it has long been considered the US backyard and the one from which the United States, in the spirit of the Monroe Doctrine, has been the most determined to exclude other powers, Washington's disposition to cooperate with others here in the settlement of regional conflicts or the solution of other problems will be less than in such areas as the Middle East or Asia. The other side of the coin is that because it is an area far removed from and of little real interest to the Soviet Union, US-Soviet cooperation in most cases will not be vital to the solution of Latin American problems.

Latin America is not the best region, then, in which to see the portent of, or come to conclusions about, future international cooperation. Precisely because it is a region of such traditional interest to the United States, however, it may represent an excellent test tube in which to gauge US responses to such problems as economic development and establishment of a new international order.

With these caveats in mind, let us briefly examine how the end of the Cold War has affected responses in Latin America to some of the challenges listed above.

Peaceful Settlement of Regional Conflicts

As was brought out in Part 3 of this book, dealing with Central America, the United States eventually did bring itself to discuss the Central American conflicts with the Soviet Union, and cooperation between the two superpowers played a minor role in bringing about a peaceful settlement in Nicaragua and in getting one on track in El Salvador—if only in removing East-West rivalry as an impediment to the peace process. Credit for the success of that process, however, belongs largely to the Central Americans themselves, and principally to Oscar Arias of Costa Rica. Here I would disagree with Sergo Mikoyan, who in Chapter 10 expresses the opinion that the US Congress rather than Arias should have received the Nobel Peace Prize. In my judgment, the prize was correctly awarded. To the extent that any entity in the United States played a key role, however, it was Congress, which finally refused to give any more military aid to the contras. To that extent, I agree with Mikoyan.

All that aside, what stands out in the Central American case is that the United States was far more reluctant to discuss the conflict with the Soviet Union or to involve the latter in the search for peace than it was in the cases of Afghanistan, Cambodia, Angola, and various other lesser regional conflicts.

Further, as discussed in Part 4, we see this same disinclination manifested even more strongly in the case of Cuba. The Soviet Union has already begun to reduce its military assistance to Cuba and has signaled its willingness eventually to consider complete withdrawal if the United States, for its part, will but begin a negotiating process with Cuba aimed at resolving the disagreements and conflicts of interest between the two. As the Soviets see it, this would be but a matter of adjusting US policy toward Cuba to the post–Cold War spirit and mind-set. So far, however, the United States has flatly refused, although as suggested in Chapter 12, this could change if the United States comes to the conclusion over the next few years that the Cuban revolution, albeit in modified form, is likely to survive.

Given the US reluctance to engage with the Soviet Union in conflict resolution in Central America, nonetheless, and its outright refusal so far to reach an accommodation over Cuba, one cannot but conclude that US-Soviet cooperation in the peaceful settlement of regional conflicts is not likely to prosper in Latin America to the same degree that it may in other regions of the world.

Latin America and a New World Order

President Bush and various others in the US government have spoken much of a new world order, especially since the beginning of the war in the Gulf. They have been less than precise, however, as to the principles on which this order is to be based. Is it, for example, to be based on rule of law and full commitment to the Charter of the United Nations? Or is it that the United States will define what is acceptable and what is not as suits its interests in each individual case?

For its part, Moscow has already given its answer: President Gorbachev has stressed that henceforth the Soviet Union will conduct its foreign policy fully within the parameters of the UN Charter. This would seem to open the way to a similar US commitment, for the United States had long argued that it would pledge itself fully to abide by the Charter if the Soviet Union would but do the same.[1] Rather than any such pledge, however, the response of the Bush administration in December 1989 was to invade Panama, a blatant violation of the Charter condemned by the United Nations and by the Organization of American States. Perhaps the invasion of Panama was an aberration. We must hope so. Latin Americans, nonetheless, were understandably concerned that what it meant was that with the end of the Cold War, the United States, with no further need to worry about Soviet reactions or possible retaliation, might become more rather than less aggressive. Whether or not their concerns prove well founded, the invasion was an appallingly inappropriate way to indicate the outline of a new world order.

The United States needs to reflect carefully on the fact that the end of the Cold War leaves it in an unprecedented position in Latin America. Not only are the Russians not coming, neither is anyone else. There is no nation in the world today that has both the capability and an interest in threatening the United States from Latin America. US leaders have never feared a threat emanating from the Latin American states themselves. But since the earliest days of the republic, they have feared that the very weakness of those states left them vulnerable to the penetration and possible control of other great powers—powers that might overcome the barriers represented by the two great oceans by mounting a threat from below our southern borders. Such fears can now be put aside. None of the other powers in the world has any interest in mounting such a threat. We compete economically with Japan and Western Europe. That they would threaten us from bases in Latin America, however, is beyond fantasy. China also has no such interest, and even if it did, it has very little capability. China has a great army, but no means of projecting military power far beyond its own borders. And the Soviet Union has opted out of the East-West confrontation. There are, to be sure, still countries that might wish us ill; Iraq is but one example. But they are all regional powers lacking the capability to position themselves to our south.

Thus, the kind of strategic assumptions on which the United States has long based its policies in Latin America—the kind of assumptions that called forth the Monroe Doctrine of 1823 and the No-Transfer Resolution of 1825—are now outmoded. There is no strategic threat and therefore no need for the doctrine of strategic denial (i.e., keeping other powers out of the hemisphere). Even less is there any need to assert US hegemony. The nations of the world are moving toward a more cooperative, interdependent system. The United States should adapt its Latin America policy to that new spirit, for what it needs in the region today is not control of, but the cooperation of, the other states.

An excellent way to signal what kind of new world order it has in mind would be for the United States to pledge that even in this region it has so long dominated and in which it has unilaterally intervened so many times it will henceforth fully respect the sovereignty of the other states, will conduct its relations with them fully within the charters of the United Nations and the Organization of American States, and in fact will make every effort to strengthen both organizations. In the new world in which we live today, the United States can well afford to make such a pledge. No valid security concerns stand in the way.

A Nuclear-Free Zone

Both the United States and the Soviet Union have expressed strong support for the concept of nuclear nonproliferation. Surely the two could make a major contribution to that goal in Latin America by vowing to take the necessary steps on their respective parts to turn the region into a nuclear-free zone. The Soviet Union could pledge never again to emplace nuclear weapons of any kind in the region. The United States could make a similar pledge, committing itself to exclude nuclear devices from its bases in Guantanamo Bay, Puerto Rico, Panama, and other sites around the Caribbean. Such action on the part of the two superpowers might be incentive enough to bring such holdouts as Argentina and Brazil to sign the Tlatelolco nuclear nonproliferation treaty. Cuba has said that it will sign if all other Latin American nations do so.

And why would Moscow and Washington not enter into such a commitment? The former clearly has no intention of emplacing such weaponry in this hemisphere. As for the latter, why would it have any need for nuclear weapons in Guatanamo, Roosevelt Roads, or anywhere else in the region?

Protection of the Environment

Could the two superpowers not commit themselves to pool their technology in a joint effort to protect the disappearing rain forests and to encourage the Latin American governments to do so? Obviously, a massive international effort is required. Would not a joint effort on the part of Moscow and Washington be a good way to kick it off?

Redressing the North-South Imbalance

The Cold War ends with the quest for social injustice and an end to poverty still unresolved. As Georgi Mirsky so eloquently puts it in Chapter 1: "Class struggle in diverse forms . . . is likely to be with us until a harmonious and just society is created in the world—and we are very far from that today."

Assisting the countries of the South, including those of Latin America and the Caribbean, in their efforts to develop their economies and provide decent standards of living for their people is in the interest of the industrialized countries of the North. A world so badly unbalanced as is ours today, with some countries enjoying plenty while others starve, cannot be a stable world, and poverty-stricken nations cannot be good markets.

The Soviet Union is going through its own time of economic troubles just now and is not in a position to be of much assistance to the developmental efforts of the Latin American countries. Latin America, moreover, is not an area in which the Soviet Union is expected to take the lead—that honor belongs to the United States. But is the United States playing the role expected of it? Not really. For years the United States argued that were it not for the costly arms race that drained away so many of its resources, it would be in a position to provide very significant economic assistance to the developing countries, those to our south included. The end of the Cold War has produced no such US effort. President Bush's Enterprise for the Americas proposal is perhaps a good beginning, but it is extremely limited in scope. Even when fully implemented, it if ever is, it will not represent the kind of major effort that is needed.

Even in such places as Nicaragua and Panama, US economic assistance has been pathetically insufficient. Having spent billions to fight a surrogate war to oust the Sandinistas, now that they are out of power and the kind of democratic government we favored is in, the United States seems to have lost interest. Certainly it has if one judges by the level and efficacy of its developmental assistance to Nicaragua. That is true also of Panama, a country whose economy we wrecked even before we invaded it. One would have thought Washington would at least feel some responsibility to the thousands of Panamanians whose homes were destroyed during the invasion. But almost two years later, people in many areas are still living in warehouses.

In sum, if Panama and Nicaragua are the portent of what we can expect from President Bush's Enterprise for the Americas, then Latin America may remain impoverished for a very long time. It is strange; even with the end of the Cold War, the United States can still always find $50–60 billion for any new weapons system that tickles the Pentagon's fancy. But when it comes to efforts to build a more prosperous world in which all have bread, dignity, and opportunity—and in which we have a greater variety of healthy trading partners—we begin to count out the pennies. This is not only pound foolish but an inappropriate response to the end of the Cold War. Perhaps it simply will take more time to break the habits of the past half century.

Meanwhile, as Julio Carranza Valdes points out in Chapter 8 on Central America, the kind of socially and politically stable region the United States presumably would like to see "cannot exist until the chronic social and economic imbalances have been redressed. And Cuba is not the obstacle to that process."

One can only add: neither is the Soviet Union.

Note

1. See, for example, Jeane Kirkpatrick and Allan Gerson's argument in "The Reagan Doctrine, Human Rights, and International Law," in *Right Versus Might: International Law and the Use of Force* (New York: Council on Foreign Relations, 1989).

The Contributors _____

Aaron Belkin is a research fellow at the Center for Foreign Policy Development, Brown University. He is author of works in political psychology, theory and practice of mutual security, and the new requirements for security in a world without a Cold War.

James G. Blight is senior research fellow and director of the US-USSR-Cuba Project, Center for Foreign Policy Development, Brown University, and author (with David A. Welch) of *On the Brink: Americans and Soviets Reexamine the Cuban Missile Crisis*, 2nd edition, 1990.

Karen Brutents graduated with a degree in philosophy from the University of Baku, and earned his doctorate in philosophy from the Soviet Academy of Sciences. He was for a number of years a member of the staff of *The World Marxist Review*. Until June 1991, he was deputy director of the International Department of the Central Committee of the Communist Party of the Soviet Union, and he is now a foreign policy advisor to President Gorbachev.

Julio Carranza Valdes, the deputy director of the Center for the Study of the Americas (CEA) in Havana, is an economist educated at the University of Havana. His specialty at CEA is Central America and Cuban policy toward that region. He is author of a number of works on Central America and on internal problems in Cuba.

David Lewis, a native of Mexico City, grew up in Mexico and France. He graduated from Brown University in May 1990 with degrees in history and international relations, and also studied at the University of Rostock in Germany. He is now assistant to the director at the Center for Foreign Policy Development, Brown University, where he works primarily with the US-USSR-Cuba Project.

Kiva Maidanik, educated at Moscow University and the Soviet Institute of History, served on the staff of *The World Marxist Review* from 1963 to 1968. For many years now a senior research fellow at the Institute for World Economy and International Relations (IMEMO), he is author of such works as *The Working Class in Spain, The Third World in a Contemporary World: Paths of the Revolutionary Process*, and *The Latin American Revolution Seen From the USSR.*

Sergo Mikoyan was educated at the Moscow Institute of International Relations of the Soviet Foreign Ministry. He was the editor of *Latinskaya Amerika*, the premier Soviet journal devoted to the study of Latin America, and the author of *Mexican-Soviet Relations* and many other books and articles on Latin America. He traveled to Cuba first in 1960, when he accompanied his father, Anastas Mikoyan, on the trip that led to the Soviet-Cuban alliance. He is currently a fellow at the Woodrow Wilson Center.

Georgi Mirsky, in addition to his work at the Institute of World Economy and International Relations, is a professor at the Institute of International Relations of the Ministry of Foreign Affairs. He is a graduate of the Institute of Oriental Studies and did advanced graduate work at IMEMO. His books include *The Political Role of the Military in the Third World, Iraq: The Turbulent Period*, and *Asia and Africa: Continents in Movement.*

Estervino Montesino Seguí is a research analyst at the Center for the Study of the United States (CESEU) at the University of Havana, and a graduate of political science from the Higher Institute of International Relations in Moscow. His specialty is US policy toward the Soviet Union, and he has published numerous works on that subject.

Valery D. Nikolayenko was educated at the Moscow State Institute of International Relations. He is one of the leading Latin American experts in the Soviet diplomatic service, in which he has served since 1964, holding diplomatic posts in Cuba, Mexico, and Washington (where he was the Latin American specialist at the Soviet embassy). He was ambassador to Colombia (1987–1988) and then to Nicaragua (1988–1990). From September 1990 until May 1991 he was director of the Department of Latin American Countries of the Soviet Ministry of Foreign Relations. He is now deputy foreign minister.

Jack Perry is now the director of the Dean Rusk Program in International Studies and professor of political science at Davidson College in North Carolina. He was a Foreign Service officer from 1959 until 1983, working largely in Soviet and Eastern European affairs. He served in both Moscow and Prague and was the US ambassador to Bulgaria from 1979 until 1981. Perry received his doctorate from Columbia University.

Ilya Prizel taught Russian at the universities of Maryland and Virginia before joining the Soviet studies faculty of the School of Advanced International Studies, Johns Hopkins University. He is author of *Latin America Through Soviet Eyes.*

Donna Rich-Kaplowitz is a research analyst for the Cuba Policy

Project at the School of Advanced International Studies, Johns Hopkins University, and the editor of *CubaInfo*, an information bulletin published by the project. She was a guest scholar at the University of Havana in 1984 and in 1991, and was an analyst at the National Security Archive, where she developed a document set on the Cuban missile crisis. She has published articles on both Cuba and Mexico.

Wayne S. Smith is a former foreign service officer, who served in Moscow and was chief of the US Interests Section in Havana (1979–1982). Now director of Cuban Studies at the School of Advanced International Studies, Johns Hopkins University, he teaches courses on the Cuban revolution and Soviet policy in Latin America. He is the author of *The Closest of Enemies: A Personal and Diplomatic Account of U.S.-Cuban Relations Since 1957* and many articles on hemispheric affairs and Soviet policy in Latin America.

Thomas G. Weiss, formerly executive director of the International Peace Academy and a United Nations staff member, is now the associate director of Brown University's Institute of International Studies. He is the author of *American, Soviet and Third World Perceptions of Regional Conflicts* and, with Meryl Kessler, editor of *Third World Security in the Post–Cold War Era*.

Index

About the Book ──────────

Pointing to dramatic changes in the Soviet Union and its foreign policies over the past few years, the authors demonstrate that even before the abortive coup of August 1991 and the consequent collapse of communism in the Soviet Union, the fear of Soviet penetration in Latin America, which had driven US policy in the region all during the Cold War, had been rendered groundless. They argue that it is high time for the United States to adapt its own Latin American policy to the post–Cold War era, a process that should include normalization of relations with Cuba.